CISCO UNAUTHORIZED

CISCO

UNAUTHORIZED

Inside the High-Stakes Race to Own the Future

JEFFREY S. YOUNG

FORUM An Imprint of Prima Publishing

To my parents

Some of the material in Part One first appeared in different form in
Wired magazine.

FORUM
An Imprint of Prima Publishing
3000 Lava Ridge Court
Roseville, CA 95661

PRIMA PUBLISHING, FORUM, and colophons are either trademarks
or registered trademarks of Prima Communications Inc., registered
with the United States Patent and Trademark Office.

Library of Congress Cataloging-in-Publication Data
Young, Jeffrey S.
Cisco : unauthorized : inside the high-stakes race to own the future /
Jeffrey S. Young
p.   cm.
ISBN: 0-7615-2775-3
1. Cisco Systems, Inc. 2. Internet industry--United States.
3. Internetworking (Telecommunication)--United States. I. Title.
HD9696.8.U64 C57 2000
338.7'61004678'0973--dc21   00-067186

01 02 03 04 HH 10 9 8 7 6 5 4 3 2 1
Printed in the United States of America

FORUM books are available at special discount for bulk purchases for
educational, business, or sales promotion use.
For details, contact Special Sales
Prima Publishing
1-800-632-8676

Visit us online at www.primaforum.com

CONTENTS

INTRODUCTION

THIS IS A PORTRAIT OF A GREAT COMPANY, ITS LEADERSHIP, ITS competition, and its character. Good, bad, brilliant, pompous, pious, powerful, arrogant—all that and more applies to Cisco Systems and its people at this extraordinary time in its history.

This is not a traditional corporate profile or leader's hagiography, not a recitation of sanitized corporate facts or excerpts from memos that should be consigned to the shredder. Rarely can those tangible, traditional elements of business history shed much light on the soul of a company, its own true place in a fast evolving market, or the character of those who make the decisions that shape it. This book is an attempt to search out and uncover the pulsing heart of Cisco, to probe its strongest chambers, and to take the measure of its weakest connective tissue.

The project began with a visit to my parents living in North Carolina. I was on a magazine assignment along the East

Coast, and during the brief visit my father took me with him to his monthly investment club meeting. The group, all men, mostly retired, call themselves CHICO, for the Chapel Hill Investment Company, and each contributes a modest amount to join up. The club—part of a uniquely American grassroots tradition—invests its collective money in various stocks, basing its decisions on group research and a democratic vote. Once a month they gather at an old lodge called Roosters (it used to be a big chicken coop) in the middle of a forest, share a member-cooked steak meal, and talk, over beer, about what is happening in the investment world and whether to make a change to their collective investment portfolio.

At this particular meeting in early 1999, I was the featured guest. Years of writing from inside Silicon Valley about technology and economics in books, magazines, and newspapers gave me a barely deserved credibility. The members of CHICO were anxious to hear what I had to say. They were men from an earlier era of America, almost all veterans of the Second World War, experienced in the 1950s trench warfare of corporate middle-management at a time when employment was for life, company loyalty was no idle slogan, and the United States was on an upwardly mobile economic and social march that has never been equaled.

When the evening's meeting ended, I was peppered with questions. The club had recently purchased Microsoft stock, and they wanted to make sure I thought there was still growth in it. But very quickly the discussion turned to the Internet. A show of hands indicated that most of the club's thirty members were already online. We discussed a number of small start-ups, many of which were getting lots of ink back then at the start of 1999—Amazon, eBay, eToys. One fellow sitting on an old sofa struggled to make himself heard. "We're thinking about investing in this Internet," he explained. "What do you think about Lucent?"

Emboldened by the beer and my place in the spotlight, I launched into an answer that described how Lucent didn't get it, Cisco did, and how the world had changed—and along the way I recommended that they invest in Cisco, not the Internet wanna-be that Ma Bell has tried to make Lucent become. Filled with the insular myopia of Silicon Valley and glibly letting the acronyms of high tech slip off my tongue, I rattled on for several minutes before realizing that everyone in the room was staring at me with glazed eyes and slack jaws. It wasn't that they couldn't understand what I was describing, it was that they weren't familiar enough with the language, culture, and milieu of networking to fully grasp it. Finally, the guy who had asked me the question in the first place spoke up. "Could you try and explain the difference between Cisco and Lucent in a way that I can understand?"

THAT QUESTION started me on this book's journey of discovery, in the course of which I've learned an enormous amount, changed my opinions many times, and deepened my understanding of the Internet and the network age. At one point I was offered the chance to write the authorized story of Cisco. I almost took the offer, but it meant I could no longer write an independent book, and that was the one thing I owed to the guys at the lodge. This isn't the story that Cisco would have blessed; it is admiring, critical, honest, impartial, and unauthorized.

For years I've written about the company and its competition for *Forbes* and *Wired*, interviewed John Chambers and his team leaders many times, observed and interacted with them in numerous different settings, listened in to earnings calls, attended annual and public meetings, and spoken with hundreds of friends and foes, current and former employees, happy and disgruntled customers, and competitors. This book is particularly concerned with the period from the beginnings of the dot-com frenzy in early 1999 to the industry's winter of discontent at the end of 2000. It is a portrait of one extraordinary company, its charismatic leader, and the world it is creating, discovering, exploiting, and fashioning. But there is also a dark side to this story, a hollowness at the core of this great company that is symptomatic of much of the Internet generation, and an arrogance that afflicts Cisco particularly. Both are essential to understanding what it is about Cisco, and its leader John Chambers, that has let it dominate the build-out of the Internet. Can its dominance continue?

In the end this is a book to answer the questions I was asked that chilly winter evening in an old lodge in the woods of North Carolina. It is my version of the story of the company and its competition large and small, what I think of them now, the Internet, and the Information Age, along with my attempt to make the mind-numbing technology of the data networking revolution understandable, predictable, and even (if I've really done it right) exciting to read about.

PART ONE

THE CISCO MYTH

CHAPTER 1

THE ZEN OF JOHN CHAMBERS

RICKEY'S HYATT HOUSE DOESN'T LOOK LIKE A CHURCH. THE unprepossessing motel and conference-room complex could be one of many such places strung out along El Camino Real, the six-lane, forty-mile-long roadway that is the spine of Silicon Valley. But on this weekday morning, in the winter of 1999, the crowd that has gathered in the foyer of Rickey's conference center is definitely in a devotional mood.

These supplicants have come to listen to a prophet of the Information Age, a man whose company is touching the businesses and lives of everyone in that room. They have come to hear John Chambers, chief executive of Cisco

Systems, chief evangelist of the knowledge economy's tree of life—the network—give a sermon.

Chambers, accompanied by a phalanx of PR aides and associates, arrives a few minutes early and slips into the back of the auditorium. He settles into a folding chair, carefully clasps his hands as if to pray, and closes his eyes. He might as well be chanting. He has a beatific look on his face; he is surrounded by his handlers, and no member of the hoi polloi can get near enough to break his reverie.

Chambers, a trim five foot nine, with thinning blond hair, is not the kind of man you would notice if you passed him on the street. Nothing about his physical appearance is remarkable; nothing leaves a lasting impression. He doesn't have the laser eyes of Apple's Steve Jobs or the gawky face of Microsoft's Bill Gates or the L.A.-cool affectations of Oracle's Larry Ellison. He's an Everyman. He could be the corner grocer, the schoolteacher, the Little League coach. He could be your next-door neighbor. Today, John Chambers is dressed in the uniform of the corporate middle managers he's about to address—blue suit, white shirt, tie. The suit may be cut from a finer cloth, but it's not vastly different from the off-the-shelf brands he wore in his IBM days—twenty years and a half billion dollars ago. Yet here he is, quietly sitting alone with his thoughts, at the center of a revolution that, before it ends, will profoundly change our world.

Chambers has come to this crowded conference room to do what he has done so many times in the past, to spread the good word about his deepest passion—the network and its all-mighty power to improve our lives. And it is fitting that Chambers has chosen to give his sermon at Rickey's.

Rickey's Hyatt House is one of only a handful of true landmarks in Silicon Valley, a place that celebrates impermanence and glorifies the next new thing above all else. It sits on a nondescript corner in what passes for a low-rent part of Palo Alto. But in its heyday, Rickey's was one of Silicon Valley's most famous watering holes. This old-fashioned 1950s motor court, with low-slung bungalow-style motel rooms and parking for the car right in front, was the backdrop for nonstop parties in the '50s and '60s, when semiconductors were being baked in ovens throughout the Valley and the world was beating a path to the chipmakers of Sunnyvale and Santa Clara and Palo Alto. Rickey's was located just a few blocks away from the original locations of Hewlett-Packard, Shockley Semiconductor, NASA-Ames, and Fairchild Camera & Instruments. At these early centers of electronics innovation, the first transistor was produced and, later, the first integrated circuit—combinations of transistors on one fingernail-sized sliver of silicon. Those early engineers who unwound at Rickey's were changing the world. They were ushering in the modern age of electronics.

Today the motel, freshly painted brown, is owned by the Hyatt chain, and no one would mistake it for a temple, a mission, or a cathedral. But a congregation has gathered here today, a congregation made up mostly of white men in their thirties and forties, with a smattering of women and minorities. After they finish their coffee and Danish, they come into the auditorium and respectfully take their seats in folding chairs.

Most are corporate warriors from every stratum of the American business world. They are not chief executives or rainmakers. They are the lifeblood of American business, the middle managers in finance, operations, business development. They work for pharmaceuticals and leasing companies, banks and telecommunications biggies and wanna-bes and never-will-bes. They are the well-scrubbed, well-heeled heart of the modern business world.

They've congregated in this nondescript meeting hall, shelled out their money to hear something that will help them understand, give them some glimmer of insight, make manifest the direction of the technological and cultural revolution that is swirling all around them.

They are looking for the word, some sign, to help them understand the incomprehensible and invisible magic of broadband, to make sense of the mystery at the core of most of their business lives this bright and sunny winter day at the twilight of the twentieth century: What is the meaning of the revolution in information? How can they harness it and ride it to the promised land?

They've come to hear the leader of the one company that has tamed the Information Age, the good missionary of the data world, apostle of the Internet. They've come to hear his sermon at the predawn of a new millennium. On a crisp and clear January morning, John Chambers has come to this undistinguished place to testify about the power of what has led him—and Cisco—to embark on their latest, greatest voyage.

When he is introduced to the several hundred conference attendees a few minutes later, Chambers becomes New Age Network Man. He eschews the carefully staged elevated podium at the head of the room and walks out among the gathered attendees, using a wireless mike and staying within a few feet of the first rows, gliding up the aisles, all the while cheerfully and happily presenting his message about the hope inherent in the Internet.

The CEO of Cisco starts by going straight for the jugular. "Make no mistake about it: The Internet is nothing short of the second Industrial Revolution. Industry is going to change. You have to make the change or you won't survive. The key is how to do it without losing your existing business. And one of the toughest of challenges is figuring out the new channels. Timing is the key. Are you ready? Do you understand how it will affect your products, your company, yourself? Are you positioned and prepared to take part in this new industrial, Internet revolution? Or are you going to be left behind?"

A deeply, privately religious man who regularly attends church, Chambers has an unshakable faith in the goodness of the Internet. He's pitching a religion, an Internet church that embraces all the world's citizens. The potential for making good while doing good fueled waves of Yankee Clipper captains and

Christian missionaries more than 150 years ago. Transmogrified by the Internet, personified by Chambers, energized on a global scale, the same twin themes of God and capitalism are rising again. The difference is that the canny traders of earlier times sought to corner the market for finite raw materials and colonize the globe's limited physical space. In the new Internet world, there is an infinity of available space, no end to the territory that can be colonized, and the only raw materials needed to stake out empires are intelligence and packets of data. But the most successful traders are still the best missionaries.

In Chambers's message is a dogma whose force will overwhelm the established order and provide opportunity for all. He doesn't need to speak with the fire and brimstone of the hill country preachers of West Virginia, where he grew up; he doesn't need to infuse his vision of the shining city on the hill with fear and damnation. John Chambers's Internet is holistic, all-embracing, a California touchy-feely New Age religion that is about a state of mind as much as, maybe more than, technology.

Best of all, the message he's sending about the Internet—that the more everyone on earth connects up to it, the better life will be for all humankind—is in perfect harmony with his own worldview and that of everyone who was smart enough to buy Cisco stock already. This is a self-fulfilling message of the best kind. Not only does it sound good when preached, but it also fills the coffers with profits.

John Chambers is constantly networking himself, listening, looking for new perspectives on his company from everyone he meets. By listening hard and making that connection, he is in effect hooking those people up to his network. He is no testosterone-laced Valley madman—no Steve Jobs or Larry Ellison or Netscape's Jim Clark. Chambers wants to hear what everyone has to say. This is not an act; this is truly who he is. What he says is more than just words, more than just some empty promise cadged from a consultant in corporate executive manners. He is the perfect apostle, whose very personality matches the dominant truth of his era. The answer is the network. Apply that same principle to a life, and the result is John Chambers. This is what saints, and martyrs, are made of.

Today is no different. Here is the quintessential John Chambers—breaking down barriers, asking for feedback, treating everyone he meets as an equal, and shaping everything he says by an infectious and deep-rooted belief in the value of the Internet to enrich business exponentially. And the message is, The network is it. Make your company fit a fast-moving environment by listening hard to customers and offering them what they want, no matter how big you become—even if that means changing rapidly and nimbly to accommodate their every whim.

"We've been called the corporation of the future. Not for the products we make, but for how we use the Internet to do business. In 1997 we did one-third of the world's e-commerce. We provide 70 percent of our corporate support over the Internet. We increased our productivity by 20 percent—it was actually higher, but the board wouldn't have believed me if I told them it was 40 percent. We are the Internet experts. I'd like to tell you it is because we are smart people and visionaries. But what we are is very good at listening. And if you listen to customers, they'll tell you exactly how to move forward."

There is perhaps no better personality to head Cisco than the very malleable, ever-solicitous (perhaps too solicitous) John Chambers. The affable one. The man with the almost cloying attentiveness to others. He doesn't just say he wants to listen to what the audience can tell him; he also is certain to make time to get their input. He doesn't just tell you he wants to hear what you think of this or that decision; he also makes sure to solicit those comments at the end of an interview. He doesn't simply say he wants to listen to customers; he also seeks them out and never lets on that he's anything less than fascinated by their stories.

This is the Zen of John Chambers. He isn't a chief executive who believes he has the answers, who believes he is anointed, who believes he is better than the rest of us, who believes that he has the secret formula for success. He's one of us. Everyman.

Chambers proudly describes to his audience the process of reinventing Cisco seven times in ten years. This is conglomerate business management taken to a higher level. It is management that is mercurial, quick to change, willing to change, embracing change all the time. It is a CEO deliriously and happily listening to customers in earnest. It is Chambers inventing and rethinking and reinventing Cisco through acquisitions and partnerships, all the while spinning the company using his own brand of aw-shucks good ol' boy–cum–Elmer Gantry performance.

In Silicon Valley, where the stereotype is of table-thumping executives yelling through twenty-hour days in a culture of paranoia and aggression, John Chambers simply doesn't fit. In looking for a high-tech executive, central casting would throw him out in its first pass.

"There's an enormous business opportunity in all of this, but particularly in the move to the high-speed Internet and the advent of consumer networking. The one thing Cisco has done consistently is that whenever we take on a market in transition, we gain market share. To gain market share in normal times you slug it out forever for 1 or 2 or 3 percent growth. But if you catch it in transition, you can gain 20 or 30 or 40 percent share points. Look at Amazon and Barnes & Noble. Barnes & Noble is a well-run company with 27,000 employees, $4 billion in sales, 1,000 physical locations—huge barriers to entry. But in two years a virtual company, with 1,600 people, now has a market cap five times theirs. This will occur in every industry. People, and companies, who get their timing wrong will fail."

Now he changes roles in midperformance and plays the statesman. New turf. A political run? There's a prime-time TV network interview, Diane Sawyer doing a fluffy profile: The World's Greatest Boss. He hosts $10,000-a-plate fund-raisers for George Bush and for selected initiatives at his Silicon Valley hills home. Is he about to run for office?

"My personal passion is education. I believe that in this country it is broken. Our K through 12 system is a disaster. We are spending the third largest percent of GNP on it, yet our math and science scores are abysmal. But the Internet can completely change this. In very short order all devices that help us learn are going to be Internet-based. Business has to play a role in this. If we in the technology industry are going to create this revolution, we can't leave a majority behind. No more haves and have nots. There has to be Internet access for everyone."

This is heady stuff for a capitalist. Chambers doesn't cut a figure as a captain of industry, a wild-eyed revolutionary, or a stump-pounding politician. Chambers is quick to smile, wants to give of himself, and is blessed with a kind of frenetic high energy that lets him rush through his days. He has been married for twenty-five years to the same woman, and they have two college-age children. He is unfailingly polite, as well as generous, gregarious, and garrulous. But the real source of his good nature turns out to be the very center of his company's products: As the world adopts more networking gear—more of Cisco's gear, if he has his way, of course, but there's plenty of opportunity for all—Chambers sees not just profits for Cisco, but profits for all of society.

"Eighteen months ago, when we started talking about the consumer revolution that was going to come to the industry, no one believed us. However, the pace of acceptance of this revolution has almost always been underestimated. We're inside a tornado market already. E-mails outnumber regular mail—but projections are for there to be 15 to 20 billion e-mails per day by 2002 or 2003. That is huge. The rate of acceptance of the Internet is already six times faster than for the telephone, four times faster than for the PC itself. The pace of change is huge. The rewards are huge. But timing is essential. Too early, and an expensive roll-out won't be able to pay for itself. Too late, and it is almost impossible to pick up the lost market share."

John Chambers, despite his all-American background—the son of two country doctors, a lawyer who never practiced, a top IBM salesman for ten years, an executive at Wang Laboratories for another decade—is a Zen master. It doesn't matter that he has an Appalachian accent. It doesn't matter that he's always attired in a blue suit and power tie. It doesn't matter that he runs a $19 billion company with 34,000 employees.

In his heart, in his soul, John Chambers has found his center. He knows just who he is, and he is at peace with himself. His religion is the good of the Internet. In a time of galloping change, of technological innovation that stretches the limits of the human mind—in a time of fear, uncertainty and doubt as the Internet promises to swamp much of what we've taken for granted—his good-natured certainty about the value of this revolution is calming. And his company's undisputed success gives him the credentials to espouse it.

His mantra: The Internet will change everything. His vehicle: a company of networking superstars who are loosely integrated around the strategic theme of keeping Cisco at the heart of the data revolution. His secret: Embody the Internet Age in every cell of your being. Forget the Organization Man, emblem for the last great period of prosperity in American culture in the 1950s. In the New World—a phrase that Chambers uses liberally to contrast Cisco with its Old World brethren, the bigger, well-heeled competitors from the voice-telephony equipment market such as Lucent, Nortel, Siemens, and Ericsson—there's a new person afoot. This is Network Man, and John Chambers is the model. Call him John the Baptist. He's the advance man for the IP—Internet Protocol, the underlying Esperanto of the network age—crusade.

WHAT IS THIS Cisco religion called Internet 2, broadband, the Next Net, or, as John Chambers refers to it, the New World Network? Why is there such a buzz and vibrancy about it, such a battle to supply it, so much recent investment capital to support it, so many investors in a frenzy to get onto the roller-coaster and then just as quickly get out? What is going on here?

At its heart, John Chambers's vision is all about optimism. The creation of a completely wide-open communications system. Available to all. Everywhere. Using the Internet, this amorphous cloud of data connections that spans the globe, to link hundreds of millions—no, *billions*—of people. Is it crazy to think that virtually everyone, anywhere on earth, will be wired within our lifetimes? No technology has ever been adopted this quickly. Five hundred million users in five years. A billion in another twelve months. Maybe it will only take twenty years to completely wire the globe. In ten years there should be affordable bandwidth enough to carry on video conversations anywhere. Your doctors will be able to take a good look at you and your ailment and vitals no matter where you, and they, are located. In five years phones and the Internet and some video, both land line and wireless, will be completely intermixed and meshed together. Sooner yet, homes and offices and cars will have digital addresses, and new services will proliferate.

We are entering an era of no limits, with nothing to brake the cascade of human intelligence that has been unleashed by the Information Age. Imagine a limitless, replenishable, and essentially free source of oil. This is the future that fiber optics promises for digital information transportation. With the imperatives of massive, worldwide demand and the economies of scale that enormous capacity on single fiber strands can produce, data bandwidth is soon going to be priced like wheat, veering toward the cost of the air we breathe. And that will finally emancipate human beings in ways that have never before been possible. The Web essentially allows all the brains on earth to communicate and share insights in real time, around the globe, all the time. This kind of instantaneous feedback, completely produced by the network effect, is unprecedented. Furthermore, the speed of the feedback possible for any idea, any venture, any innovation, is electrifying. The implications of this to business are huge.

No longer does an entrepreneur have to wait weeks or months to find out what potential customers think about a new venture. With a Web site arranged in the right way, designed correctly, feedback can be immediate and the effect profound. Imagine a motorboat crossing the Pacific, with its course corrected once a day. At any given point between corrections, the boat could stray from its course by several points of the compass, wasting both time and fuel. Now, imagine the same motorboat, but this time with course corrections beamed to it a thousand times a second, with adjustments to the rudder so minor they're invisible to the eye. This constant, instantaneous feedback elevates the boat's passage across the Pacific to near perfection—beyond the capabilities of any human skipper. No wasted fuel, no wasted time.

Now imagine this same principle applied to a business. The impact of instantaneous feedback might be the most far-reaching of all the artifacts of the evolving Internet. It can shorten product and revision cycles dramatically, with multiple iterations of a new idea generated in days, not months or years. Time scales that now seem quick will accelerate. But more than that, the quality of revised versions of any business plan or idea will *increase*. Not only will things happen faster than was imaginable in the near past, but the level of expectation for quality will rise accordingly as well.

In addition, companies will require fewer employees, presaging huge dislocations in the work force as key services are outsourced and common customer service is automated and delivered in the self-service world of the Internet. Already the availability of mass bandwidth is rewriting the software and storage industries. Businesses are starting to buy software on demand from a new breed of companies that provide software for accounting, or databases, or whatever across a big-bandwidth

Internet or through a private enhanced network. This introduces a whole new distribution model into the game—an ongoing rental arrangement—in place of discrete sales by the box or the seat. Imagine tuning to the latest word-processor program when you want to write a letter. Storage area networks are going to be big business, as fiber tendrils reach out to provide connections in commercial and residential neighborhoods, not just for enterprises and Internet hosting firms. Mass storage will be cheaper to buy remotely, over the speed-of-light Internet.

The implications of the new world network beyond business are even greater. In the mind of John Chambers, this gushing, spewing hose of bandwidth and connections will somehow make us all better humans. This is the central tenet of the religion of the Next Net. This is the doctrine of the Church of Cisco. This is the credo of John Chambers.

Essentially, the Internet creates a true democracy of information. Just as no one has a bigger signpost on the Internet, no one person's voice is louder. This means that the dream of the American democracy—a world where every person is born equal—now has a chance to come to fruition. On the Internet, we are all equal. The only differences will be in the force of intellect, the power of an individual's passions, and the ability to express them. Brand name plays a part in getting surfers to a site, but not as much as the Old World media would like. And there are brand-new ways to build a name too.

Think of it. For tens of thousands of years, might has ruled human relations. On the Internet, the only strength that counts is the power of your mind. Certainly there is still a role to be played by marketing, in terms of getting participants to go to a particular Web site. But fundamentally the only reason they will stay, or come back, is that you're offering something they need or want. This ability to communicate with everyone, not just on the one-to-one model of the telephone, but in the one-to-many world of Web sites, makes the power of a mind much more potent than the power of Mars. Wars will still be fought.

But they will be wars for intellectual capital, wars to gain brainpower that can captivate and enthrall people whose primary means of communication will be through the Web. In this new society, information dexterity and fluency will be as important as a driver's license. If you can think better, smarter, faster about how to take advantage of this new sprawling, formless, evolving thing, you'll win.

The Internet might provide the ultimate global congregation. No matter how smart one person might be, a single intelligence cannot equal the combined brainpower of tens of thousands of Internet users. This means that the hierarchical world that we've known for centuries might give way to a new kind of organizing principle—one in which the opportunities are even more individual, where all people really do have control of their destiny in a way that has never been contemplated before.

If everyone can share insights and can create personal groups of friends and acquaintances and colleagues without having to rely on the chance encounter and the tyranny of geography, what is it going to mean to the gene pool? Instead of human relations based on location and language and country of origin, this new world order might be based on intellect, shared interests, and passion. In a generation, the geography could be replaced by something much deeper, something more powerful, a human ecology of the intellect.

The impact of this revolution on the human race could be profound, or it could be trivial. There's simply no way of knowing yet. But it is in the implications of this new set of organizing principles for human communication and relations that men like John Chambers find their good book, their text, their sermons. Think of the Internet as a giant, living, evolving, shared, collective brain. It has all the power for good and all the potential for darkness that are inherent in the human race itself. Understanding it, becoming completely familiar with it and its implications, is crucial to being able to navigate during the next millennium on earth. Predicting exactly what this extraordinary living, seething thing will change is impossible. But change everything, it will.

And at this moment in time, one company stands almost alone in the midst of this ocean of change: Cisco.

FOR THE BETTER part of an hour, John Chambers has been running up and down the aisles, talking with the crowd. The time has come to finish it off.

"A few months ago I stood in front of 300 of the world's largest company's telco executives and had to tell them the truth about voice. My message was simple: In the coming few years not only would the area where all their profits came from be commoditized, but it would be given away free by the IP companies. The ability to price products differently, in different geographies around the globe, was going to disappear as the Internet flattened distance and changed the rules. Education was going to change from something that was done in rooms like this to something that individuals did in their own time, at their own pace, over the Internet. Service was going to improve dramatically. And the playing field will be leveled between big and small companies in ways that we haven't even begun to imagine yet. It might well not be an advantage to be big going forward. The one thing that is certain? The fast are going to beat the slow."

In the Q&A session at the end of the half-hour presentation, Chambers runs all around the auditorium with a microphone to get questions. This is a CEO whose stock holdings make him worth more than $575 million acting like Jerry Springer.

In a masterful, almost beatific touch that would be coy from anyone else, he asks for business cards from anyone interested in partnering with Cisco—no matter that his company is the 800-pound gorilla of the networking space and the engine behind much of the Internet's craziness, whereas the audience is composed of low-level managers who've spent a few hundred dollars to get out of the office for a couple of days. This isn't the archetypal chief executive with limos and trappings of power and self-importance. This is a disciple at the peak of his form, a man whose pride and ego have become sublimated to the company's story, a story that perfectly fits his outgoing, outwardly directed personality.

Add church bells and incense, and the religious illusion would be complete. But Chambers's message was every bit as mesmerizing as any psalm to this audience. In his presentation the ideas are unimaginable. Business opportunity galore. A world of limitless riches. Change without precedent. Accelerated time that makes every year in Internet time worth seven on the calendar. A better world. All through data. The kicker? You have to seize it. Now. No time for equivocation. And the sure path to satori? Buy Cisco gear end to end.

Amen.

CHAPTER 2

AN EMPIRE BUILT OF BITS

FROM THE AIR, LITTLE ABOUT SILICON VALLEY CAPTIVATES THE eye. It is a place where landfills have transformed intellectual energy into physical location—a place where in the great suburban sprawl of the 1960s and '70s, orchards gave way to low-slung, tilt-up concrete buildings. Now many of them are emblazoned with banners heralding new company arrivals or abandoned, their parking lots empty and waiting for the next enthusiastic start-up to fill the space before either moving on, being subsumed by a competitor, or blowing away like the fallen leaves from ornamental trees that landscape the parking lots. Yet beside those abandoned edifices, new building continues apace as wave after wave of corporate and executive egos fill every square foot of space with more indistinguishably ugly buildings. And they too will be abandoned in the next cycle of boom-and-bust that characterizes the California economy.

Off to the very northern edge of San Jose, just south of San Francisco Bay, in a tangle of constant construction and reconstruction, there's a small sea of low-rise, mock-Italianate buildings, windows gleaming in the California sun. The land was once scrub, not good for much. Today, it's the world headquarters of Cisco Systems, the most successful network and Internet infrastructure company in the universe.

The corporate headquarters building looks like all the others—except that it has a collection of flags flying on poles spaced evenly around its semicircular forecourt. All the hallways look the same, all the cubicles are the same size. The only marks of status are private conference rooms for executives.

Nothing about the physical location or the look of Cisco hints at its dominance of the Internet transmission business or its win-at-all-costs culture or its focus on customers. This is just another version of cubicle hell. There are no restaurants for miles; there are no gas stations, no corner markets, no visible vending machines with newspapers. On tables in the lobbies there are copies of the company annual report and Cisco's own slick magazine, *Packet*. Nothing else.

What is it about Cisco? Where is the corporate culture that drove IBM to dominance a generation ago? How about the crusading counterculture of Apple or the brash, unveiled aggressiveness of Microsoft?

What is the magic that has driven the company's stock market performance to outstrip that of every other publicly traded company, rising in ten years to make it one of the most valuable companies on earth, neck and neck with General Electric—an old-line behemoth with nearly 100 years of history?

It was Apple Computer's charismatic leader, Steve Jobs, who, twenty years ago, first put into words the idea at the heart of Silicon Valley's zeitgeist: "Let's make a dent in the universe." Let's change the world through computing. The problem, however, was that a computer does no more than help us do the things we already do: write books, calculate numbers, send letters. It can't take us places we've never been before.

Think about this in a different way. What makes an automobile truly valuable? It's not the engine or the leather interior; it's not the sound system or even the nameplate. It's the roads, the system of interconnecting roadways, that take us from point A to point B to point Z to wherever we want to go. It is the freedom of movement, not the convenience of comfort, that has made the car so important to so many.

Likewise, it's the network, the electronic connection to millions of minds the world over, that increases the value of the computer exponentially. The reason Cisco is one of the most valuable companies in the world, with revenues growing at an unheard-of rate, is that it understood better and before anyone else that in the Information Age, the network is king. And he who controls the network controls the future.

NETWORK. It is not a word that inspires awe or quickens the heart. You don't expect to hear it come tumbling from the lips of poets or lovers. Its first recorded use was in 1560, in a Bible published in Geneva by Gutenberg: "Thou shalt make unto it a grate like network of brass" (Exodus 27:4). Not an audacious beginning.

But no matter how it was first used in the Western world, the word is now at the very heart of the New World economy, the center of the Internet ecosystem. It is a rallying cry for bewildered old-line investors and gee-whiz dot-commers trying to get in on the new gold rush. But the real masters of the Internet are the companies selling the picks, the shovels, the jeans, the bread and eggs—the network infrastructure—to these modern-day miners. Companies like Cisco.

But what *is* a network? The *Oxford English Dictionary* defines it as "Work in which threads, wires, or similar materials are arranged in the fashion of a net." That definition is coldly precise—perhaps too precise, perhaps too cold. *Network* also can be defined more broadly as, essentially, an instrument, any instrument, that connects human beings with one another, enabling them to communicate, to trade information, to understand better the world in which they live.

Wasn't the Nile a network for the seeds of civilization that sprouted along its banks? Down that river traveled not only goods to trade but also tantalizing bits of information, ideas, and insight from other communities a day's—sometimes even a lifetime's—journey away. Likewise, the Pony Express, the railroads, the shipping lanes, the telegraph have all served the intrinsic human need to connect, to "network."

Why this basic need? In a word, survival. Throughout human history, those civilizations, those communities that were most connected with the world around them flourished; those that did not, withered. In short, the network—in whatever form it takes—is like a system of blood vessels that nourishes an organism, that makes life possible.

With the advent of the telephone, that power of connection first entered the home and finally was in easy reach of the masses. People used the telephone to connect with lost relatives, with new loves, with worlds they had never known. This new device, which connected people in mundane, sometimes mysterious ways, was, in some sense, the first Internet, but it was all about one kind of service: voice, over wires. Important, yes—and it has profoundly changed human society over the past hundred years. But when all was said and done, it was still only about voice calls and maybe call waiting and perhaps 800 numbers. The entire network was controlled by the phone companies, and they doled out its benefits to us at a price and on a schedule that suited them.

The result, however, was that one company became the largest business on earth by the 1970s. It was AT&T, Ma Bell, keeper and controller of all the phone lines in the United States. This one business, authorized by U.S. government fiat, had the transmission lines and the telecommunications services and the phones themselves in its tight fist. By 1980 AT&T carried $135 billion in assets on its balance sheet. In today's dollars that would be a *trillion*-dollar corporation. Even in this era of nosebleed market caps, no company has assets that can compare. It's not hard to imagine, however, that the next trillion-dollar company will be in a business similar to Ma Bell's—connecting people. And if any company would seem to have a shot at that, it is Cisco.

TODAY'S NETWORK HAS moved beyond voice and the limitations of telephony. It has taken all of our civilization's previous networks and bundled them, focused them into one easily accessible resource via a computer. And this new network has assumed a power equal to the millions of minds it connects.

Today, information is transported via electronic pulses racing at the speed of light on strands of glass, within an interconnected Web of copper wires, or through the ether of wireless communication. Modern networks communicate by breaking down every bit of information into packets—envelopes containing headers describing the data enclosed, an address for where the data is coming from and where it should go, and the data itself.

Packet networking had its start in the RAND Corporation think tanks of the Cold War in the late 1950s. There, researcher Paul Baran was searching for a way to build a communications network that would be less susceptible to a nuclear first strike. AT&T's phone networks—upon which this country's communications were dependent—were built on the concept of a single-network, highly optimized pathway for all calls.

Economically it made sense for a monopolist with a charter to collect, transmit, and complete every call in the United States, to aggregate them all together and carry them over a single network. But there was a huge drawback to this architecture: Destruction of a single link in the chain could put the system out of commission.

In a packet architecture, however, calls would be divided up into packets of data that would follow any available pathway to reach a destination, and only when they reached their intended destination would they be reformulated and reorganized. Think of it as a vast spider's web of interconnected points, any of which is capable of forwarding packets via any open strand. Who cares which route the data take, as long as the packet ultimately gets to where it is supposed to go and is then reassembled? This design wasn't perfect for voice, since the time of arrival of different packets couldn't be guaranteed. But for data, where timing wasn't crucial, it worked perfectly.

This notion had a powerful effect on network design. In a packet network any available intermediate stop—a routing stage or, in datacomm lingo, a network "hop"—could be used to get to an ultimate destination. In the traditional phone network, however, a phone call between any two places opens up a dedicated and devoted circuit between the two telephones. Any interruption in the circuit breaks the connection. In a packet network, any interruption is simply a cue for the network to find the next best path to get the packets through.

This was described as "stupid networking" by David Isenberg, a former AT&T planner who was fired for espousing such a heretical network architecture within Ma Bell. Because of the way voice circuits are specified (with explicit routes and pathways for most traffic), traditional backup systems are idle, waiting to kick in after some catastrophic failure. "Packet architecture, however, is designed so that all the multiple redundant systems can carry traffic during normal times," Isenberg explains. "If one machine goes down, they automatically route around it and keep going. In the stupid network, all the gear helps carry the load all the time, where in the voice world it doesn't. What does that do to the economics?" It lowers costs dramatically.

Not surprisingly, AT&T fought to bury packet networking, and the technology languished for years. Then a group of scientists working for a secretive U.S. government agency called the Defense Advanced Research Projects Agency (DARPA) and its computer arm, IPTO (Information Processing Technology Office), dusted off the ideas and incorporated them into their fledgling effort to link government and academic computer labs around the nation. It was cheap. It was reliable. It didn't require end-to-end homogeneity. Needless to say, packet networking caught on in a big way.

This new technology, however, required the development of an infrastructure more complex than the highway system. In short, the floods of packets broadcast over the wires needed to be directed, managed, massaged over dozens, if not hundreds, of hops. The first two kinds of important network equipment were hubs and bridges. Hubs allowed a number of devices to connect together to the network—imagine a city train station with a hub-and-spoke arrangement connecting numerous railroad lines. The hub aggregates the traffic and brings it together for easier, and centralized, management.

Bridges link hubs together. Imagine the underground hallways and elevators and stairs that allow a subway passenger to go from one line to another in a big urban underground station. In the early days of networking, both of these were simply brain-dead devices that forwarded all packets broadcast over one segment of the network to all other segments connected, or "bridged" together, by these devices.

But it wasn't long before two challenges became apparent. First, network traffic, and the storms of packets that were generated, swamped early-generation bridges. Traffic backups and delays were common. What was needed was a way to determine which packets went to which sector of a network and to forward them accordingly. The second challenge was that the world of the 1980s was characterized by many incompatible computers: Mainframes, minicomputers, and numerous flavors of PCs. There was little standardization and no dominance by one format over another. Each spoke a different language. Simply put, these different computers wouldn't communicate with one another. In order for them to function, networks had to be filled with homogeneous equipment. The answer, developed originally by a couple of graduate students at Stanford—Leonard Bosack and his wife, Sandy Lerner—and a top-flight engineer named Bill Yeager, was a product called the router, which would become the backbone of the company Bosack and Lerner went on to found: Cisco.

The router was essentially a specialty computer with a set of connection links—stored in a special database called a router table—for the network upon which it sat. When a packet showed up, the router read the address information on the data, scanned its router tables to determine the best routing path, and shipped the packet along its way.

Besides being a superior packet-traffic cop, the early router also offered cross-platform compatibility to the Tower of Babel created by all those different computers and operating systems. If a packet from a PC network was destined for a DECNet minicomputer network, the router could reformat the packet to fit its destination's network before it speeded the data along.

For all of its advantages, though, the market for this technology wasn't exactly hot. A few early users started playing with the gear, but there wasn't that much call for routers—at least not in comparison to the demand for hubs and bridges. Most networks were exclusively local—constellations of computers and workers clustered in company offices or campuses and called local area networks, or LANs—so adding sophisticated routing wasn't often called for.

Then everything started to change. Routers had another feature that was little noticed in the early days of the market but that grew exponentially in importance in the late '80s. In addition to being able to connect two different computer types, routers also offered telephone line connections for data that needed to go out of the local area—a window, if you will, to the world, or, as it was called, the wide-area network, or WAN (ultimately the World Wide Web).

Initially, this feature was geared primarily toward the few brave souls willing to use telephone lines for remote access purposes—road warriors linking to the corporate network, a select few employees working from home, branch offices with data links to the home office so that daily cash register receipts could be centrally gathered. Since telephone access time was expensive and metered by the second, routers enabled network managers to carefully restrict the traffic that used the phone lines to get to the wide-area network.

This combination of intelligence—the ability to look into the packets and determine what to do with each—and a gateway to the outside world made the router the crucial device for the growth of the Internet once the World Wide Web appeared in 1993. As the groundswell of interest grew and the online community mushroomed, the router became *the* central controller for the entire Internet generation.

And the central router that controlled the entire Internet generation was Cisco's. Other companies, such as 3COM and Synoptics and Wellfleet and Cabletron, also made routers, but they all offered a complete collection of hubs and bridges as well. Cisco, at least in its early days, stayed tightly focused on routers and made sure it built the very best ones in the world. Later on, when the rise of the Internet turned the tables on the network industry and the router became the only part of the data equipment market that offered enough of a value add to retain high margins, it was Cisco that had the last laugh.

STILL, NO MATTER how interested in data networking one might be, this is all about plumbing. And plumbing isn't very exciting. What is it about networks, and the biggest of them all, the public Internet, that is generating all this attention, the extraordinary economic growth rates for Cisco, a sense of limitless possibilities as sketched by Chambers, and an unprecedented explosion of opportunity in every corner of the business, consumer, and political world? Toilets and sewer pipes might be important to modern life, but they are not sexy. And they certainly don't power the stock market the way Cisco and its brethren have been doing.

Much of this revolution is based on a single explosive quasi-mathematical formulation that defines the potential, perceived, and actual value of a network. Sometimes loosely called Metcalfe's Law, after Bob Metcalfe, a researcher at Xerox's legendary Palo Alto Research Center, it is really more of an observation: The value of the network grows by the square of the number of nodes connected to it.

Metcalfe himself laughs at the way his off-the-cuff observation has achieved the status of Newtonian physics in the age of the network. "I never professed to have discovered something profound," he says. Indeed, his main claim to fame is the development of the Ethernet networking system, which was devised at Xerox. Once he and his colleagues had invented this simple packet networking scheme (based on an earlier ham radio system originally developed for communicating among the Hawaiian islands and called, appropriately, AlohaNet), they discovered the intrinsic, and expansive, useful value of adding more nodes to any data network. "It just seemed obvious that the more who signed on to the network, the more valuable the network became."

While Metcalfe's "Law" might seem self-evident, it had only limited value in the earlier generations of network technology that brought together students on a single campus or employees in a single company. While there was definite advantage in allowing employees of a particular company to communicate among themselves, that arrangement nonetheless essentially represented a closed society. Knowledge and information could be disseminated, and groups could share files to work together, but this activity was still restrained within a relatively homogeneous population.

The appearance of the World Wide Web in the mid-1990s changed everything. With the creation of a simple format (HTML, or hypertext markup language) that allowed Web pages to be shared, combined with a simple programming environment for almost anyone to create those Web pages (a kind of tabula rasa or, less poetically, a blank Etch-A-Sketch for computer-based information to be placed onto), a wide-open magic slate for communications was unveiled. No matter what system a person was using for a browser, or what make of computer, or how sophisticated the user, or what the user wanted to share, there was suddenly no barrier to communication for anyone who could get a connection onto the Web (which was almost always a wide-area, or WAN, link). The consequences of this were extraordinary.

To start, very few natural resources are consumed in using the Internet, a fact that alone changes not only all the dynamics of networking but also commerce as a whole. For the first time the path to wealth and riches isn't based on cornering some scarce commodity or moving some valuable resource around the globe to supply it to other businesses that need it. The only ingredients of this revolution are brainpower and raw mental effort, combined with some electricity and a phone line. Bits of data—the electrons and pulses of light—are essentially free: There is some value in moving them—which is just what Cisco helps do—but the real value is in manipulating the bits and bytes and figuring out how to use them to get people to part with their money. In other words, the value is in delivering services—whether they be Internet services, application services, or end-user services—and that is exactly where Cisco and its fiercest competitors are moving. After all, if you really understand the transmission game, why not make the much more profitable value-added part of the equation—the delivery of services that people will pay for—yours as well?

Today, around the world, more than 300 million people have Web access. There are 300 million people who can now interact with one another in ways both mysterious and banal. Three hundred million people who previously lived in small communities defined by work, neighborhood proximity, family, and friendship. Clusters of humans whose means of communicating were limited to geographical proximity, mail, the scope and scale of the telephone network, and chance. Estimates are that by 2004 one billion people will be online. All of those people will need a WAN connection to the Internet, a connection that requires, in the current architecture of data networking, a router somewhere along the path to move requests for Web pages and to fulfill those requests by delivering the Web pages back to the user's browser. The Internet has only scratched the surface of its possibilities.

And so, perhaps, has Cisco.

MOVING DATA AROUND in a network or through the Internet, like sharing word-processor or spreadsheet files among colleagues, is inherently better with one standard. In networking today, that standard is IP, or Internet Protocol based on Cisco's software: IOS. The primary profit maker in this business is Cisco. Microsoft and Intel have both benefited mightily from the masterful exploitation of their standards in the consumer computing space. But both were handed their monopolies when anointed by IBM. IP, on the other hand, is an offshoot of the work done by a loose constellation of computer scientists financed by the United States government. When they built the first nationwide packet data network in the 1970s—called ARPANet—they created an underlying protocol, or language, called TCP (for Transmission Control Protocol) that specified how data would be prepared, massaged, and transmitted. It would be the common tongue of many networks. Today it is generally called simply IP, and it is a worldwide standard that has proved remarkably resilient so far.

Thus Cisco's monopoly is entirely self-created, in a rough-and-tumble standards-based world with lots of competition in routers and data switches, the essential plumbing gear of networking and the Internet. Through powerful marketing, strong products, careful strategic thinking, and relentless execution, the company has grown to dominate the Internet. There was nothing stopping any of dozens of networking companies from attacking the same market problems. But none did. And then came the most important single factor: chance. Cisco had exactly the right product for the Internet when it burst upon the world's stage.

Call it luck, call it smarts, Cisco gear makes up more than half of all the equipment transporting the information economy. Networks. Plumbing of the data age. The railroads of the digital age. Commerce. Content. E-mail. E-conomies. Almost all of it at one time or another rides within Cisco's plumbing.

And forget Metcalfe's Law; there's a new kind of calculus at work here: If 1,000 customers are connected to the Internet using dial-up modems, and all are online at an effective speed of, say, 19.2 kilobits per second, that requires about 20 megabits of bandwidth per second total—easily within the range of today's routers and switches. Even so, Internet brownouts frequently occur during peak working hours. If those same 1,000 people upgrade to higher-speed DSL lines, each of which can carry data in the range of 2 megabits per second, the infrastructure needs to increase 1,000-fold, to 2 gigabits per second of bandwidth—just within the range of the latest gigabit routers. Move up to video at 6 megabits per second, and the bandwidth requirements rise accordingly, to much higher capacity gigabit routers, to terabit routers. Vast switches and cross-connectivity. Unimaginable volumes of packets roaring everywhere all around the world.

Now, increase those 1,000 customers to 300 million. In a couple of years, make that 1 billion. In short, the world in which Cisco competes and, at this moment, dominates seems essentially limitless. If routers remain the elemental way for data to get moved around, Cisco's dominance of this part of the network is not only going to remain profitable but may also become a stranglehold.

Examine the data.

Ten years ago there were 100 million e-mails sent each year versus 135 billion pieces of first-class mail. In 1997 the two reached parity, at about 190 billion each. Ten years ago data traffic was barely 5 percent of all telecommunications traffic. Today, with Internet traffic doubling every 100 days, it is more than 50 percent. The cost of moving a packet of data has fallen from $60 per packet per second in the late 1980s to less than one-tenth of one cent today.

On every front Cisco is expanding to embrace the new. It is buying companies at a feverish pace (seventy-five since 1993), and it is creating new entrepreneurial groups within the company. It is marketing and selling Cisco-engineered cable TV modems and technical-support centers, even pushing into China with "Cisco Academies," company-sponsored sales teaching the Cisco Way. It is buying network telephony vendors like Selsius for network PBX products and JetCell for wireless business telephony. It is wiring up experimental IP communities like Playa del Rey in California and delivering sales force and customer contact solutions in partnership with Oracle.

All of this to fuel the expansion into the next frontier. Voice—the entire world of Ma Bell and party lines and switchboards—is about to disappear forever, subsumed by the digital world. And Cisco wants to be the Ma Bell for the Next Net.

The worldwide data-networking equipment business is worth, by some estimates, about $50 billion a year today. By contrast, the much larger voice equipment business that makes up most of today's PSTN (publicly switched telephone network) is worth more than $100 billion. Add the billed prices for the world's telephone calls, and Gartner Inc., a technology research company, calls the voice business a $500 billion annual marketplace. This old-line market is groaning under an out-of-date cost structure, hobbled by technological limitations and slowed by installed-base inertia that makes it effectively a dead end. Worse, it is about to see a new wave of data and optical Internet-working equipment, combined with a surge in fiber bandwidth capacity, make so much data capacity available that it will swamp the voice networks. In addition, the single searing truth that sends shivers down the spines of the telecoms is that, in data networks, voice can be carried for free. Bits is bits.

Home networking is emerging. Wireless broadband is looming. Voice and data and video networking are converging in a digital free-for-all. Jupiter Communications, a company that tracks Internet commerce, estimates that within the next five years data will account for nearly 75 percent of all telecommunications traffic. As fiber reaches farther out from the backbone network, moving closer to end-users, bringing its almost unimaginable quantities of data throughput, things like hard-disk storage no longer need to be placed where the computer is located but can be across town, on the other side of the country, around the world. High-quality video is only a dream now, but it has the potential to blow all projections out the window. Who's to say that everyone on earth won't want to do video phone calling when it is as easy as hitting the keypad? Doctor No, George Jetson, Flash Gordon, Dick Tracy—get ready.

The implications are mind-boggling. Office buildings bathed in an ether of high-speed wireless data. Plummeting long-distance rates. Voice, Internet, on-demand video, CD-quality audio, interactive gaming—all coming down the same pipe.

And this is only the beginning.

THE NEXT NET, which will offer high-speed access to everyone at any time, will necessitate an end-to-end beefing up of the existing public data infrastructure (the "infranet"). All along every line. Everywhere.

This technological commandment explains why Cisco Systems, which commands about 50 percent of the data-network equipment market (and nearly 90 percent of the key router segments), is poised to explode. Never mind that Cisco is already the fastest-growing company ever listed on the Nasdaq exchange or that, today, it is the second most valuable publicly owned company on the planet. That was only the first act.

"It is our goal to be the largest computer player ever in terms of changing the way people work, live, play, and learn," says Chambers.

Chambers's unshakable faith in the coming age of data networks and the boldness of his predictions for Cisco are softened with a disarming and self-deprecating manner that makes him a sensational salesman. "I'm not talking about numbers of employees, but about profitability and being the industry's driver. In this market, at this moment, we can accomplish exactly what IBM accomplished forty years ago in mainframes."

What is it about Cisco that has let it roll over innumerable competitors, acquire and integrate a string of small networking innovators without breaking stride, to seize the burgeoning data-networking business with a vengeance? It is not just salesmanship and a place at the heart of the IP explosion that make Cisco poised to grow exponentially. It is also having figured out exactly the right way to build its business in a market that is growing so quickly no one can possibly manage it.

The secret is to move faster than anyone else. Listen to customers. Make acquisitions. Bet the company on every move. Make a decision; don't be paralyzed. Sell.

For all the company's strengths, for all its market-maker power and aggressive execution, Cisco by no means has the market to itself. "The telco equipment market is thoroughly multivendor-based," explains Joseph Baylock of Gartner Inc. "This is no slam-dunk for Cisco. No matter how much the company may preach end-to-end Cisco gear, in the IP world everyone's equipment works with everyone else's. Cisco hasn't been very good at selling the advantages of an all-Cisco market, except to corporate data managers who were in the first wave of networking. In the new telco IP space, the buyers are a lot less afraid of mixing and matching boxes. That should keep opportunity hopping for all sorts of start-ups. And in the consumer space, who cares if it has Cisco inside?"

WHEN ASKED WHAT he fears most—big companies or the start-ups—Chambers's answer is immediate. "I have a list with a dozen little companies that I'm tracking very closely," he says, although he refuses to share it. "Guys who can start from a fresh sheet of paper have an enormous advantage technologically. We have to carefully integrate new capabilities into our existing product lines and that is tougher. They keep us on our toes."

There are also big, well-financed telecom companies aiming at the same space and unlikely to give it up without a fight. And the suppliers of components in the new broadband Internet of tomorrow will come from a fertile patch of start-ups, most of whom already sell chips to Cisco. Crucial parts of the new calculus of broadband include unified messaging products, faster routers, wave division multiplexing, personalized billing, DSL and cable speeds, virtual public networks, infranets, gigabit and terabit routers, customer premises equipment (CPE) that combines traditional PBXs with routers and fiber optics everywhere. It is all happening so fast that there's no telling which sectors will ultimately prevail and which will be consumed. All of these sectors are filled with tiny companies trying to gain traction with their venture money and PR firms. Some will. The ever nimble Cisco hedges its bets by investing in many early-stage telecom start-ups with esoteric technology.

Cisco is by no means indomitable, and as the data world rapidly shifts and lurches forward, new opportunities are emerging that could limit the company's growth in some new sectors. Being forced to buy companies early in their development in order to stay ahead makes it easy to buy wrong in a market with so much ferment. With so much VC money available for every team of smart engineers, lots of new companies flourished. With countless companies to choose from, the chance of buying wrong when you're a big, rich company is great.

In some ways the new network changes the locus of power from the router, which handled all data transportation out across the WAN in the old world, to a new breed of devices that provide subscriber management systems, combining fiber with IP natively. These systems allow network service providers, or ISPs, or telcos to individually manage, provision, deploy, bill, and deliver differing services to each individual subscriber over thousands of high-speed connections and, in many cases, to offer multiple types of service simultaneously over each individual connection.

Since routers are fundamentally designed to let all data traffic share their services equally, they have to be rejiggered in order to handle hundreds of high-speed access lines passing through their gateways, each with its own guarantees of service and speed. This has led to a series of complicated workarounds designed to enable IP traffic to move through constellations of routers at guaranteed levels of service and to create ways to individually bill each IP stream as it uses up network resources.

Known generically as QoS (for Quality of Service), these somewhat proprietary schemes have been pushed by Cisco and other router vendors in order to keep the primacy of the router. But companies like Redback Networks are effectively challenging that hegemony, and with the explosion of deployment in high-speed access, they are making a strong run at Cisco in this no-longer-so-niche area. Even more threatening to the continued dominance of routers is the deployment of fiber optics all the way out to the edge of the network. If a router was essentially designed to limit the use of an expensive resource (that is, telephone long-distance lines), what happens when there is suddenly a glut of that resource and its cost drops precipitously? Bandwidth is on an explosive growth curve as the capacity of glass fibers is doubling every few months. So in this new world, why limit throughput and access by going through routers? Doesn't it make more sense to dedicate as much throughput bandwidth as every user needs? Isn't it possible that metering usage will be unnecessary? Developments in optical switching, which will let any user directly connect to a destination, are likely to make routers soon seem like quaint throwbacks to the good ol' days of networking.

Each individual sector of the high-speed networking space will end up with Lilliputian competitors who may—or may not—find a niche, depending on the way the new network develops. But all of this is only the technological underpinning for the data telecommunications *business* explosion that is about to hit. In all this chaos of opportunity, IP has won. Telephone company standards and protocols, built for another era when all was controlled by a handful of telcos and carriers, have been defeated by the simplicity, ubiquity, cheapness, and flexibility of the IP language that was devised by a band of very smart computer scientists thirty years ago.

The truly significant part of the victory of IP is that these new networks of Internet and data have grown up outside the regulated and tightly controlled world of the traditional phone companies. As such they are chaotic, barely manageable, and under the control of corporations and Internet service providers and universities and individuals who have no reason to be beholden to the existing voice carriers. Better yet, these owners of the data networks have no reason to want to protect the existing voice networks.

Why does this matter so much? After all, voice is very good, universally available, and cheap in the United States.

It matters because for years trying to put in complex new telecommunications applications like call centers, follow-me phone numbers, toll-free lines, or branch-office leased lines meant negotiating with the carriers, waiting while they worked through their backlog, and then finessing the dozens of service orders and records updates and equipment provisioning requests that were needed to make the highly structured circuit-switched networks do a company's bidding. It was also very expensive. T-1 lines, with the equivalent of twenty-four individual business phone lines, take about a month to install in California and cost $1,000 a month.

Even so, in recent years these roadblocks to self-provisioned capacity couldn't hold back the creativity of business people looking to use telecommunications in new and exciting ways, and the telephone has become increasingly central to many businesses. But imagine just how much more entrepreneurial creativity will be unleashed when instead of having to work with the phone company, a business can unilaterally decide to field a new telecommunications-based application on Monday, set some World Wide Web– and IP–savvy engineers to work on it, and deploy it a week later without any contact whatsoever with the incumbent local exchange carrier.

Today new-breed suppliers—a crowd of attack carriers like Yipes, Telseon, Cogent, Luminous, and others—are guaranteeing 10-megabit data dial tone to business users, for $1,000 a month. This is the equivalent of 200 phone lines for the same price that phone companies are offering T-1 lines. Need more capacity for a particular sales promotion? Forget about weeks of back-and-forth provisioning and visits by pole climbers and linemen in trucks. Send a request from a Web browser and the bandwidth is dialed in remotely. And just as quickly, de-provision it. Pay for only what you need, when you need it. And do it from the convenience of a Web browser anywhere on the World Wide Web.

Decentralization of the control of all telecommunications will fuel the first great economic opportunity of the new century. Prices for bandwidth will fall with fiber capacity burgeoning; new carriers will put in gear that directly links data networks to it, and in the process they will cut the legacy voice carriers out of the loop; control of telecommunications will move to business from the incumbent phone companies. Sprint is already moving control and intelligence out to the edge of its ION network. The stage is set for the real start of the Information Age. Individuals will take control of their own access.

"I used to talk about technologies such as frame relay and ATM and IP," says Chambers, "but in the past year that has stopped. Now, whenever I talk with the chief executive of another company, we discuss network applications, what you can do with a network. The Internet has made everyone wake up to what might be possible if they rethought their business along these lines."

None of these transitions have required magical technology. All have been about selling the right products—products defined by "listening to customers, who always get 51 percent of the vote" according to the Chambers mantra—to solve a business need. The same idea buttresses the latest transition to data-voice-video integration.

Data traffic is already growing rapidly, while voice is stagnating, and this is so even before new high-speed-access technologies like cable modems and DSL services are widely deployed. While the end-user part of the high-speed equation (the equipment to get it) will be an enormous commodity market, that is not where Chambers is aiming Cisco. "We'll supply high-end equipment for telecommuters and home offices," he explains, "and our [DSL] boards will soon start to ship in Dell PCs, and as part of Sony and Mitsubishi set-top boxes and cable modems. But the real opportunity for us is in powering the infrastructure."

Most of this gear will be Cisco's. Everyone else has to make sure its networking equipment—from start-up to giant—works well with Cisco's. That is an enormous, and defensible, advantage. But it is not the biggest one the company has. The real secret at Cisco lies with John Chambers and his clear-headed understanding of just what it is that Cisco is selling: Cisco's Internet business model. By selling its unique and entirely New World way of doing business, Cisco is ensuring its own future while just naturally selling lots more of its own gear.

This is a virtuous cycle of business that explains the geometric growth of the company and represents a serendipitous confluence of business, philosophy, and timing that has rarely been seen. But can it last forever? The stakes to ensure that it does are so high that they are almost unimaginable. Cisco thus far has played this high-tech poker game almost flawlessly. But make no mistake, Cisco by no means has the game sewn up. In fact, it is in a battle for its very life with a ruggedly individual and ornery Canadian giant called Nortel, an old-line spin-off from AT&T called Lucent that is trying desperately to remake itself into a New Age telecommunications supplier, and a passel of well-funded start-ups in every conceivable (and inconceivable) niche.

And most troubling of all for Cisco, the telecommunications market is in the midst of a technological paroxysm that threatens to turn the tables on the entire industry several times before all is said and done. A revolution in capacity so vast that it makes the accomplishments of the semiconductor industry over the past several decades look like child's play. And all of it in the hands of a new generation of entrepreneurs who have little respect for their elders.

CHAPTER 3

RIDING THE UPDRAFT

MONEY IS AT THE HEART OF THE CISCO STORY.

Ronald Fox* is an obstetrician in Carmel Valley, California. In his early sixties, prosperous, with thousands of deliveries behind him, he knows what he's doing, and it shows. Chief of Staff for Obstetrics at a well-known hospital, he's building a second home near Lake Tahoe, on the California side. His kids are grown; he is able to take time off and likes to play golf.

One morning he was paired with a young man who looked to be in his late twenties. It was a glorious summer

---

*Name changed

day, and as they prepared to tee off the doctor wondered who this fellow might be. But Fox has a bit of the old school about him and was reserved about asking anything too personal.

The golf course is set in a residential development—a very snooty gated community with expensive lots. As they played through a few holes, the doctor found out that the young man owned a couple of the lots along the course and was building a house for himself and one for his relatives. He had retired at an apparently young age and, since neither the land nor the houses were cheap, apparently wasn't hurting for cash.

Fox couldn't contain himself for long. "What exactly do you do in order to support all of this?" he finally asked, letting curiosity get the better of him.

"I was the original mail room clerk at Cisco Systems," the young man said.

One thousand original shares received as a grant. More bought as options at friends and family rates, two cents or less apiece, before the initial public offering in 1991.

At the offering, those egalitarian sit-around-the-mailing-machine deals inflated to 100,000 traded shares. With splits and appreciation, every dollar invested in Cisco back then is worth $25,000 today.

The mail room clerk is a billionaire. Last spring another Cisco zillionaire went to the Napa Valley Wine Auction and bid $500,000 for an Imperial (the equivalent of eight bottles of wine in one) of Screaming Eagle cabernet sauvignon. The 1994 vintage was a good one, and the label is prized because of its highly regarded winemaker, Helen Turley. Still, even with the charity angle, that was $400,000 more than has ever been spent on a single bottle of wine. At the dinner after the auction, he popped the cork and proceeded to quaff it with his friends and family.

There are thousands of such stories floating about Silicon Valley, the tales of low-level clerks turned seemingly overnight into millionaires. It is just this type of mythology that has created a golden sheen around Cisco, where today an estimated 2,000 millionaires go to work each day. That is one rarefied atmosphere. Giving those employees an extra few thousand shares, or dollars, in bonuses is not quite the same motivator it might be for others.

Perhaps being rich liberates the senior management to react rationally, to think for the long term, without being restricted by how their decisions will affect short-term profits. But being that rich can also cut management off from its customers. Money changes everything, but it also makes people arrogant. It is easy to think that it is your particular personal skills and qualities that make the tides rise. It is hard for the rich to be humble and circumspect. A big part of John Chambers's role is to make sure Cisco remains grounded, a part of the mainstream, unaffected by the personal wealth of its employees.

John Chambers knows he doesn't have all the answers. He doesn't present himself as an omniscient clairvoyant with his finger on the pulse of the future. He's no genius on the order of Bill Gates. He's a regular guy, with a regular guy's demeanor and a cheery attitude. What he does present is a clear way of viewing the future, a mantra, a chant, a prayer that makes sense of the unimaginable: IP will conquer everything. He has been transfixed by it. If *he* can get it, if *he* can understand the astonishing implications of this invisible world, this torrent of data that will make voice free and bring full-fidelity video literally to every place on earth, then so can everyone.

This regular-guy persona is important to the message he carries. In a world of almost unlimited opportunity, a world rewritten by the movement of invisible, and free, bits of data, we need a common man as our guide. John Chambers is that guide, a guy who had to struggle with dyslexia as a child, who didn't go to the finest graduate schools, who failed in his first big chance and had to lay off thousands at Wang Labs—a few days before Christmas no less. Surrounding him is an aura of earnestness that befits a midlevel sales rep, not a corporate king. He's not a superstar like Steve Jobs but a guy who could sit down to dinner with the family and listen to news from the high school. He's a leader who doesn't inspire awe. His common touch makes his message of revolutionary change—of data re-creating society in a better image, of data improving the human condition—acceptable. In John Chambers we can believe.

Chambers comes by his modesty genuinely. A kind of Southern aristocrat, he grew up in the little state capital of West Virginia, Charleston, population 50,000 in its best years. In the 1950s, this Charleston of John Chambers's boyhood was an idyllic place. Leafy streets, streams for fishing, and polite, quasi-Southern gentility—very much the proper town. For John's family, it offered a comfortable life of affluence with enough politics to spice up things. The Chamberses were a prosperous, even prominent, family in the small-town aristocracy of the capital. Grandfathers were a bank president on one side and a construction company captain on the other. Dad was society's ob/gyn. He delivered all of the children of Jay Rockefeller, the Democratic governor. June, his mom, was a psychologist. They were Methodists, not Baptists. Enlightened and witty. John was the only boy in the family.

This son of two exceptionally bright parents found school a struggle. Because of his learning disability, John had to work harder than anyone else—put in more book time, more hours studying. John drove himself to be better through perspiration. It made him very serious. He married his high school girl, Elaine, and went to West Virginia University for both undergraduate and law degrees. This was a sheltered, nearly cloistered life.

Things in West Virginia started to change for the worse in the 1960s. Suddenly John Kennedy discovered the rural poor of Appalachia. Through the 1960s more and more programs targeting the state were launched. Then came black lung and the health hazard issues, environmental pollution from pits and the big chemical plants along the Ohio and Kanawha Rivers. After all the mining and union wars of the 1910s and '20s, now

came this. West Virginia became the heel of the United States.
Hillbilly stupidity. Backwoods inbreeding. Poor white trash.
Pollutants. Dirty industry. The population plummeted. Folks
moved on. Between 1960 and 1980, the population fell by
nearly 15 percent.

How quickly things changed. From the mid-1950s, when
John Chambers was in grade school, to the late '60s, when he
went to college, West Virginia became a ghost state, a back-
water stuck up in the Appalachian Mountains. Chambers became restless and decided to look around for new horizons
beyond the local country club. He wanted out of West Virginia.
It was stifling to a smart guy like him, even if he couldn't have
quite put his finger on the reason back then.

His solution was to take his bride and head for Indiana University, where he was accepted for business school. Bloomington
might not be New York or Silicon Valley, but it suited the young
married couple just fine. John was in his early twenties, from a
very small and insular world, and had never really ventured out
into the real world. He'd originally thought he wanted to be a
lawyer, but by the time he finished the degree at West Virginia
University, he already suspected he didn't want to practice. Business school seemed like the right thing for a very sheltered and
straight young man, and the combination of degrees wouldn't
hurt either career. It was the turning point in his life.

When the two-year MBA program ended, instead of return-
ing to Charleston and the comfortable life of his parents—a life
he would inherit and ultimately be subsumed by were he to return—he took a job offer from Big Blue, IBM, in 1976. At that
moment, even with the Justice Department antitrust probe
about to be pursued by the government, IBM was still on a
value and growth curve that seemed exponential and never-
ending: It started in the 1930s with its punch-card revenues; by
the 1960s, mainframes and other computers and peripherals
and everything else had made IBM the greatest technology investment story of all time. Now there was a new generation to

sell: The System 360 had just been released. It was a great sales opportunity, and the soon-to-be-dad took the job. Chambers went out on countless sales calls as one of a team of interchangeable IBM salesmen, selling the most successful computer IBM ever built.

Joining IBM was crucial for young John Thomas Chambers. It was safe. It taught him how to be a salesman—"but I didn't want to be a salesman," he claims he told the recruiters. What's more, he was very good at it. All that empathy. The Southern accent. The toughness that a smart kid who works hard all the time, diligently, can muster.

But it wasn't enough to get the young Chambers noticed. For seven years he kicked around the IBM sales hierarchy and ended up pounding the streets in China trying to sell IBM gear to a country that was at that time firmly determined to stay in the past. He wasn't getting the plum assignments, and it was obvious that he didn't quite fit the right mold for the Waspy IBM of the time. He didn't have the right stuff to break out of the ranks at the company—to make it big at IBM, you had to have engineering experience, as well as sales. After all, IBM research was world class and one of the company's strongest competitive advantages. Chambers could see the writing on the wall. When a headhunter came calling, he took a job at Wang Labs, a much smaller company that was busting out all over with orders and the delirious problem of trying to figure out how to handle lots of demand.

"The most impressive man I've ever known, other than my father, was An Wang," John has said. Even before taking the job with Wang Labs, the young IBM exec had seen its legendary founder speak. When he had a chance to pitch his case to Wang himself, John T. Chambers, the ever so earnest and hardworking West Virginia boy, convinced the Chinese American patriarch of the clan to let him handle Asian sales. "It was the trust that he put into me, that he gave me, the belief he had in me, that I'll never forget." A white American, John T. Chambers was put in charge of Asian sales for Wang Labs.

Chambers thrived in the new, smaller, less hidebound and more freewheeling company and stayed for eight years. He used his gentle, nonconfrontational personality to great effect in the Asian marketplace, and Wang grew its Asian business sevenfold during his tenure. His success didn't go unnoticed. He eventually became executive vice president for sales worldwide. That was an era when the American technology market was far ahead of the rest of the world. Wang had a business modeled on the minicomputer model: high-power specialty, but proprietary, workstations and software. This continued to succeed after it had become apparent that the standards-based PC was going to subsume it. But in the rest of the world the Wang model stayed strong for several additional years.

In hindsight it is easy to see the error that Wang Labs made in missing the transition from the era of proprietary office workstations, where it excelled, to the age of the PC. But that is only partly the cause of the dysfunctional and chaotic mess that the company had devolved into eight years later when Chambers resigned. Part of the reason for the chaos: The elder An Wang, a truly brilliant innovator and part owner of the seminal patents on random access memory, had extended his business far beyond its origins as a professional, digital desktop calculator company. Too fast. He missed the PC revolution. And he held on to a stubbornly Chinese traditional succession plan: Number One Son.

In its heyday, the mid-1980s, Wang Labs made high-priced—$10,000 to $20,000—word-processing workstations that offices would use for the typing pool and filing. But, as the PC-compatible market grew through the '80s, the days of proprietary equipment were fast ending, and Wang never figured out how to make a transition to the new world order. Chambers jumped ship to Wang just as the IBM PC was going ballistic, and ironically that product would ultimately spell doom for his new company.

But this outcome was unknowable to the thirty-something John Chambers. He was a good foot soldier, looking for a chance to excel, for someone to "trust" him. His feelings about An Wang are very strong. "I think he is one of the *best* men I've ever met," Chambers recalls. Then he pauses, one of the few times he ever pauses in an interview, and seems almost overwhelmed with emotions. "He was a great man. He trusted me with Asian sales and together we made a great success of it."

Unfortunately, Wang, the inventor and eponymous founder of the company, died of cancer in 1990. The revelation of his illness and subsequent death brought everything to a head. It spooked the stock market; and then his son, Fred, aided and abetted by a weak board and weaker executives, completely bungled the transition. Sales plummeted as customers waited to see what would happen with papa gone. The company was already in deep trouble in the face of a withering assault from Microsoft and Apple and WordPerfect and the PC troops. Holding on to its proprietary hardware and software model for too long, Wang Labs propped itself up with sales overseas, where the market was several years behind North America, as the American pipeline dried up. John Chambers was by then one of the trusted inside circle, an executive vice president. He and the crew turned a $2 billion profit in 1989 into a $700 million loss the following year. The speed of the shortfall and turnaround was what ruined the company's credibility. Had the sales channels been stocked? Were the books cooked? Was it all innocent incompetence? The inevitable litigation was eventually settled without any clear evidence of wrongdoing on anyone's part.

Investors lost their shirts, though. And employees lost their jobs. In John Chambers's last set of official acts in the fall of 1990, he fired—"I laid off," he corrects—over 5,000 Wang Labs employees in the weeks before Christmas. At the end of it, he himself resigned as well. It was a nice touch. But the real stripes he earned by maintaining the executive's stiff upper lip and following orders were noticed in a very different place, on the other side of the United States. John Morgridge, the president of a small networking company, and his main investor, a venture capitalist in northern California named Don Valentine, were looking for a few good executives when Chambers mailed out several dozen letters in his search for a job. It was the end of January. He'd been out of work for a month. He flew out to meet the guys at Cisco.

They were the only ones to respond to his letters.

IT IS A Monday night meeting sponsored by the Churchill Club, a kind of public-affairs forum in Silicon Valley. A year after his speech to the midlevel managers—seven years in Internet time—Chambers has returned to Rickey's Hyatt House in Palo Alto to give another address, this one to an evening crowd of Silicon Valley managers who pride themselves on being informed about public affairs and politics. This crowd is well dressed, ready for the dinner and the chance to hear the Cisco CEO speak about the future of the Internet.

But tonight Chambers isn't just speaking about the Internet or the World Wide Web. He's also here to further perpetuate the mythology of Cisco, the company that is leading all others into the Next Great Net adventure. He stands before a rapt audience. It is as though they can see standing behind him the thousands of millionaires his company has helped create. To the audience, filled with managers and executives from other Silicon Valley firms, this Everyman is what they can become. Listen to him, take his knowledge and put it into action, and—who knows?—perhaps they and their companies can breathe the rarefied air of success the Cisco way. March forward with quarterly revenues and profits up in the 50 percent range for years on end. Ride the eternally cresting Internet wave into financial glory. Master every competitive challenge. Vanquish every foe. Follow the Cisco path.

Cisco's is a remarkable and enviable management history, a casebook study in riding the tide of a technology groundswell on to fame and fortune. But one big chasm separates Cisco from an appointment with destiny, from being able to prove that it really is a great company with truly masterful management and the staying power to be not just a great exploiter of a rising tide, but also a navigator of its own ship. Cisco, and John Chambers, and the whole panoply of vendors and buyers and suppliers and staffers that make up its entire ecosystem *need* to weather a downturn. Until this company is tested, Cisco is going to be lucky and smart. Greatness requires adversity.

Or does it? If there really is anything new in the New Economy, maybe perpetual over-the-top success is part of the equation. After all, if the Internet really is limitless, why shouldn't the sun keep shining on the righteous? As he gives his speech, early in 2000, the dot-com revolution is nearing its zenith. Barely two months later the first paroxysm will hit, and valuations and stock prices will start a free fall that will call into question much of the canon of Chambers, of Cisco. But today, with hope and hype still rampant and tech stock prices still defying gravity, John Chambers is the Elmer Gantry of a new world order.

But behind his words, behind his cheery, friendly Southern boy style, is a secret that fuels Cisco, something that almost no other electronics industry company can copy. It is what has created the company so far; and, when the Internet economy hits the wall, it is what will keep Cisco minting profits as its colleagues, customers, and cohorts stumble. The company preaches a revolution to those desperate to grab on to it and uses the tools of the Internet to maximize efficiency on every front, but it operates like the Big Four railroad monopoly of a hundred years earlier.

Cisco's real secret is not in the Web or in a New Economy, but in its ability to price at a premium. Push the margins in routers to the max. This is the financial engine under Cisco's continuing balance-sheet success. Price is the unspoken secret at Cisco. The company's bids are typically 50 percent higher than the competition's. Because today it essentially holds a monopoly on routing Internet Protocol packets and because more than 90 percent of router revenues go to Cisco, it can raise prices and does so. Constantly, quarter after quarter, the price of routers has risen. Forget all the mumbo-jumbo of a new way of doing business and the big picture of the Internet. Cisco gets the kind of financial results it does because it is feeding an unceasing demand for data-networking gear and has the unique, remarkable, and unbelievable opportunity to keep raising its prices in the midst of an industry where every other sector constantly sees prices eroding. This is the only sector of the high-tech landscape where such price increases are occurring. This is not New Economy; this is New Monopoly.

The real story at Cisco is about perception: convincing customers that it has an almost mystical insight into this New World of the Internet and that buying Cisco gear will rub some of that magic off onto the buyer. This is exactly the strategy IBM used to build its empire in the '60s and '70s: Build products that do a very good job of solving the technology riddle for business folks. Use the systems internally to run the business efficiently. Provide massive, dedicated, and over-the-top customer contact and support. Create a brand name and aura of invincibility and solidity in a fast-evolving market. Deliver solidly predictable high-growth results, no surprises. Then price at a premium. IBM pulled off the same trick in both its glory days—in the 1930s with the punch-card monopoly and in the 1960s with mainframes. IBM shareholders were, not surprisingly, very satisfied with this state of affairs; Cisco's stakeholders feel the say way.

How could a Fortune 1000 executive not like doing business with Cisco? There is that wonderful technology syndrome at work here too, the famous FUD factor (fear, uncertainty, and doubt) that overcomes company managers who may understand all the technical ins and outs of their own business but are at sea in the mystical packet world of networking and computing and infrastructure. IP is not a mature technology, but a wildly disruptive one that is rewriting all sorts of customer and vendor relationships. In this Wild West where everything is changing, the one safe bet is to go with the leader. Yes, it may cost a lot more, but at least Cisco's gold-plated financial results and big sales force will be there to hold your hand.

This fear avoidance, built on by rigidly controlled message marketing, a fawning media, and a superb financial engine that keeps delivering fabulous results, lets Cisco get away with its monopoly pricing strategy without much notice or comment. Call it the Cisco Factor. Poking holes in Cisco's operations or strategies, in the face of its relentless financial success, seems churlish. But the average selling price of routers keeps going higher, while everything else in the business moves the other way. Can this really be the sign of a New Economy business?

ON THIS NIGHT in January 2000, Chambers starts right off soaring in front of Silicon Valley's young believers. He's flying, but for those who've watched him in action in recent years, the message is starting to sound a little tired, even canned. Characteristically, he goes so fast that few can catch what he's saying. "I'll share with you what we see on the global economy. When we talked a year ago about the second Internet Revolution, even though we had been doing that for four years, last year was the first time that people really started to realize that it probably was going to be a revolution. And in the last twelve months the pace of that has picked up dramatically.

"We said a year ago that we were experiencing overwhelming acceptance. But a year ago it was still isolated in business, and we said at that time government and consumer sectors were dragging behind. This has changed. Today executives in business the world over get it whether that comes from their kids surfing the Web, the press making noises about the Internet, or their business partners demanding an online strategy. Now that your CEO gets this and understands that corporate survival depends on grabbing the Internet and making it work for you, not against you, how many of them think the information services community can deliver?"

The room, filled to the rafters with Information Age cognoscenti, is silent. It is the gauntlet that Chambers is throwing down. Not just "Are you ready?" That has been his—and the company's—mantra for a while. Now he is going further, much further. "Are you good enough?" This is really the heart of his message. Cisco not only is ready, but has also been mining this opportunity for several years. Is the rest of the high-tech industry good enough to make it work? The real unspoken question: Are you as good as we are?

"But the very pleasant change in the past twelve months is how quickly government leaders get it. When we talked a year ago we talked about Blair in the UK, and President Clinton in this country, and a couple of Asian leaders. Now almost without exception most government leaders around the world get it. They understand the correlation between how they use high technology and the strength of their economies—which means the competitiveness of their businesses big and small, which relates back to preservation and creation of jobs, which relates to keeping themselves in power.

"So the government uptake has been even stronger in the past twelve months in terms of understanding. Not just from places like the United Kingdom, China or Singapore or Korea or Australia, but from areas that might surprise you, like Jordan. And Romania. These countries understand that they have a chance to participate in the second Industrial Revolution as near equal partners if they can catch onto this wave."

He pauses. There is a bit of a dark cloud floating above this sunny horizon, however. Countries get it; corporations get it; the individual consumer market, though, hasn't yet caught on. "It's lagging a bit behind the other two sectors," Chambers has admitted in several comments over the past year. Furthermore, the service provider/carrier/Internet host/application services marketplace, the booming Internet network infrastructure delivery business, has been all hard slogging for Cisco and is still by no means an unalloyed success. It is in addressing these two recalcitrant markets that Cisco has encountered the only cloudy days in the past two decades.

There are four crucial market segments for network transmission equipment today: carriers and new Internet-style service providers, businesses from enterprises down to small and midsized companies, governments, and consumers. In the enterprise/business sector, Cisco reigns supreme. It is likely to extend that lead into the government arena as well. Governments are a perfect market for the FUD marketing scheme that is deep into deployment at Cisco. Nowhere is it more important to be safe than in a government purchasing agent's world. As we all know, government pork offers the perfect opportunity for a preferred vendor. This seems like a natural next market for Cisco—hence the Chambers emphasis on it.

The real trouble is in two critical developing markets where Cisco has little value add to offer to counter its very high pricing: consumers and carriers/service providers. The former, likely to be the biggest single sector in coming years as every household is outfitted with its own Internet server and gateway, is concerned much more with price than with any other single issue. This makes it hard for Cisco to get its historical margins. And in the carrier and new service provider markets, filled with sophisticated network engineers, comes the most significant resistance to Cisco as an end-to-end solution. Here the biggest and greatest demand is for interchangeable and intelligent "hot boxes" from whoever supplies them. This is a market of constant one-upmanship, with big prize purses for the victors—but no rest for anyone.

The carrier and service provider market is where state-of-the-art optical developments are reshaping the landscape daily, where wireless data networks are being built all over the world. Cisco used to be in two major product lines, both of which were highly technical and geeky: routers and switches, sold to enterprises. Today, it has made billion-dollar bets in optical transmission gear that will mostly be sold to carriers and service providers of all stripes; it is readying a bevy of wireless transmission equipment for the fast-approaching untethered data market that has no current true market and uncertain prospects; and it has a strong position in cable modems and network management software for Cisco gear end to end, differing parts of solutions for voice over the Internet, video, unified messaging, firewalls, security, gigabit and now 10-gigabit Ethernet, and even cellular phone equipment. It has a consulting business on the one hand to help customers build their own networks and on the other is starting to sell turnkey services to customers who don't want to bother with their own plumbing. This is now a company with its fingers in just about every corner of the digital data universe, a universe that is growing at breakneck pace—no matter how good, or bad, Cisco performs.

Are there cracks in the Cisco edifice? Yes. But when Chambers is on top of his game, as he is on this night, he can sell his story like almost no one else. His soft accent, his self-deprecating manner, his cheery insistence on listening to whomever he is speaking with—all make him a superb spokesman for Cisco. The much deeper, unspoken question is whether this is a man who can direct and skipper a brand-new super-tanker of a corporation that is still being built . . . while it is already sailing through the icebergs.

When Chambers took over the reins of the company in 1995, sales had just cleared $1 billion. Today they have crossed $20 billion on an annual run rate. But there is a dark side to all of this. The folksy persona of John Chambers hides a barren and cynical fact of life at Cisco.

This is a company that is extraordinarily secretive. For all its talk of New World values, it demonstrates anything but. Every single contact with the press is highly controlled, regimented, and prescribed. Only a handful of people at Cisco are allowed to speak with a reporter—and with John Chambers's time booked for months in advance, don't expect a quick response. At this company, the secret isn't in its labs but in the story that it tells. Closely allied with all this is an extraordinary focus on investor relations, managing Wall Street and the e-traders by making sure that nothing uncontrolled ever emerges about the company and that quarterly earnings are always (at least for the past four years) exactly one penny better than the consensus of estimates from the Wall Street analysts. This is a company where complete control is the order of the day. That it works is indisputable. Whether it can continue to do so is another matter.

DEFINING, UNCOVERING, elucidating the character of a corporation is no easy matter in this post-twentieth-century world of spin doctors and PR firms; stock options; fresh-faced venture capitalists with sheaves of nondisclosure agreements; incompetent, co-opted, and outsmarted journalists who covered the oil industry now assigned to high-tech; mind-numbing technology that is as close to magic as our age can experience; and money, lots of money. The money swirls around everything, and everyone, and corrupts every relationship.

Maybe most of all, the search for the heart of the Net is about greed and the promise of riches. Forget the rhetoric about changing the world, forget about the noble cause of making the world a better place, and forget about inventive engineers out to push the envelope forward for the glory of science. Maybe that was the high-tech world of the 1960s and '70s, when men were men and semiconductors were baked in ovens—but the rosy glow of history tends to burnish all memories. Then came the days of the personal computer, when a coterie of hobbyist enthusiasts drove a stake into the heart of the mainframe world, created a new universe of personal software, and got rich along the way. That era seems to be ending with Bill Gates, Steve Ballmer, and the Microsoft witch-hunt.

Now the Internet seems to be writing a whole new chapter, if not a new book. The world of the Net is different because of the giant divide between the passionate users who are fueling the revolution and the coldly cynical network geeks, entrepreneurs, opportunists, and evangelists who are profiting from it. The true believers pretend that the Internet's plumbing is every bit as important as the passion of its use. It is not. The extraordinary diversity unleashed by the Internet has demonstrated the amazing creativity of human beings. But the infrastructure to deliver the Internet and whatever else it becomes is not nearly as interesting. The contrary position is especially prevalent in Silicon Valley, but the entire high-tech industry is riven with a highly inflated sense of self-worth. The industries in sum contribute about 5 percent of the jobs in America and around 8 percent of the GDP. That is significant, yes, but not exactly overwhelming.

The plumbing of this new technologically enabled world is necessary, but boring, and highly profitable, which is why it has attracted the best and the brightest—and the torn and twisted. There's little pure scientific passion in today's telecommunications marketplace, for all the action and Sturm und Drang. Who really cares about accelerating electrons to the speed of light or cramming dozens of wavelengths of light into a single strand of glass? This isn't the kind of thing that people dedicate their lives to accomplishing. The passion is to get rich. And for those who are already rich through luck, serendipity, or, in a very few cases, hard work, the goal is to get richer still.

Today at Cisco, the game is all about protecting, polishing, and propping up the market cap in order to finance ever more acquisitions. It is acquisitions that are the R&D of the new Silicon Valley. Acquisitions mean never having to actually create a soul at the heart of a company. See where the market is moving, find a company that is in the path of the movement, and get it in under the Big Tent.

Getting acquired is the endgame for every million-dollar start-up—this is the big payoff for the venture capitalists who don't actually have to make a business successful and for executives who believe that it is the point products that count, not the process of getting a company built—a process that can knit people together and create a team spirit—and along the way create a soul at the heart of a new company. After all, it is hard work selling products, extending sets of new products incrementally, keeping costs under control, building market presence and share, and finding profits. For the venture capitalists and others involved in the start-up, the message is clear: Get out now while the going is good. Don't rock the boat. The market cap for the company that acquires is what finances the wealth that will set you free. Acquiring is the skill set for the twenty-first-century up-and-comer. Acquiring is the metric by which the world judges companies today. Over and over the new conventional wisdom holds that outsourcing everything—including R&D—is the smart way to play the game.

This is the ethos of the conglomerate, but with a difference. In the conglomerate companies were acquired for opportunistic, purely capitalist reasons. Profits could be taken. In the New Economy, acquisitions are done for synergy, for creating "an ecosystem" of interrelated companies that can deliver a suite of products to customers. The problem is that by depending on acquisition for R&D, there's no core of anything left at the company. Use a supplier long enough for a critical part of the network, and those skills disappear from the company. It is as though the New Economy has taken to heart the slogan of the virtual corporation and, in the twisted logic of Silicon Valley refracted through the prism of the Internet, decided that a company is simply an empty vessel for selling products created by others, manufactured by others, and installed by others. All of this is central to the Cisco Way, and is proudly described by John Chambers as being at the "core" of the company's success. By extrapolation, he contends that this is the right business model for every company and that it is at the heart of the New Economy of the Internet.

But it is not. This model has worked for Cisco at this extraordinary time, with the gold rush in full swing and a wholly virgin emergent market spread out before it. Add the missteps of all its main competitors, and Cisco can easily be excused for believing that it has its hands around a momentous new way of running a business. This is very treacherous territory, especially since John Chambers and his colleagues at Cisco are seeing the world through the most dangerous rose-colored glasses any company can ever wear: the binoculars of market dominance.

Becoming dominant in a couple of market segments is great for the corporate ego, but usually disastrous for the long-term health of a technology company. Competitors disappear, innovation slows, and new technologies come out of the woodwork to rewrite the value equation for customers. Worse for a technology-driven company, when stagnation occurs in a core business and there is no heart of innovation and R&D inside the business, no kernel of technology and technologists who are guiding the ship, a destructive cycle of acquisitive fervor can emerge. Call it the Cisco syndrome.

Fueled by relentlessly rising market capitalization based on the rising tide of a market sector—in this case, geometric growth in Web usage—and brilliant marketplace execution, the prices of acquired companies are ever more expensive in an unending spiral, even as they show no profits and solve only a portion of the new technology riddle that is emerging. Bet wrong, and billions are spent in the wrong place. Bet right, and billions buy only a portion of the solution. Don't bet at all, and miss out on the Next Big Thing.

All of this, and more, is now afflicting Cisco, which today owns more than 90 percent of the key market sector of packet manipulation—routers, which decide what to do with every IP data packet. These were the hot boxes of yesteryear. With routers still the most accessible part of the hard-to-comprehend universe of broadband data, the journalists and investors who try to understand the market continue to see its monopoly market dominance as evidence of brilliance. And it is. But it is not a brilliance of technology or better products or cheaper prices.

Cisco leads on few of those fronts. Cisco's success comes from the confluence of a market that has been exploding exponentially for years with a sales and marketing organization finely honed to solving the business data needs of enterprise customers and the extraordinary gift of inept management at the competition. This market won't go away; it will grow as corporate data infrastructures get beefed up to support ever more extensive data flows and video and voice and data all over a single wire. And while Cisco's genius is in its ability to sell its products to enterprises, its underlying weakness is precisely that extraordinary success.

At root Cisco's real business strategy is the same as IBM's of many years ago: Buy from us, and feel good about this wild and crazy world of the Internet. This is a powerful marketing message, extremely effective in the corporate market. But there are changes afoot in the world of routing and networking, changes being endorsed by Intel and IBM and Motorola and Samsung and Nortel, that should completely shift this market in a few years. And these changes may not be good for Cisco's current business model. Worse, the company's need to see the world through the router lens fundamentally shapes its competitive view of the market, for better and for worse.

But that is only a portion of the challenge that Cisco is facing as it struggles to make sense of a data marketplace that is shifting and growing and changing on every side. This is a market that is maturing, where second- and third-generation network architects have little time for the fear, uncertainty, and doubt marketing ploys that have kept enterprise customers in thrall to Cisco (and before it, IBM). As it buys its way into fiber optics and the world of photons with supercharged prices and questionable purchases, Cisco is spending its inflated capital drunkenly, wildly, trying to buy its way into a future that it can't see. Worse, the company has missed the impending wireless data revolution almost entirely. As it glories in its complete victory in routers, it is in danger of missing the developments in garages and by competitors—in the sweatshops of Asia and the Far East, all over Europe—that are changing the ground upon which this empire was built.

Today's Internet is only a pale shadow of the bandwidth extravaganzas that are being planned for the next few years. We are at the front edge of a torrent of data capacity that will make today's 56-kilobit-per-second modems seem about as modern a way of communicating as the telegraph. Already there are credible and significant efforts to build a next-generation Internet—called Internet 2, among other things—that will provide massive bandwidth end to end. Canada has one. A consortium of U.S. colleges and manufacturers is building another. The idea is to start attempting to experiment with the services and applications that could be hosted on massive networks like these: instantaneous videoconferencing, large-scale database navigation, real-time medical diagnosis, virtual reality for design, and enormous audio and video libraries. But if there's one thing that the explosion of the World Wide Web demonstrates, it is that trying to predict what a massive increase in available capacity will produce is a mug's game. The network, which started out as an academic idea and evolved into a public free-for-all, is about to grow exponentially again.

All of this is so completely incomprehensible, so vast and nearly inconceivable, that John Chambers's gee-whiz attitude feels like a safe haven. Cisco has routers that handle millions of packets per second, and somehow that seems like a comfort zone in a Brave New World of optical revolution and wireless data and opportunity without end.

IN PALO ALTO, Chambers seems to be moving faster about the stage. He's taking his listeners through the Cisco Way—all in a soft West Virginia accent. He looks different from a year ago, when he came to Rickey's and talked to a similar crowd of middle managers. If anything, he is moving and speaking even faster than he did then. Chambers is wearing a simple blue suit, black loafers, and nondescript tie. Only his ever-present retinue evokes the image of a captain of industry. Indeed, if anything, this night he looks less powerful, seems to be perspiring more than usual; and instead of taking his jacket off, rolling up his sleeves, and mingling with the crowd, he stays on the podium, buttoned-up. Is he a little uncomfortable?

This audience wants to eat out of his hand. A few days before, a young woman, a twenty-something high-tech multimillionaire, had gushed, "John Chambers? He's my hero. He's a god!" In this room, this night, in early 2000, everyone in the room believes—these are ground-zero shock troops ready to go out and fight the crusade for a New World ecosystem. With their glazed eyes and slack, adoring faces, the people in the audience look like nothing so much as cult members. John Chambers is their guru. They don't see the bead of sweat on his upper lip.

"Now let me switch directions for just a moment and talk about product development within the high-tech industry as a whole. In periods when the industry ran slower, and different business models worked, the vast majority of product development came from internal teams. As the market begins to accelerate, you can't keep up with the customer requirements; everything moves too rapidly and you begin to see companies who were successful at this last decade understand how to develop products both internally and how to acquire them. As I've said, most acquisitions in this industry will fail. But the companies who are going to be leaders will have to have a new focus totally on acquisition as a core competency."

Cisco is the acquisition king of American high tech. By early 2000, when Chambers was speaking, the company had acquired seventy-five companies in a matter of seven years. Already widely fêted for its ability to make acquisitions work, Cisco has accelerated the pace in recent years. Chambers talks constantly about the ability to make acquisitions a core competency, and he never fails to point out that most of these fail for his competitors. Central to this argument is his belief that it is the people in the acquired company, not the products, that Cisco is after. Chambers firmly believes that products in the pipeline are only a small piece of the story. It is the skills to build new products and to integrate them with Cisco's other gear that will make the difference in the long run. Just one little problem with this view. Salesmen aren't good at motivating and inspiring engineers to make a breakthrough innovation. Design a product that customers already know they want, yes. But to create a product that was previously unimaginable requires engineering insight, an inventive spirit, genius, and perspiration, along with a bit of vision. And inspired leadership.

The master salesman listens carefully to his customers and is superb at identifying what they want to buy and making sure he frames the product as the answer to that desire. However, figuring out the product that they need to buy to stay in business tomorrow is entirely another matter. Doing that requires technology and engineering greatness. It requires vision. And one other thing: courage.

Cisco is the ultimate salesman's company. Find out what the customer wants to buy. Go out and acquire it. Sell it back to the customer at a higher price. This is why acquisitions are so important to Chambers. According to one famous story about the CEO, he has an official rule that before anyone from an acquired company is fired or laid off, both he and the former CEO of the acquired business have to sign off on the action. Or how about the acquisition team that sets up shop in the lobby of the new acquiree—in thirty days both personnel systems are merged and the new employees are fully integrated into Cisco. This isn't some kind of magic that has been discovered by Silicon Valley, although you'd be hard pressed to find any break in the gushing coverage the company gets. This is basic vertically integrated economics—but without the R&D expense. Buy a new company and its products, reduce overhead by merging redundant systems into the economies of scale that the larger company can get, drive the products into the already-developed sales channels, and satisfy the customer, who really only wants to buy from one supplier anyway.

Chambers will do almost anything he can to accommodate acquirees. The reason is simple: There is no kernel of technology leadership at Cisco. As a result, the company must be able to add new technologies as they become important to its customers. It is this chameleon-like quality, a customer-driven dedication to adding whatever is needed to make the sale, that is possible only in a company where there is no vested interest in one particular technology or another. That Cisco is greatly successful in an era of rapidly expanding demand is indisputable. Whether it can weather downturns, or market setbacks, without losing its lead is another matter. And whether it can continue to guess right, in fast-moving and evolving data markets where it has little basic knowledge—markets like optics or wireless—buying fast and assuredly without the underlying research labs that underpinned IBM and GE and AT&T, is anybody's long-term guess. Because for all the company's belief that it is leading a new revolution, this is no great innovator with a business structure designed for the future. Cisco is a great sales company, at a time when demand for its products has never slacked off. And it is a company blessed with incompetent, myopic competition so far. But if there's one other law of the high-tech age beyond Moore's Law (which refers to the doubling of semiconductor capability every eighteen months), it is that the market stands still for no one.

In some ways, Cisco's emphasis on acquisition might demonstrate both the core strength and the biggest potential weakness at the firm. For a company like Lucent, with a proud history of internal development, acquired technologies are seen as a way to jump-start internal teams with new technological skills. Cisco's core competency isn't a central kernel of defensible technology—after all, the IP world is standards-based, and there is little to differentiate Cisco's gear from any other company's router, save for marketplace momentum, hype, and perception. It is the ability to graft new teams onto the conglomerate as new areas emerge that becomes the central defining tenet of the company. For Cisco, acquisitions are not just a way to bring new technologies into the heart of the business for internal teams to exploit. They are essential to creating the company itself in its own image.

Cisco has created itself out of fielding a superb customer support and sales team and acquiring people and technologies that can add to the collection of gear the sales side sells. At bottom, Cisco is not a "traditional" high-tech company with a core technology base that separates it from all the rest of the field. And by not having a defensible core technology, the company can embrace acquisitions in an egoless way—a purely rational way. It also risks being hollowed out by suppliers who take over out-sourced mission-critical parts of the product line.

Who is leading the charge? The salesman or the engineer? Imagine Bill Gates without his allegiance to Windows. A technologist will perhaps be too committed to one or another technical solution. A corporate entrepreneur is looking only for fast growth and hockey stick opportunity all across the technical landscape. But the deep difference is that perhaps a company president who is a technologist can see the scientific trends idiosyncratically, even intuitively, through familiarity with the science. The biggest risk for a corporate executive without technology chops but with a financial juggernaut like Cisco beneath him is to know when to jettison the old way of seeing and doing things—with the router as the center of the universe—and leap onto a new horse. And to know how to do it without causing a train wreck.

Getting ahead of customers and creating powerful families of products early is the best way to create defensible territory. But that is by definition impossible if the entire corporate strategy is reactive and acquisitive. Q.E.D.

This is the heart of Cisco's opportunity and its liability. Without a technology-vested interest, it is free to reorient and remake itself repeatedly. Chambers is proud of saying that he has remade the company seven times in ten years. But for all the reactive power that implies, it also demonstrates a fundamental weakness: This is a company that has only rarely innovated on its own, almost always reacting, not leading. Cisco is very specifically not following any particular god—except the god of mammon. Give the customers what they want. Over and over, and better and better, than anyone else. What is wrong with this?

Maybe it is the secret to success in a crazy-quilt industry that is changing as fast as it is born.

CAN CISCO SURVIVE in a world where pricing for its products is tumbling, not rising? Routing will never be the same again. The irony is that routing could be important only in a world filled with voice circuits, where data had to be shoehorned in. In the coming world of almost unlimited fiber bandwidth, routing needs to be done only a few times. This means the market will be for bigger and bigger, hotter and hotter boxes that do routing—but fewer and fewer of them. In this tough market it will be hard to keep making sizzling revenues.

However, in the short term, for most enterprise customers it remains much safer to select Cisco's high-priced gear. The company has a lock on the corporate data universe, and it will not lose it for years to come. But the more businesses buy monthly data services from carriers and service providers of every ilk, the less these same companies will need to buy (versus lease or rent) hot boxes themselves in order to get broadband data services of all kinds. And as Generation X managers at companies and service providers rise up, as network geeks who know that every IP packet looks the same no matter whose router is forwarding it ascend to the levers of power, this assault from below on the pricing scale puts a lot of tension on the wire for Cisco. Intel is bringing out ever more sophisticated lines of network processors that are optimized to perform routing cheaply. Chipsets. So are Broadcom and Motorola and PMC-Sierra, suppliers and competitors at the same time. On the horizon is a new market idea for routing and telecom switching that is built around the steep pricing slope of the semiconductor industry. Routing becomes a commodity function, done in chips and slivers of silicon, not in purpose-built, high-margin routers that are mostly software, as Cisco's are, except at very large central routing centers near the heart of each region of the Internet. At the core of these new-generation routers is a different approach: on the low end, a generic routing software supplied by Nortel's IP routing software, among others, that is cheap, works with everybody's equipment, and is open and extensible; on the high end of the scale, in the monster terabit, petabit, yottabit, and zettabit router hot boxes that are just starting to show up in prototypes to challenge Cisco's top-of-the-line 12000 series, all the routing functions have to be hard tweaked anyway—and unless Cisco can keep outdrawing the young bucks, it is going to be gunned down eventually.

Could this be the beginning of the end for the router monopoly? If there is a glut of bandwidth, why not do a little basic routing, and switch everything else through the regional optical net to a few very big iron routers—BFRs in nethead vernacular. Instead of the current network topologies that make most Web page requests take twelve hops and pass through about that number of routers, in the new commodity routing model there would be half as many hops, or less. And that means fewer and fewer routers. Why bother making routing expensive when the solution is to throw cheap bandwidth at the user?

For years the company has been trying to sell its products as a family, with better performance implied, if not out-and-out suggested, if the customer chose an end-to-end Cisco network. But in a standards-soaked world such as IP, that improved performance has yet to be demonstrated. And, indeed, the company's acquisition strategy belies it. If it is relatively easy to buy companies and integrate their products into Cisco's end-to-end solution, why can't the same be done with competitive products? Currently, the reason is Cisco's proprietary operating system software, IOS. As long as the company hangs on to the idea that closed and proprietary is better than open and extensible, a day of reckoning will come. The eerie part of this is that it echoes the fatal flaw that brought down Wang Labs, where John Chambers had his own personal wrestling match with abject failure. Wang hung on to a proprietary software and hardware environment for far too long in the face of a clear customer preference for the standards-based PC model.

The answer and path out of this one might lie with technology: developing the kinds of interdependencies and advanced features that can justify end-to-end Cisco gear and higher prices. Or it lies in acquisition fervor: Keep buying new technologies and companies with overheated stock and P/E ratios to add to the Cisco comfort blanket, the lifeline for enterprise and government customers eager to avoid making a misstep. But if you buy your R&D, you will ultimately come up short as the astronomical multiples needed to buy early-stage tech companies come back to haunt you in the wake of a couple of failures—which are inevitable in this fast-evolving market. Or are they? Is this New World voodoo economics, where success is guaranteed?

Perhaps the greatest gift John Chambers brings to the Cisco story is that he is more than just an enlightened businessman. Like all great preachers, he is able to create a bridge between the tarnished reality of everyday business life and the shining city on the hill that beckons to us all, the place that can be entered by those who not only believe but also act on their faith.

And make no mistake, Chambers believes in action, has faith in competition. For all his talk of a New World, he is a ferocious Old World competitor. While the sermon he's preaching is about getting a jump on the competition, it is also about how to think in a way that can't be defeated by a competitor.

He talks of paranoia—at one point saying that maybe his team had learned the lesson too well and that in the wake of the most recent quarterly results they were too paranoid. Fifty percent growth in net income every quarter, like clockwork, is an exceptional performance on any level.

But getting the jump on the competition and staying ahead means more than innovating once. For Chambers it means taking change, and the love for change, to heart—and then grafting that onto a willingness to listen to customers. The fact that Cisco operates in a world where there is very little to differentiate it from the competition makes it an ideal player in an Internet-enabled world where there is very little barrier to entry if another company almost immediately starts to copy any Net-based innovations. This gives Chambers's comments a great deal of currency. He talks repeatedly about speed, change, and flat organizations. This is what Cisco has used to succeed. It is exactly what he preaches.

But at the very center of Cisco is a tightly wound, carefully controlled, very proprietary core. A strange balancing act, this. One side talks about the New World and a new world order and opportunities galore. The other side works to shut out any other company from enhancing Cisco products while fervently buying every new company with a product in the pipeline that can be sold and that can extend the Cisco family of products. Sell the handholding and the products, soup-to-nuts, in one big package with a bow on it. Just do it, and follow the Pied Piper of Networking's pitch, and all sorts of New World benefits will magically befall you. This is a very Old World tactic.

"How many people in this room like change?" Chambers asks the audience gathered at Rickey's Hyatt House. "On the Internet, change is all the time. And the important thing is that even though nobody likes it, you've got to build a culture that embraces it, so that each time your customer changes how they buy, you can change your organizational structure to help them buy more from you. And better. It is going to happen. When I get asked about what mistakes have you made at Cisco, as a leader, I always say one thing. This is going to surprise you. Many people think we move at lightning speed and get numerous products to market. But almost every mistake we've made has been because we moved too slow."

All this talk of speed can make your head spin. For Cisco— a company built around routers and switches and an IP packet technology core, as well as strategic acquisitions—swift reaction to customer needs is the crucial operating principle. This dependence on customers—"listening to our customers is our best R&D," says one Cisco minion proudly—is both the cause of the company's great success and the heart of its weakness. Fundamentally, this is a reactive strategy, in a technology universe that is being invented, in real time, play-as-you-go. We've come to expect that great companies will lead the market. Has that changed in the New World economy?

Then there's still that Silicon Valley blind spot. The glib reference to change. And the offhanded way to get it done: "outsource, outsource, outsource." If you contract out the crown jewels, what are you left with after all? Outsourcing is one of those ideas that sound good on paper around the conference table in the entrepreneuring fantasyland of Stanford's business school. But the real world is all about actually selling something or delivering some tangible service to a customer and doing it better than anyone else can. It is hard to see how a crowd of freelancers can deliver what the real world demands. For companies with core businesses that are essential to their success, core businesses that are critical to their value add, and bricks and mortar that separate them from the competition, all this talk of rapid change may be moot for another reason as well. Change requires resources. Of course, not changing might consume them all.

So, IS THIS a company that is growing through inspired management with the kind of creative vision to anticipate the breadth of possibilities the future holds for technology? (Think Andy Grove and Bill Gates.) Or is it a business led by a top-notch salesman that is playing the rising tide for all it is worth? (Think Steve Jobs.) Is there little difference between the two?

For all its talk of New World economics, Cisco is an Old World company masquerading as a New Age force. This is one of its secrets. Keep margins high and reduce expenses by slashing costs with Internet streamlining. Sell the benefits of a sparkling new technology. Offer a safe and powerful migration path to take advantage of the new technology. Sell products that are very highly priced but that solve the business problems of customers. Cut costs and improve efficiencies in every possible place to enhance the balance sheet. Fuel continuing growth by buying, buying, buying as new technologies appear to attract customers' dollars. Sell comfort and a business model in the midst of massive change.

One of the truly remarkable things about John Chambers is that he talks about this bigger picture. Not only is he at the helm of the company that is charting the path into this New World economy—an Internet Age of unparalleled opportunity for the explorers—but he also sees clearly the need to bring the Old World into his New World. Because without these customers, the Fortune 500 customers who buy from him, he won't have a business to run.

This is one of the most phantasmagoric aspects of the network universe. Always before, the new replaced the old. Electric power replaced coal as coal had replaced water. But in this New Network World, every company can survive if it can just grab hold of this new communications opportunity and make it central to the company's basic business: improving how it sells to its customers. Sure, there is a whole new industry here, a whole new Internet and data communications industry led by Chambers and Cisco. But what is really happening is the creation of a new way of doing business—and that transcends any individual or company and opens up vast new vistas for anyone willing to embrace it all. At least, this is the mantra.

There is no doubt that John Chambers has heart. He demonstrates it over and over again in the way he talks and the way he interacts with his audiences. The key unanswered questions are whether *Cisco* has a heart—and whether it is about to be mortally wounded by one of the many competitors coming at the company from all directions.

There is only one sure thing in the business world Chambers and Cisco operate in. The phrase is a standard closer to his stump address. It is a big part of his chant, his message, and every bit as much a part of the fabric of Cisco as any of the slogans Apple has used for years. "There's only one thing I know for true," he explains, heading into his finale. "The quick and nimble will win no matter how big or small. And the fast will beat the slow."

It may be more prophetic than he wishes.

PART TWO

COMPETITION AT THE SPEED OF LIGHT

CHAPTER 4

HOW FAST IS FAST?

THERE ARE FEW CONSTANTS IN MODERN LIFE—AND FEWER YET have withstood the onslaught of the twentieth century and survived relatively unscarred. In fact, at the heart of the Quantum Age, only one fundamental constant has defined the most powerful forces of the past hundred years, and it also promises to redefine communications in the next millennium. It is c, or the speed of light. Although there have been recent experiments that have demonstrated "supraliminal" —faster than c—velocities for light in certain circumstances, the fundamental quantum implications of Einstein's equations have not yet been challenged. The speed of light is the most crucial factor in the most crucial equation of the last century: $E = mc^2$. Einstein's formulation changed the course of modern history.

Now, in an entirely different form, light is going to create a new technology and economic imperative for the next millennium.

Light is fundamental to life itself, yet it is only dimly understood by the most advanced physicists and theoreticians. The speed of light is beyond human understanding—186,282.4 miles (299,792.5 kilometers) per second. Put a different way, a single beam would travel more than seven times around the earth in a single tick of the clock. In addition, light is unaffected by basic forces like gravity, magnetism, or electricity in most cases. It behaves like waves in some instances, like beams of particles in others. Controlling, harnessing, capturing, or directing light is the single most important endeavor in the age of information. It is the new frontier through which the modern world must move in order to realize the potential for the Next Net.

Aside from its unimaginable speed, light has another attribute that is perhaps just as important: capacity. One of the fundamental rules of communications is known as Shannon's Law, after Claude Shannon, an MIT theoretician who was instrumental in laying the foundations for binary logic in computing during the 1930s. The law states that the carrying capacity of any wave-based medium, such as radio, electricity, or light, is directly proportional to the frequency of the wave. The higher the frequency, the more data capacity—or bandwidth—the wave has. Light waves oscillate at about 900 trillion hertz (terahertz, or THz), or cycles, per second, and these wavelengths are measured in nanometers, or one billionth (10^{-9}) of a meter. Therefore, each wavelength of light has the ability to carry *trillions* of bits of information if—and the key word is *if*—these waves can be controlled: deconstructed and reconstructed, modulated and demodulated, routed and switched, coded and decoded, pulsed and dimmed.

The principles of wave-based transmission have been around since Marconi figured out how to propagate radio waves to send voices over the ether, and applying them to light shouldn't be too challenging—except for the size of the physical frequencies and wavelengths involved, which are many orders of magnitude (powers of 10) greater in the former case, and smaller in the latter. In the radio world a carrier wave provides a reference baseline—like the string that connects a pair of tin can telephones—through which the transmitter and a tuner/receiver link up. Along the carrier wave, another set of waves is introduced that varies by amplitude (the size of the signal itself) for AM radio, or frequency (the rate that the wave fluctuates, or oscillates) in FM radio. The carrier wave locks the transmitter and receiver together, and the varying physical component of the signal actually delivers the information, voices, or music.

But because of the need to make radio comprehensible to human ears, it was much more complicated than the systems devised to deliver data down light waves. Imagine an even simpler system whereby the carrier wave (light) is simply turned off and on sequentially, and fast enough, to deliver a digital version of the drive-time talk show. This turning off and on—like some super-fast six-year-old flicking a light switch at superhuman speeds—is what the circuit boards in top of the line Nortel laser equipment are doing. This is the semaphore taken to the digital age and pumped up on steroids. Machismo engineering in the realm of light waves.

The magic of capacity is in the nature of light. And the entire future of communications is contained in the physics of light. The bandwidth capacity of any given signal is directly proportional to the frequency of the wave. For nearly two centuries, electronics has been involved in manipulating oscillators and crystals and other exotic human-made objects to increase the frequency of electronic equipment. The limits of human-made wavelengths are currently in the microwave area, where tens of billions of cycles per second are possible. These include microwave ovens at 2.4 gigahertz, or 2.4 billion cycles per second, up through various esoteric microwave systems that operate at around 30 gigahertz, or 30 billion cycles per second. The radio spectrum itself, which has yet to be tapped and where wavelengths are about 1 millimeter, ranges up to about 300 GHz.

This is a lot of bits, and in the world of electronics it is an extraordinary achievement. Struggling up the technology mountain has led engineers and scientists to ever more arcane solutions, finer and finer micron architectures for transistors and microprocessors, and bigger and bigger cooling solutions to mitigate the high levels of heat generated when something oscillates, or vibrates, billions of times each second. In the human-made world, tens of billions of cycles per second is pushing the envelope. But in the world of Mother Nature, light rips the electromagnetic envelope to shreds. A simple, natural wavelength of light oscillates at 900 trillion cycles per second—100,000 times faster than the fastest human-made waves, radio waves. And light packs another secret: With very slight variations in wavelength, dozens, if not hundreds, of wavelengths can be packed into a single thread of glass without interfering with one another. That translates to an upper limit potential for about 900 trillion bits of data (the actual number is marginally higher, but for most purposes using the carrier wave frequency as a guide is close enough) per wavelength, times many wavelengths in each fiber, each of which in turn is as fine as a spider's thread. What this means to capacity—or bandwidth in the language of the digital broadband world—is a breakthrough of profound proportions. We are quite literally on the threshold of being able to send from coast to coast, in one second, more data volume than passes today across the entire Internet in a single month—and this across a single glass fiber.

This conceptual possibility explains why broadband is a revolution in the making. If capacity rises to encompass this kind of extraordinary volume and does so at the pace of optical innovation in the past few years—where data-carrying capacity has been doubling every nine months or so at Nortel, which is leading the charge—all bets are off as to both the possibilities of the Next Net and the structure of the industry that will arise to supply the components and services for it. Imagine that instead of the basic power that now comes out of the plugs in every home, each household had access to the amount of electricity generated in the hydroelectric plants at Niagara Falls. The impact of this available power on economics, invention, and services would be unimaginable. But the effect would certainly be profound on the structure of society. This is what even a modest upgrading of telecom bandwidth will unleash.

In some ways this technological revolution in light and capacity overthrows all the old rules, which were designed for a world of scarcity and cacophony. Bandwidth was constrained and relatively expensive, so it had to be carefully parceled out and controlled. Data-capable machines sported all sorts of different operating systems and characteristics in order to operate efficiently in this constrained world. This was the raison d'être for the router as well as Cisco's foundation—to manage the expensive wide-area bandwidth available over long-distance lines and to allow lots of disparate machines to interconnect.

But now we are on the verge of a universe with essentially unlimited bandwidth, with new network suppliers appearing every day. It is easily predictable that in ten years every middle-class home in the United States will have access to telecommunications connections 200 times as fast, and wide, as the fastest modems of today—and at lower monthly prices. And with the World Wide Web making differing and incompatible computer systems a thing of the past, or at least irrelevant as long as every data device can talk HTML or some variant thereof, the entire underpinning of the world that Cisco so artfully exploits is about to shift massively. It is this earthquake, this exponential and elemental change in both technology and economics, that is driving the Next Network and that will power much of the next millennium.

The difference between the human-made world of electronics and the natural world of light is one of magnitude. The former requires enormous effort for small improvements in capacity; the latter starts from the most capacious wave structure known to us and is the fastest thing we've yet discovered in our corner of the universe. It is much easier to slide down the slope from the highest mountain than to climb up. But first human intellect had to conquer light, in the quantum dimension—a feat that was beyond rocket science, as much a breakthrough for our age of materials sciences as the Egyptians' accomplishment with the huge building blocks of the pyramids was for theirs.

Engineers who understand the history of technology know that in the beginning of the twentieth century Marconi manipulated so-called long waves, which were measured in kilometers and hundreds of kilohertz, and fifty years later FM radio was broadcasting over wavelengths measured in meters and at frequencies in the millions of cycles per second—or waves that were 1,000 times smaller and 10 times faster. Next came the step down to the microwave and the millimeter—now 100,000 times smaller than Marconi's waves, but it took only twenty-five years this time. Now the best and the brightest have learned how to manage, manipulate, and direct light waves, offering an almost certain view of the future, where bandwidth is wide enough and cheap enough to do anything imaginable—and if history is any guide, much more that is completely unimaginable, that will astonish and surprise all of us.

So it is almost a cruel joke foisted on the human race by a tribe of superior beings: After millions of years of moving beyond stones, after eons of learning to forge metals and craft crude tools and implements of bronze and iron and copper and tin, after a millennium of chasing after rare earth metals like gold and platinum for wealth and prestige and figuring out how to extract atomic power from infinitesimal molecular quantities of uranium and plutonium and a whole host of more arcane and dangerous rare earths and elements, the human race has finally learned to master its environment in a way that makes almost all of its efforts irrelevant. What are the odds that the most sophisticated and advanced technologies of the twenty-first century would be based on two of the most plentiful substances on earth: sand and air?

WHEN THE HISTORY of the Internet and the technologies of the new millennium are written, one compound will be the lodestone, the golden bough, the alchemist's stone for the age. In the future we won't be calling this the Bronze Age or the Iron Age or even the Information Age. The new twenty-first century, and the last half of the previous one, will be called the Silica Age—not so much for the silicon that sits at the heart of transistors and semiconductors, but for the most abundant chemical compound on earth: silica, the combination of silicon and oxygen—sand, really, those trillions of grains on every beach, in every desert, in every corner of the world. All of the crucial technology behind the Internet is based on learning how to manipulate silica. In fact, the entire modern age was built using silicon as a transistor, pouring electrons by way of electrical current into blocks of impure silicon in order to amplify microcurrents. But transistors, and the binary age of electronics and information that they created, were only setting the stage for the real revolution that was going to come—fiber optics.

The fundamental building blocks of fiber optics and the state-of-the-art science involved in using light itself to convey data for hundreds, if not thousands, of miles began in the Victorian era at expositions in London, Paris, and Chicago. A series of nineteenth-century inventors started delving into the nature of optics and light waves. Along the way they discovered a strange property of light, known as total internal reflection.

Light entering water from air is bent as it moves between the two media because of the differing refractive densities of air and water. This difference in density causes the light to bend. For instance, a straw appears to be offset inside a glass of water compared to its appearance in the air. The cause of this difference is the relative speed of light in the different media—light travels faster, and closer to its ultimate speed, in air than it does in water. Controlling this variation in speed is how lenses work in eyeglasses and other optical devices. The refracted—bent—waves can be focused in different locations depending on the exact alignment of one or more lenses.

But while much light that strikes a surface between two transparent but different media is refracted, a large amount of it does not make it through the surface at all. The issue is the angle at which the light strikes the surface of conjunction. Waves striking outside a particular angle from 90 degrees—known as the critical angle, which varies for every medium—do not enter the surrounding substance but are reflected back. This is why from certain angles a glass window will no longer be transparent but will appear to be a mirror reflecting an interior scene.

Discovering this quality of light and calculating the angles kept many a scientist at work, but it was in a kind of parlor-trick application that the public first saw the impact of this law of nature. In the great expositions of the late nineteenth century, lights were fitted underneath the water in a number of big and opulent waterworks. Because of total internal reflection, light that was shined into a column of water would stay inside the column and illuminate it as if from within. This created spectacular displays and wowed the crowds in Paris, contributing to the city's nickname, the City of Light.

Although crowd-pleasing, this fountain trick had little intrinsic value. Over the following several decades and into the early years of the twentieth century, however, a number of researchers started trying to use flexible glass fibers to carry light and images—mostly in medicine, where, for the first time, it might be possible to use a bundle of fibers to view the inside of the human body. But getting the glass pure enough to transmit the image without dissipation proved very difficult, and several fledgling efforts to create fiber-based imaging schemes were of no avail by the time of the Second World War. Glass fibers, called spun glass or referred to by the trade name Isinglass, were used as insulation but couldn't be mastered for image use by the technologies and scientists of the time.

The key technological insight that would further the science of light was called cladding, and it came about in a series of overlapping discoveries in the United States, Holland, Denmark, and Great Britain at about the same time the transistor was being developed at Bell Labs, AT&T's research branch—the early 1950s. As it turned out, the man who advanced the idea of cladding never received much recognition for his brilliance, although he had a distinguished career in optics.

His name was Brian O'Brien, and at the beginning of the decade he was president of the Optical Society of America and director of the department of optics at the University of Rochester. The school, due to the largess of Kodak and Bausch & Lomb, was generally considered to be the finest place to study light at the time.

O'Brien discovered that the answer to getting light to stay confined within a glass fiber was to coat the fiber with an outer surface—a process known as cladding—made of a substance that refracted light *less* than the glass fiber itself. The result would be that much of the light bouncing along the walls of the fiber wouldn't be absorbed but would be reflected back into the fiber, entirely due to total internal reflection. In this way glass fibers might be able to transmit images.

Unfortunately, the scientist never published his results and told only a few colleagues about cladding. One of them, a

Dutchman, Abraham van Heel, followed up on the work and proved O'Brien's theories. But, by that time, O'Brien had become distracted by a new venture. As America's leading optical physicist, he had come to the attention of Mike Todd, a Hollywood producer, one of the many husbands of Elizabeth Taylor, and a showman convinced that the future of the movies was in wide-screen formats. Todd launched an audacious scheme for a single-projector process using a large-format film—65 millimeter versus the standard 35 millimeter used in the cinemas of the day. To do this he enlisted American Optical, a leading commercial lens venture, and together they formed Todd-AO. But in order to fulfill his vision of enormous screens and massive projectors, Todd needed an optical genius. The man he pursued and won over was Brian O'Brien.

When van Heel's article on cladding finally appeared in *Nature* in 1954, O'Brien was furious, especially since there was no mention of him or his work. Because the American Optical patent team misunderstood the European format for dating and consequently filed for a U.S. patent too late, O'Brien never received a penny for discovering the crucial method that made glass fibers capable of transmitting light.

With the publication of van Heel's paper and an accompanying letter from a pair of British researchers describing a similar technique for cladding fibers to use in a medical imaging system, the cat was out of the bag. A number of optical researchers began work on creating the best-clad fibers possible. It involved sliding a high-quality, highly refractive glass fiber inside a tube of glass with a much lower refractive index. Heating the combined set of rod and tube and then drawing a fiber from the combination resulted in a glass fiber with a core of one refractive index surrounded by a glass cladding with a lower index. The result was that much of the light introduced at one end of a fiber remained inside the tube as it traveled several feet.

At this point, glass fibers were being used only in gastroscopes, medical instruments for peering into the human body.

Since these medical instruments were limited in length and needed flexibility, light dissipation was less important than the fact that a physician could see a distinguishable image. Dark, yes, but useful—the first generation of internal imaging systems were a big hit by the late 1950s, although finding other uses for the exotic fibers proved somewhat troublesome. IBM adopted fibers for its soon-to-be-obsolete punch-card readers in 1960. There were also attempts to use the fibers as Christmas decorations, and NASA tested the fibers in its Saturn rockets. But aside from their short length, the expense of the fibers was outrageous, and their brittleness made them very difficult to work with. Creating them involved gigantic and slow-turning exotic Rube Goldberg contraptions with wheels where the molten threads could cool as they were extracted or tall cooling towers where the extruded fibers could be *pulled* with the help of gravity. Without a clear and compelling economic need for them, glass fibers remained a technological footnote.

In any case, in the 1950s electronics were all the rage, as a wildfire of innovation and invention sparked by the development of the transistor threw the established tube-based electronics industry into ferment and turned the economics of technology upside down. Start-up firms appeared at an unprecedented pace, and since the techniques of manipulating semiconductors were being invented on the fly, there was no particular advantage to being big. It was the second great wave of electronic innovation after the days of vacuum tubes and radios and television in the 1920s and '30s. It would not be the last.

THE IDEA OF using clad glass fibers as conduits for information—data—was not immediately obvious. After all, transmitting an image along a bundle of fibers seemed a straightforward idea. Passing data along light had nothing very intuitive about it. The credit for the basic idea goes to a British electrical engineer by the name of Alec Reeves, who spent his entire career working for the labs at the International Telephone and Telegraph

Company, or IT&T. Although Reeves was an eccentric who spent much of his free time investigating paranormal phenomena, by 1938 he had already patented one of the most important concepts of the digital age—before the invention of the transistor or the first computers.

It was called pulse code modulation, or PCM, and it is at the heart of Napster and all of today's Internet-traded music recording, compact discs, and every cell phone call. In the 1930s Reeves realized that by using digital tools he could remove the noise and static that occurred in a prewar telephone conversation as a call passed through dozens of switchboards and switches. What he did was essentially "sample" the voice component of a call at the very beginning of the call and convert it into a digital string of zeros and ones. These zeros and ones were transmitted down the line to the other end, where they were reconstituted as intelligible speech. However, the noise that was introduced along the line was not part of the listener's portion of the conversation because it had not been present initially when the voice was recorded. This produced extraordinary fidelity for the 1930s. The basics of PCM worked out by Reeves, including sampling rates and encoder/decoder calculations, have made possible the modern world of digital music and telephony.

IT&T filed for the patent for Reeves's invention but never used it. Nevertheless, key IT&T executives realized that they had an exceptional thinker in Reeves; and after the war, they named him senior research director at the firm's Standard Telephone and Cables Laboratories in Great Britain. STC Labs was IT&T's equivalent of Bell Labs. His assignment was formidable: the development of the next-generation network for the British phone company.

Even then, in the early 1950s, it was apparent that telephone use was growing exponentially. Wires were fine for carrying signals in local neighborhoods, but when it came to creating nationwide networks, something new, with greater capacity, had to be devised and deployed. The new radio-based transmission systems that had been developed at MIT during the Second World War seemed promising and had several great advantages: Radio transmitters and receivers could be set up anywhere within line of sight, thus eliminating the need for rights of way and the laying of cables; and the capacity of radio waves for carrying data, once the microwave (or centimeter) band was reached, offered enormous potential for ramping up traffic as demand grew. For example, a 100-MHz-frequency FM signal was three meters long; moving up to 1 GHz, a tenfold increase in bandwidth, reduced the wavelength to thirty centimeters. Climbing up the capacity scale by 100 times meant using waves that were only three centimeters long. The idea was to beam a highly focused radio signal between antenna towers placed about twenty miles apart—and to encode voice calls onto the radio signal itself. As traffic increased, the radio systems would move up the spectrum, using ever-higher frequencies and smaller and smaller wavelengths, while cramming more and more traffic into the same basic infrastructure. The physics of this was ruled by Shannon's Law: Bandwidth is directly proportional to the frequency of the waves.

In order to pack more data onto the first generation of radio links, smaller waves were required. In a vacuum, or on a clear day through air, this was no problem. Thirty-centimeter microwaves could carry ten times as much data as three-meter-long FM radio signals, and they were also more tightly focused and thereby required much smaller antenna dishes for reception. The problem was the weather. Droplets of water in fog, or haze, even smog or smoke could stop centimeter waves, while the larger meter waves were unaffected. The only solution seemed to be to use microwaves, for their massive data and voice traffic capabilities, but to send these waves through some kind of controlled environment, a pipeline. And by the middle of the decade, Bell Labs and STL were hard at work devising pipes for millimeter waves. The solution that many of the world's finest scientists had decided on was hollow pipes filled with air—called waveguides—which could theoretically carry the radio-frequency-based microwaves.

The plan proved to be completely unworkable for several reasons.

First, in order to bend radio waves around corners, a pipe needed to follow a very slow and carefully prescribed arc—in practical terms, this meant buying or leasing large swaths of land on which to route the waveguides. Worse, the straight stretches of the pipe needed to be almost exactly—100 percent—straight, which made laying the waveguides prohibitively expensive. Furthermore, tiny surface inconsistencies and irregularities on the inside of the pipes caused a great deal of signal loss. Some kind of amplification was needed every few miles, and this only added to the expense and the complexity.

It wasn't long before the creative Alec Reeves decided that waveguides were unlikely to work no matter how much money IT&T and AT&T poured into the projects on both continents. At the same time, over-the-air microwave was pursued anyway, and the environmental limitations were accepted as the price to be paid for the much larger data capacity. However, Reeves was fascinated by the paranormal and dreamed of a time when he could decipher the secret of telepathy. He thought that ultimately this would be the answer to the telecommunications networks of the future. But in the meantime, he let his mind wander over the electromagnetic spectrum and came to the conclusion that the best portion of it to use in order to get vast transmission capacity was light. If only highly controlled light waves could be created and transmitted, then data—including voice in digital form—could be encoded into the light. With an average light wave oscillating 900 trillion times per second, there was enough capacity potential in a single wave to make microwaves seem like clipper ships in comparison.

By the end of the 1950s Reeves had gathered a small team of engineers to investigate how light could be used as a transmission medium. Initially, they thought of waveguides, but they quickly dropped that idea in favor of thin glass fibers. But as they investigated and studied the issue, there were two problems. First, the glass fibers of the day absorbed far too much light, making it impossible to even theoretically use them over long distances for transmission. Second, there was no available and readily controllable source of coherent—single-wavelength—light waves; and without single-wavelength light waves, the idea was dead in the water.

The development of optical transmission could have been stymied had it not been for the work of a physics professor at Columbia, Charles H. Townes, who came up with a new way to generate microwaves in the mid-1950s. Although Townes's device, called the Maser, for Microwave Amplification by the Simulated Emission of Radiation, ultimately had little economic advantage and never amounted to much more than a novelty, it nonetheless did excite a number of researchers with the possibility of using similar techniques of controlled electronic stimulation to generate light waves. The original idea was to pass a current through a crystal at just the right voltage to generate coherent microwaves of radio frequency energy. It turned out to be an interesting scientific trick, but much cheaper sources of microwaves were available from well-established companies. However, in 1960, Theodore Maiman, a scientist working for Howard Hughes's secretive think tank in Malibu, succeeded in using rubies peppered along a reflecting tube, in combination with a light source, to produce pulses of coherent red light waves, not electromagnetic (radio) waves.

The Laser (for Light Amplification by the Simulated Emission of Radiation) Age was born. While rubies were useful for proving the possibility of generating a single-wavelength light wave, they could work only in very short pulses and generated enormous heat, all of which did little to solve transmission issues. A continuous source of light was needed so that data could be modulated or encoded within the beam. But it seemed only a matter of time before lasers would be perfected.

In late 1960 Bell Labs demonstrated the first gas laser, developed by an Iranian-born scientist, Ali Javan. Javan's device consisted of a tube of helium mixed with a touch of neon, stimulated with an electric current passing through it. In just the right arrangement, the tube emitted a continuous wave of infrared light at very low power. Scientists at Bell Labs further refined the gas laser, and within a couple of years the highly focused beams were being investigated as alternatives to sending microwaves through waveguides. Surprisingly, the tiny nanometer—0.001-millimeter—waves of laser light were not interrupted by most kinds of atmospheric disturbance. On the other hand, the highly energized beams of light would drill through the head of anyone unfortunate enough to get in the way. So while the beam had the potential for carrying a great deal of data, it needed to be directed into some kind of advantageous pipeline to have any hope of transmitting data for phone companies. With reliability the benchmark of the monopoly phone companies of the time, lasers looked promising from a potential capacity point of view, but they were far too finicky for day-to-day use.

Then, in 1962, the first semiconductor lasers were demonstrated by a trio of researchers at MIT: Robert Rediker, Tom Quist, and Robert Keyes. Most transistor devices—consisting of a sandwich of negatively and positively charged semiconductor material—emit energy when a current is passed through them. In a transistor made of silicon, energy is released as heat, an unfortunate by-product of the device's fundamental operation. Could that energy be turned into light in the right circumstances?

In the 1960s, just after the golden age of the transistor, when the integrated circuit had been devised, every electronics researcher was studying semiconductors. The IC, which allowed numerous transistor-based devices to be integrated, or combined, on a single "chip," solved the "tyranny of numbers" that had promised to stall the electronics revolution in its tracks. (Attaching hundreds of electronics components together by hand was not only tedious, but also introduced enormous opportunities for hard-to-locate human errors in very sophisticated gear.) By integrating lots of electronic components onto single microscopic chips, it was possible to debug one single device, interconnect hundreds (by now millions) of components, and save space and power. As a result we were able to conquer space and set in motion the electronics revolution that continues today.

Researchers started looking into other substances, similar in molecular composition to silicon, that might be manipulated into performing semiconductor-type functions. The three MIT researchers were working with gallium arsenide, which in a particular formulation and at exceptionally low temperatures—minus 321 degrees Fahrenheit—emitted single-wavelength coherent light as a by-product of its transistor function.

Because of its complexity and the tribulations involved in working with cryogenic temperatures, the research project had little practical application. However, within months of its announcement, bands of researchers at GE and IBM improved on the innovation, and the semiconductor laser was born.

It would take fifteen more years to perfect the gallium arsenide laser so that it worked at room temperatures. At first, generating a single pulse of laser light took as much current as that needed to run a freezer, piped into a tiny sliver of a semiconductor device smaller than a child's fingernail. The power problem was solved by more sophisticated semiconductor technology, called heterojunctions. First discovered and perfected by a Russian team led by Zhores Alferov in St. Petersburg, the procedure "grew" further layers within the semiconductor block that effectively isolated the light-emitting portion of the semiconductor, trapping the light in a single band and allowing it to be concentrated more efficiently. This made semiconductor lasers viable for the first time.

By the mid-1970s, small start-ups began to sell room-temperature lasers that were guaranteed to last 10,000 hours. These tiny blocks of semiconductor had tightly controlled light-emitting characteristics and a narrow range of wavelengths. The laser could now provide the light waves that could be used to carry data. What was still missing was a way to transport them.

The man who would ultimately change the way that data were transported was born in Shanghai, educated in Hong Kong and England, and came to work at IT&T under Alec Reeves. Charles Kao was an electrical engineer given the unpromising task of coming up with an alternative to waveguides by the ever-thinking Reeves. By the early 1960s Kao was digging into the literature on glass fibers, convinced that brand-new developments in lasers might provide a way to fulfill his boss's dream of using light waves as the means of moving data. The missing piece was some kind of pipeline for the light to pass along, and Kao thought glass fibers fit the bill. The finest glass of the time, however, was incapable of transmitting more than 50 percent of the light introduced at one end any farther than ten feet. After seventy-five feet nearly 99 percent of all the light had dissipated. This clearly wouldn't work for any kind of transmission scheme.

But Kao was a theoretician and also an empiricist. He refused to give up on the idea of using glass fibers and set about trying to solve the problem of light dissipation. He soon discovered that the dissipation was the result of two essential quantum, or molecular, factors: First, there was scattering caused by light waves hitting atoms of the glass, which then reflected the light in a direction other than straight ahead through the fiber; second, there was absorption of light by impurities in the glass. To the eye, glass may appear clear, but it is never completely optically perfect. Pure sand, or quartz, melts at very high temperatures—over 1600° Centigrade, or 2900° Fahrenheit—which is very difficult to achieve and manage. Glass blowers add potash, lime soda, and other compounds to lower the effective melting point of the silica. These compounds are invisible to the naked eye, but to a light wave that is measured in nanometers, speeding along at nearly 300,000 kilometers per second, they are roadblocks.

After discovering that theoretical work by scientists at glass manufacturer Corning had resolved the scattering problem, Kao decided to focus on the absorption problem. What was required, he concluded, was a new level of glass purity, one that, up to that time, had never been achieved. He announced his findings in January 1966 and called on the glass industry to create optically pure glass fibers.

His suggestion dropped like a lead goblet into the science world and disappeared without a trace. Kao's theoretical musings about glass and the level of loss that should be possible if impurities were reduced made little impact. However, Reeves believed in his young protégé and sent him on a five-year quest around the world to try to sell the idea of contaminant-free fiber-optic cables as a better solution than waveguides and to convince one of the world's preeminent glass makers to supply optically pure glass fibers.

While Kao's research and tireless globetrotting brought him some visibility, scientists at Bell Labs were sure that pure glass was impossible to produce, and they weren't convinced that getting it pure enough would solve the light loss issue. AT&T was deep into testing its waveguide solutions and didn't want to see glass fibers get in the way of what was likely to be an extremely lucrative contract to build light pipelines—light waveguides—all over the United States. So, even though Bell Labs had pioneered the first working lasers, and had even built a fiber drawing tower on its New Jersey campus to make optical fibers, the company management cut back funding and lost enthusiasm.

Unlike AT&T, Corning Glass listened more attentively to the Brits, especially the scientist whose theoretical work had been fundamental to rejecting scattering in the first place: Corning's Robert Maurer. By now a research manager, Maurer decided to see what he and a small team could do about producing optically pure glass. Taking two kinds of specialty glass manufactured at Corning—pure fused silica and titanium-doped ULE, or ultra-low-expansion glass—he and a few associates started creating clad glass fibers with the titanium glass on the inside and the pure fused silica as the cladding. In glass, titanium is converted to titanium oxide, which has the singular property of not absorbing any light whatsoever. However, titanium oxide also raises the refractive index of the glass, so in order to keep the light from departing from the fiber, it had to be the inner component of the fiber. For a number of reasons, it proved very difficult to make it work.

The project started in 1967, and three years later the Corning scientists had created only a single roll of glass fiber, but it showed astonishing transparency. Tests indicated that these fibers absorbed very little light and were within the parameters that Kao had calculated were necessary for loss per kilometer in order to make the project viable both technologically and economically. The loss, or attenuation, was measured in decibels per kilometer, and Kao's numbers required a loss of no greater than twenty decibels (20 db) per kilometer. Corning's new fibers actually tested at four decibels per kilometer—the laser age was about to start. The venerable glass company was careful to patent its process before revealing to the world that it had solved the light loss problems. While it sounds simple, this level of purity was an astonishing feat of engineering and manufacturing. Today the best glass fibers have an impurity level that is equivalent to one atom in billions of molecules of glass. This is the equivalent of a single grain of sand on a mile of beach. The result is that laser signals can now travel for hundreds, even thousands, of kilometers without needing to be refreshed and with only minimal loss.

Kao and Reeves were ecstatic. By the mid-1970s coupling the new lasers with these very-low-loss fibers made the possibility of using light to transmit data over medium distances not only demonstrable, but feasible. One more thing was needed: a way to amplify the light waves without having to turn them into electronic signals, where they could be regenerated but at a great cost. By the early 1980s light amplifiers started to appear, based on the rare earth metal erbium. They were first developed by an academic researcher at the University of Southampton in Great Britain—David Payne—who chanced upon the effect when he "doped," or treated, a glass fiber with the element erbium. These amplifiers effectively took in light waves on one side, amplified all of them collectively as they passed through an enriched section of fiber, and then shot them out the other side. Amplifiers allowed light waves to be transmitted for hundreds of kilometers before expensive, and complicated, regeneration of the signal was needed.

The development of the erbium-doped amplifiers was the final piece of the puzzle. However, the combination of parts was expensive, which meant that early optical transmission schemes were suitable only for long-haul transmission networks where lots of traffic was being sent. Low-loss clad glass fibers carried the signals, semiconductor lasers generated the light waves, erbium amplifiers kept the signals pumped up at high enough levels to get to their destinations, and optical sensors based on selenium converted the on-off pulses of the light into binary bits at the pace of millions of bits per second. The market timing was right too, and fiber optics was the right product for the changes that were roiling the telecommunications marketplace.

In 1984 AT&T was split up, and competitive carriers like Sprint and MCI were finally free to install their networks across the United States. Fiber optics was the preferred technology, and the industry was ready with the right products for the time. Continuous improvements were made to lasers and amplifiers, and nanometer wavelengths became standard for low-loss glass fibers as thin as a strand of hair.

After long-haul networks were equipped with fiber, the next step was to move fiber into regional areas, in order to link big customers and various telephone switching centers together. To do so, a new local area standard was formed, called SONET, for Synchronous Optical Network. The idea was to create a way for local "loops" (the communications traffic rings of fiber cable that supplied junctions in cities and office parks) to use optical fiber locally and—by supplying the interfaces—to interconnect photonically to every big long-haul and data network. One essential component of SONET was a way to ensure redundancy, so that if part of the "ring" was cut by a backhoe, it would be "self-healing." The answer was to use two optical rings, both connecting to all the same points, with sophisticated equipment to sense any break or outage and the wherewithal to instantly reconfigure everything. This made the SONET rings highly fault-tolerant but also very expensive. It was classic telco thinking. Just as the big voice switches were always installed with million-dollar backups sitting next to them, SONET was designed with a similar fail-safe—and exorbitantly expensive—architecture.

Because SONET was created in the old world of telecommunications, it was hamstrung by one big flaw that would become apparent only many years later: SONET connections were not designed to be filled up incrementally, or in a modular fashion—in other words, in the "bursty" traffic patterns that characterize the Internet universe. An entire pipeline had to be dedicated to each end-user and was always dedicated once configured—a long, complex, expensive, and typically phone company bureaucratic process. As long as the traffic was predictable and came from one location, this arrangement worked fine. But with the rise of the Internet and its chaotic and on-demand usage patterns, the SONET environment proved inflexible and too expensive. Nevertheless, the first company to deliver equipment that conformed to the standard was Northern Telecom—Nortel—which had been eyeing the digital telephony market for a while. Already the leader in digital telephone switches, Nortel had aggressively moved into small and mid-sized office phone systems with its Meridian line. At the same time, IT&T decided to divest itself of its STC Labs operation in England.

Nortel, with only a small optical contingent, bought the lab where fiber optics was born. Renaming it the Harlow Lab for its location in that English town, the company completed the purchase in 1991.

It was just in time. Until the early 1990s the fiber industry was growing along with the rest of the telecommunications industry. Long accustomed to well-planned-out schedules and predictable growth rates, the business was nothing if not methodical. With fiber equipment selling only to the largest telecommunications companies in the world, there was little pricing pressure to reduce costs or extend innovation. But looming on the horizon was the "cross-over" point, as Nortel's CEO John Roth called it—the place where faster-growing data traffic was going to overtake voice on the world's networks.

It was going to happen around 1995. And one company looked as if it had the business by the tail. Bell Labs was a marketplace leader and laser innovator and was ready to step out of the shadow of AT&T. SONET, the big telco data-transmission standard, couldn't help but win as the world's existing carriers retooled their big voice-oriented networks. Bell Labs gathered itself up with Western Electric, the manufacturing arm of old Ma Bell, and packaged itself for a spin-off as the new Lucent. It had a very successful IPO in April 1996 and became the darling of the market, roaring to new stock price highs as revenues grew at a 40 percent rate, from $25 billion in 1997 to $40 billion by the end of the century. The Internet Revolution was all about supplying the gear for the world's big existing telephone companies and a new generation of enterprise and smaller business customers who were already buying telephone services from the old AT&T.

Lucent, and its smaller and weaker cousin Nortel, had the market to themselves. How could either one fail?

CHAPTER 5

LUCENT LOST IN THE FOREST

IF A TV CREW HAD STOPPED A FEW DOZEN PEOPLE ON THE streets in the mid-1980s and asked them who was going to lead the world into the new Information Age, there is little doubt what the answer would have been. One American company was not only dominant in telecommunications but also moving heartily into computers; and although it was having a few problems related to a government-decreed breakup of its monopoly, there was little doubt that it would ultimately prevail. After all, it had the world's preeminent research institution, owned the U.S. long-distance market, and provided the only data service that global corporations could depend on. It wasn't a funny little band of ponytailed netheads out in Silicon Valley who would lead the data and optical revolutions and create the seminal products that would define the Next Net. It was surely going to be AT&T. Ma Bell.

By combining American ingenuity with a congressionally mandated monopoly, Ma Bell created the finest telephone system ever known. It stretched from one side of the United States to the other, and from the beginning its high rates for businesses subsidized telephone service for others: for the 50 percent of the population who rarely made calls and for those in locations so remote that stringing wire to their farmsteads or homes otherwise would not have been economically feasible. This near-universal telephone service made the telecommunications revolutions of the second half of the twentieth century possible.

It was a marvel of American can-do attitude. But it was also a poisonous and lugubrious bureaucratic swamp. As the single largest employer in the country, with an army of lobbyists in Washington, Ma Bell became very good at having its way. What was good for AT&T had to be good for the nation. And until the Second World War, when the American population started to abandon the hinterland in droves and headed for the new and shiny suburbs, it probably was.

The 1950s were the heyday for Ma Bell and especially for Bell Labs, its research arm. There really was no other place like it on earth. A private research institution of unprecedented size, funded by a regulated gargantuan of a corporate parent, with a charter to do both "pure" research—that is, fundamental physical and chemical investigation—and "applied" work that related directly to the world of telephony. Run by a series of enlightened technocrats with a very free hand, Bell Labs had more Nobel Prize winners than did any other institution in the world.

But its real mark of distinction came with Nobel Prizes for the two most important technology inventions of the twentieth century: the transistor and the laser. Both were feats not only of intellectual insight but also of extraordinary practical and mechanical

skills. Both would create enormous wealth, beget entire industries, fuel stock markets, and shape society for years to come.

This legacy of world-class research is one that the current
owner of Bell Labs—Lucent Technologies, the equipment maker
spin-off from AT&T—is justifiably proud to advertise. Indeed,
the company's logo displays a large-type subhead right underneath the name of the company: Bell Labs Innovations.

NEW PROVIDENCE IS an idyllic township in northeastern New
Jersey. It is a suburban oasis, a comfortable bedroom community with wood and brick houses and the tidy lawns and leafy
streets that characterize the prewar New Jersey of Nancy Drew.
Progress discovered New Providence in the 1940s, when the
largest corporation in the world decided to build its research
facility on Murray Hill, a green, wooded hillside just outside of
town. A portion of the Watchung Forest, which tops Murray
Hill, was cleared for the construction of state-of-the-art labs.

Today, the research facility has grown over several square
miles of hillside but has the pastoral appearance of a sleepy Ivy
League campus, with thick, green lawns shaded by tall, leafy
trees. Cut into one of the lawns is a helicopter pad. In another
are a couple of soccer fields. In a third a baseball diamond. Set
back about half a mile from the road, down a private winding
lane, is the main quadrangle, a cluster of yellow and brown
brick buildings.

Newer structures surround the original one, where most of
the pure science is still performed, and together they create a
massive six-story atrium, with walkways all around. The entry
to the buildings, the foyer, is vast. On one side a giant bust of
Alexander Graham Bell stands watch over the thousands who
stream through this portal every day. In another part of the gargantuan lobby, a series of glass cases highlight over a hundred
years of Bell Labs innovations and are passed each day by every
one of the thousands of employees who work in this facility.

The achievements highlighted here include the discovery of the fundamental wave nature of matter, which was a key proof of the quantum theories of the early part of the twentieth century; the transistor; condensed matter theory, which was essential to understanding magnetism and other phenomena on the quantum level; the existence of cosmic background microwave radiation, which led to radio telescopy; the laser trapping of atoms (which involved ultra-low-temperature physics); and the fractional Hall effect, which moved quantum mechanics forward by demonstrating the existence of partial charges on particles. All of these developments won Nobel Prizes for the labs; and, along with hundreds of less fundamental but equally important innovations such as the cellular phone, the UNIX computer operating system, communications satellites, digital signal processors, touch tone telephones, and even the charge-coupled device (CCD) at the heart of nearly every video and digital camera, they are celebrated in these glass cabinets. All these paeans to the past are reverential, and for good reason. The unending string of scientific achievement is unequaled anywhere else on earth.

But inside, the ediface is confusing and complex now, with a mishmash of staircases and corridors stretching for what seem to be miles in each direction. The place would bewilder any terrorist bent on destruction, but no matter how modern most of the place is, all paths seem to lead back to the original building, with its six stories of scientific warrens.

The one original building is where the wave nature of matter, the transistor, the laser, radio astronomy—all of these components of modern life—were invented, perfected, developed. It consists of floor upon floor of quarter-mile-long white corridors, set with yellow doors, each with a glass panel giving onto a warren of small labs. Some of the door windows are papered over for privacy; many have printouts and research papers heralding new breakthroughs taped to them; others emit strange orange and purple light or odd humming noises that promise extraordinary experiments; and some doors are open, offering glimpses of lab-coated scientists and exotic equipment.

Inverted eyewash units hang from the ceiling, while breathing devices and fire extinguishers are never, it seems, more than an arm's reach away. What is striking about these corridors, however, is their sparseness, which makes the intellectual force of what went on here in the last century so powerful. It wasn't money spent on luxurious quarters that made Bell Labs a preeminent research center. It was a collection of brilliant minds and a commitment to pure science. Products were an afterthought, a possible benefit of the research these scientists embarked on, but never the goal.

Today this complex, including the original Bell Labs buildings and several more traditional office units that have been built to mesh with the original campus, makes up the corporate headquarters of Lucent, the heir to Ma Bell's throne, the world's largest telecommunications-equipment manufacturer.

DOWN IN ONE of the building along one of the corridors in the original Bell Labs, David Bishop can hardly contain his excitement. Bishop, a tall, bespectacled man in his late forties, is the kind of scientist who has been attracted to this place since its heyday. "We're going to ship our first commercial optical switch today," he explains volubly. "It has been a very hard few months."

The product Bishop has been developing has been given the mellifluous product name of LambdaRouter—a refrigerator-sized device that looks like any other big piece of iron you can find inside telephone switching centers. What makes Bishop's device important is that it is the first optical switch. (A lambda, in optical parlance, is a single wavelength of coherent light, crammed full of data.) Long one of the holy grails of the optical industry, the switch connects the light waves from one fiber of glass to another, entirely in the optical domain. Today, data and information traveling on light waves must be converted to electronic bits before they can be routed and switched to their ultimate destinations—a costly and complex step for carriers. Optical switches will allow carriers to make better use of their fiber capacity in case of breakage or in case they need to change available optical pathways and routings in response to daily or hourly fluctuations in demand. Better yet, because the LambdaRouter can perform these switching functions on up to 256 light wavelengths simultaneously, it solves one of the giant problems in the optical arena. Currently each separate wavelength of light, with its own data, requires a separate set of receivers, amplifiers, routers, and regeneration equipment in order to move the light wave, crammed with data, from one route to another. This is extremely expensive.

Working with a single wavelength wouldn't be such a big deal, but in the 1980s Bell Labs devised another innovation, one that has revolutionized the optical arena in recent years. Called initially wave division multiplexing, WDM, this was the ability to split a single beam of light into a number of very closely separated constituent waves. Think of this like the prism—separating white light into its rainbow of colors—but done on the nanometer frequency level. Essentially, optical scientists could separate 980-nanometer from 982-nanometer wavelengths. To the human eye they are indistinguishable, but to a finely tuned laser receiver, all but one particular target wavelength are invisible. The result was a massive increase of capacity inside existing optical fibers. Multiple wavelengths could each carry trillions of bits, and the more wavelengths that could be isolated and used, the more capacity a given strand of glass could carry. More innovation led to *dense* wave division multiplexing (DWDM), the state of the art today, where 80 to 160 different wavelengths can rocket down the same fiber. On the horizon, through the use of esoteric "gratings" (called Fiber Bragg Gratings in the optical world), thousands of wavelengths, each of which can carry gigabits of data each second, can be packed into a single thread.

However, the limiting factor for all this innovation has been the current necessity to move the wavelengths, and their data, out of the optical, photonic domain in order to reroute, switch, and reamplify them electronically for long-distance transmission. This expensive step has made it prohibitive to bring the capacity of fiber optics unleashed by DWDM technology into regional metropolitan ("metro" in the lingo) networks, where lots of routing and switching and demand-based chopping and changing of capacity are required as demand rises and falls minute by minute with thousands of users requesting Internet Web pages and sending e-mail and using server-based applications, with little predictability. As a result, dense wave division multiplexing, with its slightly different frequencies of light allowing multiple wavelengths on a single fiber, has been economically viable only in the very largest long-haul networks. By getting optical switching into the networks at the local and regional level while solving one of the biggest expense problems for all optical networks (costly individual equipment sets for every wavelength), Lucent might be on the brink of something very important. If this product could really work, optics might become the standard way to route data and voice traffic all the way to most end users. This is the dream that fueled the run up in optical company share prices in the first half of 2000.

At the heart of Bishop's LambdaRouter is a series of 256 tiny mechanical mirrors that can move on two axes. The mirrors are created by techniques derived from the semiconductor industry—layers of various substrate compounds are built up on wafers and then etched away by various acids and compounds. The result is an array of tiny mirrors that sit on a semiconductor wafer that is about one inch square. Multiple chips like this can be ganged together to create switches with the potential to handle a thousand or more wavelengths altogether. On every mirror chip, each of the input mirrors can be focused, or tuned, to any of the other mirrors. The idea is that up to 256 input and output fibers are trained on various mirrors. The light wavelengths coming down the fiber bounce off the mirror, which can be adjusted so that it will direct that light onto any of the other 255 mirrors. In this way any input fiber can be switched to any of the output fibers—this is exactly the technology behind the so-called crossbar switches that have long enabled electronic signals to be patched and directed and that have long needed to be used to route optical signals, after conversion into electronic bits. But what is crucial in this new development is that the light and its data never change from optical to electronic, and since the mirrors can be controlled entirely by sophisticated network management software that can adjust them in less than fifty milliseconds, the device effectively provides instantaneous optical switching for a network carrier. If there is a surge of traffic on the Kansas City to Atlanta path, capacity from the New York trunk can be switched over to take care of it—all in the optical domain.

Lucent has done a great deal of pioneering work in the field of MEMS, or microelectromechanical systems—nanotechnology works with very small machines such as these, which have been used in air bags for several years and are just now gathering momentum in the world of optical switching. The mirror arrays that Bishop and his group developed are, among other things, self-assembling: Once the components are etched on a big wafer and sawn apart, the tiny microscopic arrays of mirrors—the machines—essentially assemble themselves through built-in springs and connective tissue. This assembly is crucial because the devices are far too small for human hands to manipulate. Furthermore, since, unlike transistors, these arrays have physically moving parts—the mirrors—a great deal of testing in the field has been undertaken to ensure that they won't wear out quickly in operation.

Today, in the summer of 2000, that period of testing is about to come to an end. Bishop is ready to head out to the loading dock to supervise the crating of the first actual production model of the machine, which is being sent to Global Crossing, one of the new breed of telecommunications carriers building all-optical networks. By replacing the much more cumbersome combination of routers and switches that are now deployed by the carriers to reroute and switch their optical streams, Lucent is opening the door to a "whole new world," according to Bishop, who envisions the ability to take charge of the optical data and wavelengths—and do so relatively cheaply—as a "world-changing event."

Nonetheless, there are lots of competitors in this space. While Lucent has built the first working model of a MEMS device, Nortel bought a small company in Silicon Valley—Xeos— that promises to deliver a unit with four times the fiber capacity of Lucent's LambdaRouter within a year. There are many other experienced companies and start-ups tackling this exotic market, with highly advanced solutions as well, and they promise exotic technologies too. For instance, Agilent (formerly the printer division of Hewlett-Packard) is using bubble-jet technology derived from its very successful printer business to replace the mirrors.

Ultimately it is impossible to tell what solution is going to prevail; but optical switching is on the near horizon, and it spells the end for the deployment of numbers of routers within the carrier networks. That is bad news for Cisco and explains its rush to buy its way into a beachhead in the optical world. As the core of the backbone networks gets faster and faster, as more and more capacity is available, and as wavelengths and optical light beams can be switched and stitched together entirely in the optical realm, electronic functions—such as routing every packet—become necessary less often. Bigger and bigger routers, yes. Terabit, petabit, even greater. But fewer, not more. This is the technology shift that Cisco is trying to overcome.

For its part, Lucent understands the optical universe. Even though it was slow initially to bet on fiber-optic cables (rather than light pipes or waveguides), with its early innovations in the field, Ma Bell quickly seized the light revolution and made it a central piece of the company's modern age. It was AT&T

that installed the first fiber-optic systems in the New York to Washington corridor. It was AT&T that first developed multiple wavelength transmission capabilities—called wave division multiplexing back then—that today are called dense wavelength division multiplexing, DWDM. This is the critical method dozens of metro optical networking companies like ONI, Cerent, Qeyton, and many more are using to tackle the big current market opportunity of getting the vast data capacities in the long-haul networks, through the intermediary metro networks, out to the end-users. And Lucent, along with Corning, is the world's leading maker of pure glass fibers, the critical component for the optical revolution.

But for all this technological innovation, for all the thousands of telephone companies and voice-call exchanges powered by Lucent equipment, this company still has something to prove. In the past, new products were developed at a leisurely pace only a monopolist could afford. Research was followed by slow and measured development. After five years or more, a project emerged from AT&T's equipment sheds and was sold into the networks with a guaranteed slot. But the Bell System breakup in the early 1980s changed everything. The old, venerable monopoly disbanded, MCI and Sprint emerged as formidable competitors, and then the Internet revolutionized data transmission in the mid-1990s—and all the old equipment bets were off. Venture capital is freely available to every team of smart engineers; and the fragmentation produced by the semiconductor industry, where every part of the high-tech value chain can be reduced to a chip and outsourced for faster time to market, means that competition is ferocious, product cycles have telescoped, and there is little benefit to size any longer. In this brave new world, Lucent is trying to find its way. And with the LambdaRouter project, it is trying to prove it has the right formula.

As Bishop and his boss, Cherry Murray, the newly appointed senior vice president of research at Lucent, explain it, this is the "new Lucent" at work. Bishop and Murray came straight to Bell Labs out of college in the 1970s. He was a doctoral candidate in low-temperature physics—super conductivity—and she is a world-class researcher on the structure of colloids, a kind of human-made suspension of particles that forms distinctive crystal-like compounds. Both of them spent years delving into the esoterica of their chosen fields in the halls of Bell Labs, publishing papers in obscure journals and aiming for the day when they could announce a breakthrough of pure research that would merit a Nobel Prize—or at least the acclaim of their colleagues.

Then, some ten years ago, AT&T woke up from its slumber and put out the word that utterly pure research was no longer going to be tolerated. Even the geniuses and Nobelists at Bell Labs had to justify their research in terms of the new world of telecommunications that was emerging. For David Bishop and a number of his fellow low-temperature physicists, what had been an exceedingly comfortable and undisturbed niche for well-funded pure research suddenly got a lot hotter. Super-conductivity, if it was going to have a place in the new Lucent, had to find a way to pay for itself. It could not.

Searching for a new subject, Bishop found himself intrigued by the world of nanotechnology and minute machines. Within a couple of years he had become an expert in it. As Cherry Murray explains, "He's a very good physicist, which means he can tackle anything in the field." Soon thereafter Bishop teamed with a few colleagues and made a presentation to the management of the Labs. They proposed to create a working MEMS-based mirror array for switching light. A couple of years later they had done it.

"We were pretty proud of the four-by-four grid we created," Bishop explained, "until we took it to some of the people in the development group upstairs. They told us that to have a viable product we had to make something with a minimum one hundred mirrors."

In the old days Bell Labs would have left it at that, and perhaps the scientists would have moved on to something else until a time came when their invention had applicability. But this was the new Lucent, and in the post-spin-off days the company was looking for innovative products wherever it could find them. When Bishop told Murray about his conversation with the product guys, she listened carefully and asked two key questions: "Did they think the process they had invented [for making mirrors using a semiconductor fabrication model] was scalable? Would it be stable?"

Murray is a tall, thoughtful woman in her late forties, with a classic scientist's unwillingness to promise anything more than exactly what she knows is true. Slow-spoken, methodical, and precise, she listens intently and then gathers her thoughts for an inordinate amount of time before speaking. This is no firebrand with a marketing touch; Murray is a research scientist with a prickly personality who has been promoted to manage hundreds of top-flight scientists. As a research director, she was being pressured to create new products, but her natural conservatism made her slow to overcommit. Worse, there was no model in place for bringing researchers from their ivory towers down to the street fight of product development. There had always been a wall between the two, and AT&T/Lucent was highly compartmentalized, with lots of tightly defined niche jobs and very little willingness to cross between them.

But times had changed. Murray called Bishop and his handful of fellow researchers into her office. "I'll give you eighteen months to build a product we can manufacture," she explained. The low-temperature scientists were thrilled. But the boss quickly silenced them. "Now here's the rub. You'll have to do this like a start-up, and in stealth mode. No fancy offices, no big corporate budgets, and, most of all, no hierarchy. Everybody pitches in and does everything."

It was the new Lucent's first product skunkwork. Bishop's team enlisted a like number of development engineers whose job was to take the prototypes and figure out how to actually make the things as well as to canvas customers for the features they would want if the products were developed. Starting in early 1998, they fueled a small revolution in the heart of Bell Labs. Eighteen months later they had proved the technology and convinced Murray and her superiors that this ramshackle team of eggheads could deliver on the technology and, more important perhaps, the product embodied within it.

It then took them a year to debug the product and the processes, get the software right to control the delicate mirror array, and figure out how to route all the strands of optical fiber into and out of the unit without taking up rows of racks the way previous generations of DWDM gear had. And so, on a rainy Monday in July 2000, Bishop sat in his narrow office and reflected on what he and his team had done. He was tired, but exhilarated. Critical insights had come from biophysicists, who saw parallels between his team's tiny mirrors and the flagella of tiny multicellular animals like paramecia, and from Bell Labs machinists, who created the self-assembling mechanisms in mock-ups. This was the kind of cross-disciplinary advantage one could find only at a place like Bell Labs.

But for all the *frisson* of excitement in his office that day, as Bishop made ready to go out to the shipping dock, something else was playing out in this tiny corner of the Labs. Here was a group of top-drawer physicists, ranging far from their original specialties, engaged in a seemingly desperate effort to create a new state-of-the-art optical product.

It was a few days before Lucent management would reorganize the fiber optics team that gave the company its new name into two groups—one for long-distance, or transmission, systems, the other for metro or regional systems. Each was now going to be led, not by a long-time Lucent executive or an up-from-the-ranks fast-tracker, but by two men from outside the company, two men who had come to Lucent as heads of acquisitions. It was also a few days before a Securities and Exchange filing revealed that the new chief financial officer of the company was wooed from Boeing with a cash bonus in excess of $4 million. It was a few weeks after Lucent's chief executive, Richard McGinn, had warned Wall Street that the bad news he had announced earlier in the year—reduced revenues due to a mistake in forecasting and delivering higher-speed products to customers—was going to continue for several more quarters.

Bishop was talking about "his mission" in creating the new product that he would ship that very afternoon. When asked how he motivated his team when Lucent couldn't offer the lucrative stock options of the start-ups, tears seemed to fill his eyes. Maybe it was the emotionalism of too many late nights and too much pressure. Or maybe it was something deeper, some loyalty to another time, another era, when lifetime employment seemed desirable and the motivation for success wasn't purely economic, but something more profound. "I've got a chance to change the world," he said slowly, staring out his window at the raindrops trickling off the leaves of ivy just outside. "We all wanted to do this to help save Lucent."

A noble idea, and the kind of loyalty every company craves. But is it too late?

HAVING A GREAT history and a tradition to uphold can inspire the troops, as it did for Bishop's team. And it can provide context for a corporate story.

It can also be a big weight hanging around the neck of that same corporation: The institutionalized ways of doing business that met with success in an earlier and quite different environment might be a death knell when all the rules get tossed out the window and change is the only constant. There's nothing particularly new in this. Evolution—Darwin's theory of natural selection—explains the process in the natural world, and business follows the same rules. Or call it "creative destruction," as economist Joseph Schumpeter (and later his disciple Clayton Christianson) did. Breakthrough changes in the technologies of an era disrupt all the most carefully laid plans of man and beast.

In the era of the 1950s and '60s, when product cycles were long, it was a badge of honor to be vertically integrated. In-house R&D was a sign of corporate machismo, and no one had a better research lab than AT&T. But this advantage also led to the rise of NIH—the Not Invented Here syndrome, which holds that any technology created in-house is inherently superior to one bought from outside. Nowhere was NIH more prevalent than at AT&T. The company's argument—that reliability could be guaranteed only if everything attached to the network was an AT&T product—was specious, but until the infamous Carterfone of the late 1960s, it held sway. Tom Carter, an inventor and the owner of a small company in Chicago, came up with a way to let truck dispatchers connect two-way radio systems to the phone network so that drivers could make regular phone calls while on the road. AT&T fought it, but the FCC sided with the entrepreneur. This case broke open the customer premises equipment market and allowed the Carterfone Company (which, ironically, had gone bankrupt during the long legal maneuverings, trials, and appeals that AT&T mounted) to attach alternate telephone equipment to the AT&T network. Soon the consumer had a choice of handsets, and they weren't all black. In the face of competition, Ma Bell came out with different colors as did lots of other manufacturers. Kicking and screaming, AT&T was forced to let others make equipment for its network.

Ironically, Lucent was hobbled by having a world-class research facility like Bell Labs. Since it was obvious that no one could be better than the Labs, it followed that the Labs should have first chance to develop all the products that Lucent sold. In certain fields, especially those that were related to the circuit-switched world of telephone voice calls, this was the right choice. Nowhere was there better, deeper knowledge of phone circuits than inside Bell Labs. To this day, Lucent sells the world's most advanced voice-switching gear and the telephony computer at the heart of most of the world's networks. It is called the ESS family of switches, and each costs millions of dollars.

But the world changed.

In the New Economy, with all the hype and talk of the Internet and new ways of doing business, it is easy to think that every company can grasp the principles of the New World networks and remake themselves. But there is more to it than seeing that circumstances have changed and sensing that new competitors are emerging from behind every rock. To truly remake a big company takes a different kind of leader, one who can see the path ahead of others and who is fearless and confident enough to force the rest of the troops to follow him through the breach and into the new battleground.

Richard McGinn, the long-time AT&T executive handpicked to lead Lucent into the promised land of the new Information Age, was exactly the right kind of leader to make Wall Street— and the Main Street investors who got the bulk of the Lucent stock in the spin-off from AT&T—feel good and safe about their future dividends. But he was exactly the wrong kind of man to lead Lucent into the future.

RICH MCGINN IS a slight man with thinning hair and a quick and facile intelligence. In July of 2000, there are storm clouds all around the embattled chief executive, and the company has spent months trying to avoid letting him talk about his plans for the future. Finally, however, an interview is granted just after the company announces its second-quarter results—which are not very good. Once again, Lucent has to explain why its revenues are growing at a slower pace than for the rest of the torrid fiber-optic competition, especially Nortel. At the same time, McGinn announces that he is going to sell off Lucent's micro-electronics business—its chip-making business—which is the world's largest and most sophisticated communications semiconductor operation. Three months later, when one more quarter shows further erosion in the company's financials, the chief executive will be shown the door by the board.

But on this rainy day in summer, he is still in charge, although the hushed atmosphere around his glass-walled office seems to presage some kind of change in the air. In appearance McGinn is very similar to Cisco's John Chambers; indeed, when given a chance to slam the competition, McGinn graciously refuses to do so.

McGinn is no engineer and, in fact, makes that point in the same way that Chambers does. "I'm not a technical guy," he says. The difference, and it is a significant one, is that McGinn has the head of Bell Labs—Arun Netravali—and a phalanx of scientists whispering in his ears. This certainly gives him a powerful quorum of technologists. McGinn is a history graduate of Grinnell College, a small Congregationalist college in the middle of Iowa. One of Grinnell's most famous graduates is Bob Noyce, the man who led the team that walked out of Shockley Semiconductor to create the integrated circuit at Fairchild and then founded Intel ten years or so later. Grinnell, as it happened, had a close relationship with one of the heads of Bell Labs and was one of the first schools in the world to get its hands on a transistor. But McGinn, who was a student of history not physics while in college, probably would have named Harry Hopkins, President Roosevelt's administrator for the New Deal and arguably the power behind the modern welfare state, as Grinnell's most famous graduate.

While at Grinnell, Lucent's future CEO availed himself of few science classes and left after graduation with a vague idea of getting into business. Right out of college he joined Illinois Bell as a junior manager and worked his way up the ladder until 1978, when he jumped to AT&T. Again, his native intelligence served him well, and he moved through executive slots in AT&T's international and computer services divisions. In the meantime, the company was being broken apart by the Justice Department, and its foray into computing through its acquisition of NCR in the mid-1980s failed.

Back during that period, McGinn worked to get Ma Bell, the giant gorilla, to dance when he spearheaded an initiative to buy 20 percent of Sun Microsystems. Sun was one of the primary users of UNIX, a computer operating system initially developed at Bell Labs for telephony operations, but powerful enough to have found a home in workstations and a few commercial systems. "On the same day in 1987 that the stock market crashed 500 points we were signing an agreement to buy 20 percent of Sun Microsystems," he recalls. "We didn't get much publicity that day. But we were looking at them as an innovator and starting to look for ways to learn how to play in that game." A few years later, AT&T sold its stake in Sun.

From there, McGinn was tapped to head AT&T's Network Systems division; and in the mid-1990s, when the decision was made to spin off that operation, along with Bell Labs and most of the successor operations to Western Electric, which made telephone equipment both for end-users and the heart of the networks, he came along to join the new Lucent. The first chief executive, Henry Schacht, who had run the Cummins Engine Company but who knew little about telecommunications, quickly gave way to McGinn, and for the past few years the Grinnell graduate has been running the show. (On an interim basis, Schacht agreed to return after McGinn's ouster.) The show includes nearly 125,000 employees around the world, facilities in many places, and revenues of nearly $34 billion. From the beginning, Lucent was mired in the old world of circuit switches and voice networks—almost every dollar of revenue was generated from either AT&T or the Baby Bells.

"One of the pieces of conventional wisdom in technology business is that the leaders in one generation of technology don't lead in the next," McGinn says, warming to his subject in a far-reaching discussion of the business landscape of the telecom munications and data-networking world. His office is spartan and like a fishbowl, with floor-to-ceiling glass walls that let any passerby see what the CEO is up to. In addition, he

has a big-monitor PC and a bookcase filled with personal pho-
tos of his ten-month-old son and eleven-year-old daughter,
signed footballs, and Wall Street tombstones—the Plexiglas-
encased reproductions of the title pages of stock and bond
offerings that are distributed to principal participants by investment banks—and other memorabilia. The furniture is blonde
Danish modern, the atmosphere is hushed and sleek, and he's elegantly dressed in loafers, a blue blazer, and a yellow polo shirt.

The effect is casual, but McGinn is a wound-up executive;
and his words, like those of John Chambers, tumble on top of
one another as his mind races to get from one point to another.
However, there's a major difference between the two. McGinn
tends to use big words and big concepts, speaking with an intellectual passion for his subject, but without a deep emotional
feeling for it. Chambers, on the other hand, uses simpler, more
emotional language; in person, he's more accessible, more the
common man. McGinn has thought deeply about the changes
that are surrounding him and his company and understands the
context of the revolution. He also knows exactly where Lucent's Achilles' heel is located. At least on this summer day, before he reaches the end of his tenure, he says he understands it.

"The old leaders were always tied to the technology of the
past. Those companies that are agile enough to move from S-
curve to S-curve as new technologies come along are the ones that
have sustainable durability. We've done this before, and we are
doing it again now. We moved from vacuum tubes to transistors,
even introduced the transistor. We started with analog phone systems, then adopted and embraced digital systems. We grew up
with circuit-based voice communications, and now along comes
packet technology. We've moved into this aggressively. We had
zero position in packet technology when Lucent went public [in
1996]. Zero. Today we're the market leader in providing service
providers worldwide with packet-based technology."

In the latest market share numbers released by the Dell'Oro
Group research firm, Lucent does indeed lead in the service-

provider sector. This is due almost entirely to products that were acquired when the company bought Ascend Communications a couple of years ago. Ascend, one of the early highfliers of the Internet Revolution, had made its mark by providing access and concentration gear to the early generation of service providers for the Internet and had successfully fought off Cisco's efforts to move into this market. Lucent has been able to hold on to this business, although its market share has dwindled from the better than 30 percent share that Ascend sported during its independence to about 25 percent today.

The mantra—"invention, acquisitions, and partnering are three fundamental skills for those companies that propose to be successful"—comes from McGinn as well as John Chambers and even John Roth of Nortel. Ascend was one example, but there were others as well. Some were brain-dead, such as the early acquisition of a company called Livingstone, whose products allowed lots of dial-up modems to call into a single point-of-presence—but which were entirely analog in function just as the market moved speedily to digital connections like ISDN and DSL. But Lucent didn't always get it completely wrong. More recently, the company bought Chromatis, a metro area optical company that had no sales, but a very promising way to pack more data traffic onto existing SONET rings. Unfortunately, once again SONET was an old telco standard, not a new digital IP play, and confirmed Lucent's essentially backward and telco-centered view of the market. It went along with the company's string of ATM, or asynchronous transfer mode, acquisitions to create a bigger, but not necessarily better, product mix for the future. (ATM was another telco method for moving data between end-users and SONET rings using voice circuit networks, and while offering a step up from a previous protocol that was called Frame Relay, it also is too expensive, and too inflexible and ultimately is going to be swamped by pure IP data traffic.) But the Chromatis acquisition was a sign of both McGinn's effort at remaking Lucent somehow—any way!—and his desperation. Within weeks, he installed the president of the newly acquired company at the head of half of Lucent's newly reorganized optical business. This all fits into McGinn's macro view of the changes sweeping over the business landscape.

"There are many companies today that are coming to the marketplace with the idea that they will bring forward the fruits of their great energy, their intellectual property, but that perhaps they're not trying to create the next large company. Rather they're going to seek their place in the market, and then partner up with a larger company, and then go off and do it again," he muses, letting his words catch up with his brain.

"Do you see the General Electric of today being started in Silicon Valley? It is unlikely because there's such a reduction in sustainable, competitive advantage. Today many of these advantages are defined by distribution systems, by using other people's technology like the PC industry, where lots of parts and pieces are packaged together. Or perhaps a small company does have a technology which is phenomenal, brilliant, a nova for a period of time. But that may not be sustainable over time. And when you're small, you may have certain ways of doing things that are not sustainable when you move to a large company. If you want to give options to everyone, and you're a 100,000-person company, it challenges how many you can give to each person."

Where a big company is at a disadvantage is in grafting all of this together, the advantages of size and scale to the agility and passion of the small and tightly focused. McGinn is far too smart to be blind to the problems. "By definition it is easier to be agile when you have twenty people in a small facility all signed on at the same time, or sharing the same passions—usually for an IPO. You know each of the people intimately, know their skills, know how to map those skills to one another to create something that is truly focused. But the same holds for a large endeavor as well.

You have to have a goal, you have to have a vision for what is possible, and the strategy to execute it, and you have to communicate regularly to people and acquire the best talent that is out there on an individual basis or in the acquisition of start-ups.

"If you are self-satisfied, if you are complacent, if you are lacking in the passion to make a difference, then you will fail to succeed at either a small or a large company. The combined restlessness of the people in a company is really what makes a difference. I think of it as almost akin to the American experience, because what really happens in this country is that we constantly challenge the tyranny of the status quo. It is nothing [for Americans] to think of changing our architecture, embracing the new, looking to the future, asking 'why' five times in a row—from a political standpoint, from a technology standpoint, from a management systems standpoint, sometimes even from a religious standpoint. To constantly challenge the notions of mainstream thinking.

"That is exactly what goes on here at Lucent. There is an incredible passion about moving forward, about constantly changing, about embracing the new. It is an essential part of the DNA of the place."

Maybe he is right. After all, Lucent ten years ago had a handful of customers. Today, it has thousands. Ten years ago, it had literally no overseas business. Today, one-third of its business comes from outside the United States. And to give McGinn his due, he was trying to remake the company—this past year he announced the spin-off of both the enterprise networking systems business and the Lucent communications chip-making business—before time ran out for him. "We're so new as a company and have had to go through so many changes that I don't think we've gotten to the 'legacy' stage quite yet. The pace of change is moving so fast, it is more akin to what you see inside of start-ups. That's becoming the norm. We say that if you're an adrenaline junkie, this is like dying and going to heaven because it is constant change, constant excitement, and you really have to have a passion about accepting the new and rejecting the tyranny of the status quo.

"And I would say that this excitement is what is carrying the business right now. I was, and remain, surprised by how quickly our people have adapted to the new world. What we need here are the kind of people who enjoy coming in in the morning, kicking the door down, and going after the excitement that's out there in the market, the new technologies. How many times do you get a chance to take a $19 billion company [the size of Lucent at its IPO] and to make of it what you want it to be? We've doubled the size of the company in four years, each year increasing the speed of change."

That may be true, but Lucent has been having some very tough quarters. Sales grew in the year 2000, but not at the pace Wall Street predicted. The stock has plummeted. McGinn has had to admit that the company didn't see the demand for high-speed—10 gigabits per second—optical systems in time and saw their revenues flatten, while Nortel was able to double the size of its business. Worse, Nortel is at least a generation ahead of Lucent in deploying high-speed laser systems—a lead that it will likely extend in the near future. At the same time, Nortel is now getting very close to Lucent in overall size and, after the divestiture of chips and enterprise systems, will actually be much larger than its U.S. cousin. This may not be much of an advantage.

So if it is not the technology leader, what is Lucent's particular strength? McGinn gives an interesting answer, one that is heard at Cisco with a very different emphasis and only grudgingly admitted at Nortel: the ability to partner. "We really try to help our customers succeed no matter what equipment they need to use. We have a range of skills, a range of offerings, a range of capabilities, both technologically and from the human standpoint, that puts us in a strong position with our customers. We have the ability and have demonstrated time and again the willingness to work with others, to partner with others, where we don't have all the pieces. Rather than leaving it to the customer to get all these different boxes working together, we'll come out and do that no matter who made the equipment. We are willing to embrace others' technology for the good of our clients. And we'll be there tomorrow, or two or ten years from now, to support the networks. We have staying power.

"Those are some of our big advantages. So, of course, is our ability to develop new technologies. Right now we're working on free-space optics—the ability to transmit laser light with data through the air. And there are dozens of other technologies we're working on in our labs."

This humility is something unique in the big ego game of data networking. Cisco seems determined to create entire families of equipment that bolt together seamlessly. Selection of another vendor is only grudgingly accepted by its sales and consulting forces, and the song is always that there "are big benefits for selecting Cisco gear end to end." Nortel has made a point of supplying a complete line of gear that stretches from the long-haul backbone networks all the way to the end-user, and while it has added partners in the IP arena, Nortel equipment is carefully conceived to run in its own semi-proprietary environment. Can Lucent really offer best-of-breed products in a fast-changing marketplace where this week's garage start-up is next week's hottest product? And do so with agility and innovation? In many ways it seems as if McGinn is talking about the new IBM model. Sell the company's ability to integrate both internal and external products—in effect, become a kind of networking consultation and services house—no matter who makes the boxes. He talks about sustainable advantage, downplaying the value of technology breakthroughs. He describes reducing manufacturing operations in order to be more nimble and better able to adjust. He talks about speeding up time to market and latency but never once in the interview touts any particular technology that he thinks will give the company a breakthrough the way Nortel's 10-gigabit-per-second laser systems—four times faster than Lucent's 2.5-gigabit-per-second best effort—have accelerated that company far out in front of the rest of the industry or the way Cisco's router head start and fast-track acquired switch businesses gave Chambers the edge in the corporate data-networking arena.

There seems to be a disconnect in Rich McGinn, and it is the same disconnect that one feels in the halls and corridors of Lucent. On the one hand, the company's research is so far advanced as to be almost magic. On the other, it is selling products that are middle of the road, that don't take advantage of the company's greatest assets: its intellectual horsepower. On the one hand is state-of-the-art research. On the other is slow and plodding product development and a business model that is about cobbling together other people's equipment and offering a better distribution network as the value add.

McGinn's jargon-packed discussion goes on. "Underlying technologies of optical, of broadband, of medium band or wireless, and of packet-handling switch fabrics will really be the rootstock. We will partner with mass storage for massive storage going into these networks and for better databases. The network really forms the atomic structure, both the nucleus and the electrons moving around that. Important adjunctive pieces like the servers that support the applications all are tied together in this atomic structure."

It is a kind of gobbledygook that almost sounds right but doesn't quite gel. Worse, when pushed to show his aggressiveness, to identify why Lucent is going to win in this new world, he takes the magnanimous high road, which might again be right but won't fill the company's shareholders with confidence. "I do not subscribe to the theory that there is a winner-take-all. I think it is Pollyannish to think that. I think it is unknowable by any measure, and it implies that you believe that you've already developed a secret as to how to win, how to subordinate others in terms of your leadership. I don't believe it happens because I don't believe that there is any sustainable competitive advantage. It is transient."

This is an extraordinary comment from the chief executive of a powerful global corporation. He doesn't think his company has something special that should make customers buy from him? Where's the fire here? Maybe he's right intellectually, but emotionally this cannot be a good sign. When the board finally saw this, he was finished.

"The British probably thought they had an infinitely long duration competitive advantage in the Industrial Revolution. But it was not in fact true. Things changed. I believe that any company that believes that they've got the secret is really filling themselves with hubris. That is in fact the most dangerous thing that can bring a company down. You've got to think that you know you don't have the secret, that you've got to constantly reinvent yourself because you always have this unease about where you are. And that's a positive motivator."

Perhaps, but it seems like an intellectual's argument. John Chambers truly does believe that Cisco has the magic formula, and he wants to evangelize to the world the message of the good inherent in the Internet economy. He is a member of the elect, and if you'll just listen to his sermon, he'll get you into the gates of heaven too. After one has heard the emotion and passion of the Cisco CEO, Rich McGinn sounds like an apologist.

If this is true, what then does Lucent have? He comes back to that monkey on its back, the half of the equation that Lucent indisputably owns. "It is the intellectual horsepower that really makes the difference. It is that essential defining human ingredient to envision something new, pattern recognition, to look at disparate bits of information, to conceive of something in a different way and in doing so to shake the status quo, dramatically. And then to have that be born as a new marketplace opportunity, or a new technology, or a new product. Bell Labs is a fountainhead for these kinds of ideas.

"But nobody, no firm, no individual, no group of individuals, has cornered the market on genius. It is a uniquely human quality that appears in every culture, in every part of the world. It would be hubris for any one company or individual to think that they've got it and someone else can't take it away."

The problem is that unless you really do believe that you have something better to offer, why bother?

FIFTY MILES TO the south of Bell Labs and the headquarters of Lucent is the company's biggest single facility. Located in Holmdel, New Jersey, the building is a giant black rectangular block of glass, with a central atrium so vast that it looks big enough to have its own weather pattern. This is the heart of the company's optical operations, a vast place with nearly 6,000 employees, again set in a landscape of lush greenery, miles from the nearest commercial centers or any restaurants or stores. Inside the entryway, a huge banner proclaims: Welcome to Photon City. This is ground zero in the company's efforts to hold on to the optical market, where Lucent has slipped to second place, supplanted by Nortel in recent quarters.

The area is famous in Lucent lore because about a mile down the road is a place called Crawford Hill, one of the highest spots in New Jersey. Atop the hill the first radio astronomy studies uncovered the background noise of the universe, as well as the existence of vast amounts of electric static from the heavens. Today, the building is headquarters for Lucent's wireless operations. After all, it was AT&T and Bell Labs that first conceived of the idea of cell-based mobile telephony: dividing up a region into small "cells" that would hand callers off to the next "cell" as they traveled. Originally developed for the analog world, the Bell system was called AMPS, for Advanced Mobile Phone System; it is still widely used throughout the United States today, and for a number of years supplying the gear to support AMPS has been an important part of the company's business mix.

However, Lucent stumbled somewhat with the emergence of digital wireless. Like Motorola, another leader in early analog cellular, Lucent decided to bet on homegrown American CDMA (Code Division Multiplex Access) systems, licensed from Qualcomm, rather than building expertise in the European GSM (General Services Mobile) systems. The result was that as GSM has taken off around the world, Lucent has been left behind, although the firm has now seen the light and has licensed GSM rights as well.

All of this would be of little importance, except that the next yawning opportunity in the data space after optical systems is wireless data delivery. So-called 3G systems, based on GSM technology, are starting to make their appearance around the world, and they promise Web surfing speeds for a new generation of handheld devices that may look something like cellular phones. Missing out on this could relegate any communications supplier to also-ran status and would be particularly devastating to Lucent. In the fall of 2000, the company suffered a humbling setback when AT&T announced that it would hire Nortel, not Lucent, to install and manage a new third-generation data network for its cellular phone network. Since AT&T had the largest cellular network in the world, this was the biggest wireless data contract ever signed. Lucent was the prime contractor both for the initial AMPS and the more recent digital cellular voice installations, and this is a big blow to Ma Bell's former sister company.

So, you might ask, what is Lucent's most advanced wireless group doing to ensure the company's future? Once again, Lucent is hung up on the primacy of the new rather than the opportunity of the present. One group tries to demonstrate a new breed of interactive wireless data applications, supposedly built around a new kind of e-mail client. But in several hours of trying, the young engineers who are demonstrating them cannot make them work. That in and of itself is no mark of failure—after all, demos routinely go wrong even for Bill Gates. What is worse, however, is that the product being demonstrated is pedestrian and old and not at all innovative. It is as though the isolation of these engineers has made them oblivious to the real work being done all around them.

Next up is a new antenna technology that Lucent has developed, called BLAST, which stands for Bell Labs Layered Space Time—actually quite an interesting scientific development. Radio frequency engineers and mathematicians at Bell Labs have figured out that by using an array of antennae, not just a single one, both to transmit and to receive radio signals, they can increase data capacity for wireless systems manyfold.

BLAST really is innovative and potentially quite important. In one of the labs the team shows a demonstration of the technology using a pair of handmade antennae clusters and a passel of oscilloscopes. It is quite impressive and might one day have serious applications. But when asked how far off might be any products based on this technology, the project leader says, "I'm a researcher; I know nothing about products," and the whole group laughs uproariously, as if that were a topic that never fazes them. Then he adds, "Maybe five to ten years."

Five to ten years? What are they thinking about? And while fascinating, there is just one little catch. The world is used to one antenna per device. Making use of BLAST would require at least a dozen antennae built into every device and arrayed on every transmitter. This seems likely to be an uphill battle in a world already struggling with innovation overload.

In an office high up in the black rectangle, an optical-systems manager starts talking about the kind of work that the company is doing. She describes the next phase—what comes after light waves. Called solitons, they are pulses of energy that can travel at the speed of light. They are described as being like "standing waves"—particular waves in the sea that travel intact across vast spaces . . . only these solitons do so in the quantum energy world. Because they do not decay, or degrade, solitons have the potential to travel vast distances with no amplification, and with very little interference. Imagine a soliton as a data "packet" in the photon world.

According to her, solitons are going to revolutionize fiber optics in future generations, and no one except Bell Labs knows much about them. It is the kind of scientific insight that keeps coming at you in Bell Labs, even though research into the topic reveals that the Japanese have done some of the most important practical work in the field. And while a Bell Labs theorist might have predicted their use for communications first (another of those glass-case innovations identified in the lobby of Lucent headquarters), pockets of soliton research exist all over the world. But then, this middle-aged optical division senior manager starts talking about her real passion: the retirement house that she and her husband have just completed in Colorado. She muses that she doesn't have the energy left to keep fighting the optical battles in the new world of "lots of competitors" and waxes nostalgic about the good old days when "we were really the only supplier of advanced fiber-optic equipment in the world." Now she's counting the days until she can retire.

AFTER A FEW days of this barrage of ideas and research and thinking, it is impossible not to come away wholly impressed by the caliber of the people at this venerable institution.

But for all this innovation, there's something missing. The pieces just aren't quite adding up. Is it the difference between the go-go Silicon Valley and the pastoral hinterlands of suburban New Jersey? Or is it something else?

Down on the ground floor of the big black building, Lucent is just completing work on a state-of-the-art demonstration lab: All stainless steel and advanced recessed lighting, with racks of gear and teams of demonstrators and crews of actors for hokey skits and multiscreen projectors for gee-whiz video wall demonstrations. According to the Lucent guide, the place costs "$30 million a year in operating costs, on top of at least $100 million in capital equipment costs . . . each year, what with all the new equipment in the marketplace."

The tour guide is the manager of the $100 million facility, and she dutifully sits through the heavily sales-oriented demonstration and the product demos that go along with it. One particularly well designed presentation concerns the high-speed routers that Lucent bought when acquiring Nexabit a few years ago. The presentation is about how the Nexabit routers are better than anything that Cisco has on the market for hosting streaming video across the Internet. Although the demo does have a few rough spots—the sound disappears for long stretches of time during the movie—it appears that the Nexabit routers are competitive with Cisco's gear for a state-of-the-art application like streaming video. Finally, there is a skit where the actors pretend they are going through their daily regime, all the while using Lucent gear and systems.

It's almost embarrassing that a great American company like Lucent has to resort to this kind of razzle-dazzle to sell its products and services. Nonetheless, the setting is so slick and the pitch is so earnest that it's refreshing to sit back and watch it after days of being confounded by brilliance and edge-of-the-wave inventions. For visitors impressed by the quality of the scientists, influenced by the history that surrounds them at every corner of the company, the presentation is an effective way to drive home the message that Lucent is leading the way to the future—and that it can be every bit as hokey as any infomercial pitchman.

Finally however, the tour guide proudly takes her visitors next door, where a glass-walled lab has been built to showcase not only all of Lucent's gear, but also its interoperation with competitive equipment. The idea is to provide a flexible setting for testing any customer-equipment configuration. It is a good and noble goal, even if the place is a little over the top. As we wander through the racks upon racks of gear, there are plenty of Lucent devices, along with lots of competitive equipment, but no people. It is almost hermetic. Like a networking lab from *Star Trek*.

However, finally she takes us into the "very heart of our network. This is where we run all the lab's systems. This is the soul of this facility." As she stands and waves toward the racks of gear, one thing jumps out at the casual viewer. In the very heart of Lucent's most advanced lab, at the center of the network that drives its own demonstration facility, there are no Nexabit or Lucent routers to handle all the basic IP traffic.

At the heart of the $100 million Lucent lab are three Cisco 7500 routers.

CHAPTER 6

NORTEL IN THE DRIVER'S SEAT

IT TAKES A SPECIAL BREED OF PERSON TO WANT TO WORK WITH the fastest thing in the physical world. Operating at the speed of light is a challenge that only some kind of engineering daredevil would take on. Grabbing hold of wavelengths of light, cramming data bits into them, and then shooting them hundreds of miles to resurrect them as electrical signals is not for the fainthearted. It takes a deep understanding of the physics of matter and a healthy disdain for the normal-rules of accepted engineering. It takes teams of talented engineers and deep enough pockets to stay the course.

All of this, and more, is to be found at the company founded a few miles away from the site of Alexander Graham Bell's original telephone experiments in Canada, now called Nortel Networks.

The very heart of Nortel's attack on the foundations of the Internet, ground zero in its assault on the data-processing hierarchy of today's world, is in a jumble of buildings in the Canadian capital of Ottawa, deep along the eastern edge of Ontario province. Far from the St. Lawrence or the Great Lakes that were the pathways for the economic development of Canada, Ottawa is an overgrown farm town turned capital, with none of the worldly sophistication of either of its bigger brothers: French-speaking Montreal or Anglophone Toronto. There's little about Ottawa that would make you suspect it's a hotbed of technology and even less to make any normal observer single out the buildings with discreet Nortel logos as anything much beyond processing and administrative offices.

On reflection, the anonymity seems entirely fitting. If ever there was a company that has used stealth and its position out of the spotlight to research, develop, and market a world-changing technology, it is Nortel. Ottawa is just the kind of place where Nortel could sequester thousands of optical and wireless engineers, far away from the prying eyes of competitive neighbors and the potential for overheard secrets. Of course, in the wake of the world's recent fascination with all things optical, this anonymity is no longer a secret. Today, another major producer of laser components is also headquartered in Ottawa—JDS Uniphase, which was created as a spin-off from Nortel in the time-honored Silicon Valley tradition of departing engineering renegades.

Nevertheless, Nortel's optical research labs are located in a building that looks like any other ugly office building in any town anywhere in the Western world. Four stories high, surrounded by parking lots, set in a business park along a long straight road that is filled with other nondescript buildings. Nothing would make you look at it twice.

Befitting a big company, the place comes with a cafeteria, a company store with corporate logo items of all kinds, state-of-the-art conference and presentation rooms, and even a very fancy electronic entry system that uses wireless badges to open turnstiles. Done up in a modern panoply of colors—beiges, violets, magentas—along with polished and burnished pine paneling, and designed with corridors that are angular and twisting to reduce a sense of uniformity and regimentation, the interior is a bit better than the exterior, but by no means inviting.

Down on the ground floor, a few turns around the building from the entrance, is a wall of glass and an airlock marking the entrance to Nortel's fiber-optic labs. Entrance requires donning a strip of Velcro and connecting it across the heel of a single shoe. This is a static electricity damper, and everyone in the facility has one of these attached to his or her heel. The effect is like true Canadian chic, walk around with a piece of tape on your sole, but since everyone else is similarly equipped, nobody laughs at you.

Once properly outfitted, a visitor is allowed into the vault.

The reason for controlling every bit of errant electricity is immediately evident. Racks and racks of equipment stretch in all directions. Wiring races carry dozens of cables overhead, with fibers snaking down to individual boxes. Hundreds of technicians, engineers, and scientists in white coats scurry about, plugging in this wire or that, sticking a probe into one junction or another, or just sitting on stools, silently contemplating some mysterious fine point of data transmission in the modern age. And in every one of the thousands of three-inch-high by eighteen-inch-long boxes are several slots filled with circuit boards.

Every box has at least one pair of critical circuit boards—many have several. In each pair, one board represents a receiver, the other a transmitter for laser light pulses. The idea is simple: Wavelengths of light are generated by a laser and emitted as a beam of light. The light wave itself is turned on and off billions of times each second, and each fluctuation represents another bit of digital information. These fluctuations, or modulations in the light beam, represent a string of zeros and ones, the lifeblood code of the digital age.

Essentially, the transmitter laser takes in a stream of digital information and encodes it into the light beam that the laser generates. This beam is focused on the fragile end of a glass fiber barely thicker than a human hair. The beam then travels through the fiber until it reaches a receiver circuit card, where a tiny speck of selenium turns light into electronic signals. At the surface of semiconductors made of this rare element, billions of light pulses of data are stripped out of the beam of light, decoded into an electronic signal that can be routed (or stored in a hard disk, displayed on a screen as data, or re-encoded into another beam of light), and sent to a piece of modern-day machinery or shot off on the next stage of the journey—where the whole process starts over again with the regeneration of light in another one of the laser devices.

Inside each of the laser circuit boards populating the racks of gear is a single golden device, which contains the minuscule laser, surrounded by a number of chips, integrated circuits, power supplies, transistors, bridges, amplifiers, multiplexers, registers, and memories. All of it is encased in a cooling jacket, a big gold-colored metal jacket that acts as a heat sink, radiating heat away from the magical mystical laser in the heart of the thing that is pulsing some ten billion times every second, pulsing with a light at one particular wavelength that is so rigidly controlled that a variation of one angstrom, one ten-billionth of a meter, makes it go out of tune. Temperature variations, vibrations, a breath of fresh air, any deviation from the settings that this band of scientists make on each and every laser circuit board, will destroy the $100,000 lasers. These are no mass-produced PC products. They are highly variable and hand tuned; and each laser, once sawn from its wafer and dropped into the tiny harness, has its own particular band of operating frequencies that can only be determined by extensive testing—hence, the hordes of lab-coated scientists swarming and sweating through the research facility. Worse, the science of fabricating semiconductor lasers is still more an art than a manufacturing science, and the exact frequencies that each batch will yield are unpredictable and infrequently repeatable. This uncertainty, and alchemical imprecision, is one of the key factors that has kept the fiber-optic marketplace on tenterhooks. The supply of critical optical components is never certain; and to minimize that potential for disruption Nortel has retained its own fabrication facilities, where it makes the one crucial and essential part of the process: the lasers themselves.

Gigantic by the standards of most electronic devices today, the laser assemblies measure several inches by several inches and are fed by loops of very fine fiber-optic thread. These are then connected to dozens of integrated circuits that control and adjust the data that is coursing in and out of these machines. Nortel's best engineers have figured out how to pump 10 gigabits—or ten billion bits—of data each second along a single wavelength of light. The devices themselves are an extraordinary feat, based on indium phosphide lasers, and include esoterica like Mach Zender Modulation and gas MOSFETs and Etalons and gallium arsenide multiplexers and more and more unique, incomprehensible components to lock the devices onto particular wavelengths of light. However, what is perhaps most surprising is that the 10-gigabit systems are composed of a number of discrete, or separate, components and devices, all mounted onto a single one of the big circuit boards that fit into each machine. To the uninitiated, to the outsider, these could as easily be the circuit boards of a stereo or a videotape player.

When asked how they are going to deliver the 80-gigabit systems that they've promised, and started to show to customers and at trade shows in carefully orchestrated demonstrations, the Nortel scientist—Dino DiPerna—who is explaining the device just smiles. Eighty gigabits is 80 billion bits of data a second and is so far beyond the rest of the optical world that when Nortel engineers talk about being two generations ahead of their competition—or a couple of years at the pace of innovation in this field—they might well be understating things. Lucent, after all, has been promising 10-gigabit products for two years and has yet to deliver them—and Lucent is one of the only other companies on earth with the expertise in-house to actually accomplish something of this magnitude.

In answer to the question, DiPerna reaches inside his lab coat jacket pocket and pulls out a small opaque plastic case. Stamped on it is language designed to be dismissive: "Non Operational Engineering Sample." Inside, when he opens the clasp, sandwiched between two pieces of foam, is a semiconductor chip about the size of an Intel microprocessor, perhaps one-inch square. Holding it in the palm of one hand, he picks up the big twelve-inch by six-inch circuit board assembly he has been using to explain the science of laser devices in the other. "This," and he holds up the small integrated circuit between his thumb and forefinger, "when connected to a laser and a fiber, does everything that this big circuit card can do. And better. With less power, and less to go wrong."

The Electronics Age meets the Photonic Age. Standing in the middle of this enormous room filled with wires and red and green signal lights, silent oscilloscope probes reaching deep into the gear while their screens dance with green waveforms beside racks of equipment and in the hum of electronic power supplies, with the whoosh of massive air conditioners and the animated discussions of hundreds of white-coated scientists and engineers as backdrop, it is suddenly apparent why we are on the verge of a revolution. The photon is meeting the electron in the heart of Nortel. And while electronics might be a teenager still, with all that gawky awkwardness about to bloom to maturity, harnessing light is still in its infancy, a squalling, unpredictable, and barely tameable bundle of possibility that could turn out to be the messiah.

It is hard not to be humbled. We are only at the very beginning of the quest for speed and bandwidth. Deep in the basement of a building in Ottawa, the Information Age has lurched into motion.

With a technology like fiber optics in its very earliest days, yet its engineering already far beyond the simple rocket science of the '60s—Missiles? Child's play!—what kind of person should you select to quarterback a company facing the exhilaration—or terror—of the opportunity that confronts Nortel?

The man the board of directors have chosen is a native Canadian and a Nortel lifer. His name is John Roth, and he grew up in Calgary and Winnipeg. His dad was a radio engineer for CPAir. Like most of the men of the post-war generation, cars and speed are two of John Roth's passions. He likes to tinker under the bonnet, always has, ever since he grew up as a car-mad teenager in the 1950s in Canada. He also likes to drive very fast, either out on the long, sparsely traveled highways around his rural 100 acres in Ontario or, now that he can afford to indulge himself, on racetracks.

Roth is an old-fashioned, roll-up-your-sleeves kind of engineer, sitting atop a New Age colossus. Making tomorrow's telecom networks work is part technology and part art. The technology comes from the young turks and hotshots who are raring to tweak the carburetor for another ounce of torque—the photomaniacs who keep the optical world pulsing—but there's a new gunslinger every week and in every garage. This is a young man's game—rewrit in this age of the dot-com and the venture capitalists, to a young company's game. The art is in building that technology into products that let customers be more profitable. For that it helps to have deep pockets, wisdom, and lots of experience and knowledge about selling telecom equipment to customers who resell those enabled services to consumers. And it helps to have vision.

Cisco's John Chambers certainly has a vision—it is a vision of society made better by the advent of the Internet, and of business remade in a newly swift and interconnected networked universe. But this is less a technological vision, more a sociological one. That explains much of the appeal of his sermons. It isn't necessary to be a techie to get it, and Cisco has played that melody perfectly into the nontechnical management ranks of most big companies in the world. Nortel's John Roth also has a vision, but his is a technical vision, fed by his deep and passionate love for engineering and years of designing products for customers. John Roth believes that he can read the technological winds, the tea leaves of technology, and by marrying that experience as a working engineer to a totally pragmatic economic outlook, he can divine what will happen by the relentless, commonsensical, and predictable march of science.

In John Roth—a design engineer who started in radio systems, has worked in wireless and headed the labs, been up through the ranks, run divisions and made countless sales calls—Nortel might have found just the leader it needs to take it to the next level. A man with his feet still in the engineering of the old voice world but his heart in love with the new one.

HERE'S HOW JOHN ROTH meets his customers: in November 1999, Roth, at fifty-eight years old, gets behind the wheel of an open-cockpit Formula 1 racing car. The setting is a NASCAR track located in the Poconos mountains. The occasion is one of those corporate tribal-bonding sessions between a vendor and its customers. Roth is hosting forty of Nortel's better customers at an all-day racecourse driving program. It's a chance for the CEO to escape the onstage role he's had to play, to temporarily stop being the corporate spokesman. It's a chance for him to do what he loves—to go fast, very fast.

On this crisp November afternoon, the whir, the pitch of the race car, whines in Roth's ears. He takes his path into the turn and pushes the car up near 100 miles per hour, catching the right line, sailing along. Roth's car is literally zipping around the 2.5-mile course, lapping the dozen other cars. Sixty laps around the circuit. When he finally pulls the car into the pits, he is exhilarated, and he has the fastest time of the day.

For some people, speed is a rare momentary passion—go faster, ride bigger roller-coasters, floor the accelerator when overtaking a line of traffic, wind the motorcycle out to the red line. For others, it is more than the occasional thrill. It is, simply, a way of life. John Roth lives to go fast. In person he is quiet, reserved, a classic middle-management type who looks as if he's spent years in the trenches of the corporate world. He's about six foot two, with a full head of black hair, big ears and nose, an engaging personality.

But give him a chance and he'll uncork one of his collection of hot cars—including a brand-new Ferrari 3500, an E-type Jaguar, and a Prowler—and tear around a local speedway in Toronto at speeds approaching 150 miles per hour. Or he'll bend your ear talking about engines and how to goose more performance out of a project car, a clunker, or a Formula 1 racer.

Some people relax by playing golf, others, by lazing on a tropical beach or in front of the TV set. John Roth relaxes by trying to go faster than anyone else. Since he runs a company that can now move data at higher speeds than can any other company on earth, the racetrack might just be the perfect training ground. Nortel controls the world's fiber-optical transmission business. Within its microscopic lasers, trillions of pulses of light are being encoded, pulsed, created in every second. Trillions of pulses and packets of data, bits, are flying along at gigabit speeds—billion bits per second—that can't collide as they rush though hairpin turns and S-bends and metropolitan rings and out onto the straightaways of the long-haul networks of the world.

This is speed. Engineering for speed. Nortel is at least one generation ahead of its closest competitor—Lucent—with its optical laser systems. In some sectors of the optical business, it maintains a near 90 percent market share; overall, Nortel sold about 40 percent of the world's optical transmission and management equipment in 2000. That's $8 billion (U.S.), in a business that is more than doubling every year. When it comes to optics, Nortel is in the driver's seat. Remarkably, five years ago it was Lucent (or its predecessor, AT&T) that had that pole position.

In this digital age, mechanics and their grease-under-the-fingernails tradition of can-do and make-do have somehow taken a back seat to the clean and antiseptic and throw-away world of electronics. Cars broke down and had to be fixed. Computers break down and they are thrown away. You can still buy replacement parts for a fifty-year-old tractor. Try and do that for a ten-year-old IBM PC. Most conversations with Roth loop back to cars somehow—whether through the metaphors or the stories he tells. Here is part of his explanation for the moment of "getting it," grasping the possibilities of the Internet: "I've got some old cars, and I was always looking for parts to fix them up. I have an E-type Jag, and there was a part on that Jag that somebody had ruined in trying to repair the car. So I said, 'Where can I possibly find this part for a 1966 E-type Jag?' Well, I got on the Web, and the next thing I know, I'm on the Web site of a three-man garage up north of London, England, someplace. And he had the part I wanted. I thought it was amazing, how this little guy running a garage in England could communicate with some guy in the hills north of Toronto and sell him an obscure part.

"That was when I realized what a powerful medium we had on our hands in the Internet."

It all comes back to cars, building hot boxes and doing it the only way he knows: by getting to work on the machine itself. He explains his fascination with cars, and speed, easily, naturally, without pretense or artifice. "I've always been hooked on cars. I started off helping Dad fix up the old Chevy. Then it became my Chevy, and then I bought myself a little secondhand MGA 1600. It was a pretty quick little car."

But, as it turned out, not quick enough. One day a big Buick Roadmaster towing a boat pulled up next to him at a stoplight. The two guys eyed each other in the derring-do machismo of men all over the world, and the guy in the big Buick revved his engine to signal a willingness to race. Roth, in his small and sporty MG, was sure there would be no contest, so he roared his as well. With that the Buick's driver got out, checked the hitch to make sure it was solid, got back into the car—and, when the light turned green, left Roth in the dust.

"I went looking for a new car," says Roth. "But I couldn't afford to buy any of the cars I looked at. So I went out and got a supercharger, and over the winter I took my engine apart, got a bigger head—an MGB [successor to the MGA] head because it had bigger valves—put the supercharger onto it, and took the engine from 80 horsepower to 140 horsepower. And then I could run down Mustangs. In fact, I could run down Jags. It was an amazing little car—just a sleepy little old MGA, with paint peeling off the back—but what an awesome little speed machine."

That, in a nutshell, is the Nortel M.O.: Downplay the razzle but back up the dazzle with performance. Sitting in his elegant wood-paneled office on the second floor of Nortel's sprawling headquarters building, Roth clearly relishes the memory of those teenage years. You can see it in his eyes; you can hear it in his voice. This isn't a CEO talking PR-filtered corporate-speak. This is a man who has spent his life getting grease under his fingernails. This is a man who enjoys nothing more than making machines sing. Roth has an infectious fascination for how things work. But he also very carefully makes it clear that he was always a "design" engineer. He did the work of designing a product, a job that required equal parts creativity and "really getting to know just what the customer wanted to do with the equipment. That was the hard part. Once we really, truly understood that, the actual design was often pretty straightforward."

This is not a man you'd expect to find leading a company (a *Canadian* company, of all things) that not so long ago was a slumbering giant ensconced in a monopolized market. John Roth's executive qualities, his hot-rod drive and competitive fire, his cowboy unpretentiousness, and his rock-solid belief that he and his company have all the ingredients they need to win the telecommunications wars of the next few years seem better suited to the American business landscape, to Silicon Valley and its celebrity CEOs, to Paul Allen's yearly retreat and its group shots splashed across foldout spreads in *Vanity Fair*. This presumption, however, is deeply rooted in U.S. arrogance or ignorance or both; in the belief that cowboys can only be American; in the Cisco-centric view that the game is already up and that Nortel and all the rest should pick up their bats and balls and go home. But based on the history of John Roth and Nortel, underestimating either is dangerous.

Most Americans are surprised to learn that Alexander Graham Bell was a Canadian and that his first phone call occurred at Brampton, in the province of Ontario, not down in the lower forty-eight states. The Canadian patent rights to his new invention were deeded to his father, Melville Bell, a well-known Canadian elocutionist, or speech therapist, of the era and formed the basis for Canadian Bell.

As a result, a separate Canadian telecommunications empire was formed to exploit the telephone, and it ultimately produced several world-class equipment makers as well as the operating companies that provide telephone service around Canada. Nortel was originally called Northern Electric and Manufacturing Company, then Northern Telecom, and now Nortel Networks. The company always was an independent firm, but with a patent cross-licensing deal with AT&T and its manufacturing arm, Western Electric, the Canadian company looked like a wholly owned subsidiary of its Yankee cousin. And until last year's divestiture, most of the company's stock was still owned by the northern version of AT&T, Bell Canada.

It is easy to dismiss the company. First, it is Canadian, which makes it, if nothing else, drab and boring like so much that is stereotypically Canadian, such as flannel shirts and Canada's version of bacon. And to some Americans, there's a faint whiff of socialism to things Canadian, of perhaps not being quite up to par, and of always having to battle in the capitalist marketplace with one hand tied behind the back. Then Nortel has that long history of being a toady to AT&T, a small equipment maker with few original designs of its own. Given the vast differences in economic resources between the two companies, Nortel was perpetually a sickly sibling to its giant sister south of the border.

In the beginning of this new era of speed and more speed across the phone lines, it would have been easy to dismiss Nortel as simply another one of the monolithic telecommunication equipment makers like Lucent.

It's true that Nortel may have looked like another dinosaur, but the Canadian company was not what it appeared to be. With a captive market less than one-tenth the size of the United States, Nortel has been forced to be an aggressive international telecommunications company from the very beginning of its corporate life, a factor which has paid off as the global village prophesied by the Canadian media pundit Marshall McLuhan has come to pass, and the Internet has made the world smaller. This has given it a breadth of customers and a scope of installations that no other major telecommunications supplier today can match. Without a monopoly license to sell gear to the giant U.S. market, the company has long had to go out and shake the trees to get customers. To put it in starker terms: Nortel is a company that has had to make success, without a monopoly or luck. People facing such challenges usually become tougher, more resilient, and more tenacious. So do companies.

But there is more to this company than an outward-focused marketing effort. Nortel is made up of engineers with a frontier mentality. And, indeed, this core engineering competency, this fundamental attribute, might be the single most dangerous part of the company's makeup. One single point illustrates it best: Nortel bet the company on digital voice and data equipment in 1972, at a time when AT&T was still convinced that the analog circuitry of the first hundred years of telephony would last until well past the end of the century.

Nortel embraced the digital world first, created the first CODEC (code/decode) devices that could convert analog voice—the tinny speech from a phone handset—into the bits and bytes of digital signals. (Using Reeves's PCM ideas, of course.) On the heels of this came the first digital business telephone systems, which would evolve into the Meridian line, today the world's most successful line of small office phones. Simultaneously, Nortel created the first digital telephone switches, the DMS (digital multiplex system) product family, for carriers. In combination with SONET equipment, these boxes revolutionized the carrier architecture of the 1970s and '80s, leading the way into the digital era.

And why did Nortel take the aggressive move to digital? Because its engineers firmly believed and were willing to gamble their company's future that by converting voice into data and then treating both voice and data the same through all the gear inside the telephone network, enormous efficiencies of scale could be achieved. It might have seemed in the short term that the most profitable—and safest—course would be to continue fighting AT&T for market share in the analog world. But that would have doomed Nortel to being a small player.

By completely changing the rules of the battle, moving into the new world of digital voice and data switching where no one else had any products, Nortel could win over the long term. And win it did.

Its first major wireless customer set the tone for the contests to come. It was a small, two-way dispatch-radio-network operator called MCI, initially a Springfield, Illinois–based firm that was trying to build an alternative wireless communications network between Chicago and St. Louis. The goal was to provide a way for truck drivers hauling along the interstate to call back to their head dispatch office from the road. It didn't take long for the entrepreneur the founders brought in—Bill McGowan—to realize that there was more potential in offering a private long-distance network to compete with AT&T's monopoly. Nortel would supply the microwave dishes to do it—that is, if American federal regulators and the courts would let them. For years AT&T tied MCI up in the courts and before the FCC, stopping it from delivering on its competitive voice and data network.

MCI understood that, in the future, data—not voice—was where the profits lay. Voice, the old technology, was the means by which the upstart company could crack the door and get the marketplace to take notice of it. But the real money was going to come from clients—big companies—that were looking for ways to link and move data around their far-flung branch offices, while also avoiding AT&T's outrageously expensive tariff schedules.

Nortel's microwave transmission equipment allowed MCI to shake AT&T to its very roots and, ultimately, to topple Ma Bell. Without Nortel as its partner, MCI would never have been able to get off the ground, because the only other company in the world that could build microwave transmission equipment was AT&T. Combine microwave towers with digital switching gear, much of it supplied by Nortel, and MCI was able to crack the AT&T long-distance voice-transmission monopoly wide open, with a pricing structure that allowed for big margins, and profits, even with a rigorous 10 percent minimum pricing advantage from Ma Bell's best rates. It also created a cash cow for Nortel, one that financed long-term development.

Microwave wasn't the only technology that Nortel developed hand in hand with MCI. The upstart carrier soon realized that if it was going to have any chance of offering a viable alternative long-distance network to businesses, it had to build that network all over the country. And in very high traffic corridors, that meant going beyond microwaves and adopting the fledgling world of fiber optics, where capacities were more unlimited. Turning to Nortel, in 1983 MCI ordered 62,000 miles of fiber-optic cable and transmission equipment to beef up its service between New York and Washington. It was an audacious move, gutsy and aggressive and the first time anyone other than a monopoly telephone company tried to use photons for communications traffic. The only supplier in the world who could deliver what it needed was Nortel.

MCI is the kind of company that Nortel keeps. Tough, smart—like its CEO—and unwilling to kowtow to conventional wisdom about markets, engineering, or technologies as gospel. This might just be the right background for an apostate taking on the cult of IP zealotry that John Chambers and Cisco preach.

IN 1977 JOHN ROTH came to Nortel after a stint at RCA, which he joined after getting a master's from Canada's McGill University. He joined the wireless division of Nortel (then called Northern Electric), where he worked as a radio frequency, or RF, design engineer. (Years later, in 1992, that background would be helpful when he took over Nortel's wireless business and turned it from an also-ran into the world's number two supplier. It was this performance that won him the top job.) From the very start he was an engineer who designed products—hot boxes—and that background emanates from every pore. John Roth loves the gear Nortel makes and, better yet, understands it.

In a technology company, Roth's innate talents and his engaging personality served him well. He rose up the management hierarchy quickly, working his way through all the different parts of the sprawling mega-enterprise that is Nortel. He was given operating and research posts to provide him with a full view of the corporation. He ran equipment divisions and research groups, learned P&Ls, hired and fired. He came to know the inside of the company as well as he knew the engine of his old MGA. This broad operating experience, across various lines of business, is one thing that marks the Nortel team, especially in comparison to its Cisco counterparts. This company has weathered ups and downs in various divisions, at various times, over the long term. The experience adds character.

In the early 1980s, when he was head of Nortel's research labs, Roth made the fateful decision to push into semiconductor lasers on a gallium arsenide (GA) base—a move that would prove important to the development of modern-day lasers. "The way one of my physicists explained it was that GA always goes ten times faster than CMOS [complementary metal oxide substrate: the standard method for creating semiconductors]." Again, it was the speed that attracted him, the ability to flash and read a laser beam faster than anyone else on the planet. Today, Nortel makes most of its own lasers, and the list of exotic semiconductor materials includes indium phosphate, silicon germanium, selenium, and, of course, gallium arsenide.

Nortel bet right on lasers early and kept plugging through the SONET world of the late 1980s and then right into the data explosion of the Internet of the mid-'90s. SONET (Synchronous Optical Network) was a system of optical fibers set out in a ring in most metropolitan areas around the world, accompanied by a plethora of software protocols and fault tolerance features. (In Europe a very similar standard is called SDH.) Devised, designed, and deployed primarily by telcos—the seven Baby Bells and GTE, AKA the Regional Bell Operating Companies (RBOCs)—the system was extraordinarily fault-tolerant and great for voice, but hard to change or reconfigure and, hence, exceptionally inflexible. This was a telco big-cost and slow-to-deploy solution for the predictable pre-Internet world. IP was not native to SONET, and the basic design of the system was bad for IP traffic. SONET was designed in such a way that its sectors—or "pipes" in telco language—had to be preconfigured for particular volumes of data traffic and wouldn't work when only partially filled. This was fine for big telephone companies that had lots of voice traffic to move—they were essentially monopolies at the time of SONET's development—and could depend on scores of same-sized voice circuits. But when the data world started to explode, with the chaotic nature of Web surfing that was anything but predictable, SONET turned out to be a big economic and structural weight around the necks of the bigger telcos.

SONET also had one other fatal flaw: a ring topology, where traffic is carried around a continuous loop of fiber-optic cable between all the nodes in a regional, or "metro," network. This was good for fault tolerance, since the SONET specifications call for two loops, or rings, side by side, with traffic able to switch to the other if one is cut or breached or fails. But it meant that everything had to be supplied in tandem, in effect doubling the cost of the rings without increasing performance or throughput. On the other hand, the world of IP is based on a "meshed" architecture, which is more like a Japanese Pachinko game—a ball (the packet of data) bounces along whatever pathway it finds open until it reaches the bottom. In this way, all the nodes can reach all the other nodes by as many different paths as the system supports mathematically. Each node maintains a list of its connections—these are router tables—and so every component of the network can always be used to pass data through it. Meshed networks, like IP, where every node talks through a routing table to every other node, are inherently more efficient in a switched world. And in the telecommunications world, efficiency means lower costs.

Nortel was the first company to sell SONET equipment, starting in the mid-1980s, and it became the market leader in the space. However, at the same time the company made an important decision not to make a major push into another telco data-transmission standard. In retrospect, that turned out to be a very astute move and in many ways allowed the company to marshal its resources for what would be the much more important area of IP. While SONET was the way the telcos proposed to move telecommunications traffic around metropolitan and regional networks before handing it off to the long-haul networks, ATM

(Asynchronous Transfer Mode) was their proposal for addressing the local data-transmission crisis. As more and more end-users—primarily big companies—adopted local area networking in the 1980s and needed to connect branch offices and remote sites, data volumes coming out of these clients started to rise precipitously. The answer the telephone industry came up with was a variant on the IP/Ethernet packet networking architecture, which from a telco viewpoint was a much better solution: ATM used a "cell" structure for data transmission. Instead of using the highly flexible but inherently unpredictable architecture of packets—which could vary from a few bits of data to thousands of bytes in any one packet—the new cell system specified absolutely standard 56-bit-sized chunks of data.

ATM's rigidity had several advantages, chief among them the ability to tightly pack any data pipes with lots of standard-sized cells and to guarantee delivery times for a new generation of data transmissions that involved voice and video, which were on the horizon by the early 1990s when the protocol was being adopted. (In the older world where data, voice, and video were separate, data packets could arrive at different times and be reassembled by the end device without loss of integrity or value. Such was not the case with voice or video.) But this rigidity was itself a significant drawback. It was the flexibility of IP data networking that made it so capable of evolution and provided a kind of tabula rasa for inspired and energetic engineers to build their own product on top of. Furthermore, because of its telco heritage, ATM came with layers upon layers of built-in conformation to years of preexisting telco standards, all of which added complexity and expense to the equipment. The result was that while ATM did become widespread in voice-circuit-oriented telco networks, it never reached the kind of growth numbers that IP networking enjoyed.

Nortel, being a significant supplier of telco equipment around the world, developed a number of products that supported the ATM standard but never made the kind of commitment to it that Lucent, with its heritage as a captive AT&T supplier, adopted. As a result, Roth was later able to get the company to make "a right-hand turn to the IP world" even though there was much internal grumbling about the benefits of ATM. At Lucent, ATM was never vanquished, and it ultimately tripped up the company. At Nortel, Roth is quick to describe the advantages of ATM in the way only an engineer with deep knowledge about his products can do. But he is also just as quick to make it clear that "IP has won. Discussion over."

FIBER OPTICS AND wireless cellular and data networks are what John Roth knows, and he is taking the company in those directions. He knows speed, feels speed, exults in speed. Driving Nortel screeching through tight curves and corners, stomping on it in the straightaways, and racing as hard as in his best roadster Jaguar to catch, lap, and stay ahead is what makes John Roth get up in the morning. This fire, this passion, this scope of technologies and troops, this extraordinary time for a global data communications provider put his company in an ideal spot to knee-cap Cisco and to grow to exceptional size and power. His passion to change the Nortel that he took over in 1997 has created this opportunity. He admits that IP was something of an epiphany for him. But the question remains whether the rest of the company has truly taken the New World of networking to heart, or is only talking the talk.

"I took over as CEO in October of 1997, but it was announced in the spring. That meant I had a little more time on my hands. So I figured I'd spend some time looking at what was coming up that I should be paying attention to. I spent much of that summer on the West Coast with the people generating the traffic to see what they thought was going to happen. I talked to people at Sun, Microsoft, Hewlett-Packard, Novell. I was trying to figure out why the data growth slope was so steep. My job is to carry the traffic efficiently, so what exactly is the traffic? It's not voice anymore."

Roth had grown up in the cumbersome, long-horizon bureaucracy of the phone company. Nortel was a captive of the Canadian telecom monopoly—based on the Ma Bell model—and had been selling switchboards for years. Although this company of engineers was saddled with a giant bureaucratic inertia, it wasn't opposed to change. Indeed, the only reason Nortel had survived for so long (other than the monopoly preferences) was that it had reinvented itself several times already. In John Roth the board found a man lacking the silken-smooth air associated with corporate inner sanctums but one unafraid of change, a top-flight design engineer but also someone who could see the Nortel culture for what it was and discover its failings and, better yet, devise a way to get past them. With his too-big ears, oversized features, and shock of black hair, Roth doesn't look like executive material—but he is definitely growing into the statesman role. His grasp of the current telecommunications marketplace—and his view from inside a giant company that has recently seized a major market segment going through explosive growth—is acute. Better yet, he can articulate it well.

"By 1997, the market had already decided that the IP protocol had won out. It was the standard for the Internet and was much further along than us telco guys would like to admit. So I said, 'If you can't beat them, join them.' The industry is best served if there is a standard. Rather than debate and say we could do a better one, let's not waste our time."

In 1997, after John Roth decreed that IP was going to win, he had to think about getting that message out to nearly 100,000 employees—100,000 telco people—and getting them to take the right-hand turn with him. He hit upon an ingenious idea. Describe it to them in their own terms. "I wrote this note to everyone inside Nortel. I told everyone that we were going to bring webtone to the Internet—that we were going to give it the attributes of dialtone. Dialtone is so good we take it for granted. I said our job was going to be to build a better Internet.

"That then moved the Internet onto our turf. We know how to make the network reliable. We know how to make it scale up to massive size. IP is just another communications protocol. We're good at these kinds of things. And the organization embraced it and said: 'We can do that.'"

Inside the company, he told everyone, especially the old engineers he had worked with for years, "You have to speak IP." Many of the old-timers, who believed in the telco data standard ATM, left. These were the Bellheads, who couldn't adjust to the new nethead world of IP networking. A leaner Nortel emerged, sized down from over 100,000 people to under 80,000 today. The management suite was subject to the same winnowing process. Everyone who stayed believed in Roth's new dictum.

To prove how committed Nortel was to IP, in 1998 the company bought Bay Networks for $9.1 billion. Roth realized that Nortel had to import people who understood IP and who also understood his passion for speed. He also desperately needed customers. Even angry ones. "Customers teach you all kinds of things. That often gets overlooked. People think design is the art of applying technology. Well, it is. But the more difficult part of design is figuring out what to apply it to.

"People often jump to that second part of design, assuming they know what the product is supposed to do. But the first part is more difficult. Do you really understand what it's supposed to do? And when you acquire angry customers, they tell you what it's supposed to do—in no uncertain terms. They're really upset with it, but they're stuck with it and can't get rid of it because in our business, it's too big an investment to get rid of it. It's much easier to fix it than get rid of it.

"With Bay we acquired a lot of customers, and we acquired 7,000 people who understood the ins and outs of IP. And they also understood something else. They understood speed. Consider the time it takes to develop a product, on a continuum from short to long. And consider the life of the product—again from short to long.

"[In one quadrant] is telecom, which traditionally had a long development cycle and a long life cycle—long-long. DMS, our central office switch, took five years to develop and represents a billion-dollar investment. Twenty years later, we're still selling it. A lot of people dropped out because of the decision-making process. You had to bet the farm—a billion-dollar investment. If your decision-making process is flawed, and you made the wrong calls, you're dead.

"Now, in the other quadrant, the present and future IP universe, you've got the world of short-short, and our industry is moving from long-long to short-short. All the rules of management that we learned and made us successful were correct for the prior time, but they're not correct anymore.

"We realized, then, that we had to look at how we operate and what we value and change all that, because we didn't value time. We valued a correct decision. This was all wrong. I looked at approvals on some of the things that we went through. The time on some of the documents between the first signature and the final signature was twelve months before the decision was actually ratified. These decisions went to the board of directors. You can imagine the review that you would go through before getting it all done. That's fine for long-long, but it doesn't work here.

"So we had very, very long cycles. We would check and recheck to make sure the quality was right. Or we would say, 'Gee, I can get another fifty cents off the cost of this line card. Well, this line card is made at 6 million per year and the design will last for four years. I think it's worth it to take another six months to get that fifty cents out.'

"In essence, you would trade time for better decisions. You would trade time for lower cost. You'd trade time for higher quality. You'd trade time for just about anything—and that became a habit for the organization.

"In the short-short quadrant, you don't trade time for anything. It is nonrenewable. When the window's gone, there goes the opportunity. So it's a huge change in the culture to value time. Speed to market is critical."

This is a wrenching process that isn't finished yet. Roth admits that he has been forced to retool several of his executive assignments recently. A lot of employee poaching is going on, and the CEO is a bit prickly about the other big Canadian optical company, JDS Uniphase, which has hired a number of Nortel-trained optical engineers. And the Bay acquisition hasn't exactly been an unalloyed success. New high-end routers haven't materialized, and the Nortel IP product family is still weak on the one crucial component for anyone planning to work in this space: Cisco router protocol and software intercompatibility.

"The Bay acquisition, then, accelerated our change to this new culture, and it did so dramatically. Instead of having to invent something from scratch, we could adopt theirs. We adopted much of their reward and compensation policies, for example. It got back to how many people would stay at the company and if they were comfortable with change. When you start changing the reward structure, you reward different behaviors. People who got rewarded under the old system suddenly found they weren't getting the rewards anymore. The rewards were going to different people, because they exemplified the new behaviors that we valued. The other ones that were no longer valued got the message and moved on.

"The result was that the organization became more demanding of leadership and got intolerant of executives who were not providing it. And several hundred were invited to leave the company. So there was a big turnover in the executive ranks—people who did not get it."

It is a great story he tells, and you can almost believe it when listening to him. But there is just one ugly fact that he can't hide. For all its growth in optics, and the promise of wireless, Nortel has been steadily losing market share in every area of the IP networking market since it acquired the company that used to be Cisco's primary competitor. Can Nortel really win the battle for tomorrow's network without making a run at Cisco in the one sector of the telecommunications market that has shown unceasing growth?

TWENTY-FIVE YEARS after the early days of digital innovation and the unraveling of the traditional telecommunications monopoly in the United States, Nortel is in a serious battle with Cisco and Lucent and Ericsson and Nokia and Alcatel and Siemens and lots of hot and not-so-hot start-ups to sell the gear required to create the Next Net.

Don't tell these frontier Canadians that they can't possibly win. This is a company obsessed with winning, whatever it takes. And even though Nortel is sometimes considered an underdog in the competition with Cisco, it is determined to beat back the Americans.

The psychological power of the chip on the shoulder, the undervalued younger brother, is a driving force that can't be easily dismissed, but being an underdog, one with sales of $28 billion, is a position almost any company would enjoy holding, especially in a market that is growing as fast as the Internet and its infrastructure. What kind of underdog is this?

Outside of the IP world, Nortel is sitting pretty. It has the number one market share in optical equipment worldwide. Its sales are growing at nearly 100 percent per year. More than 75 percent of all backbone Internet traffic is carried on Nortel optical networking equipment. Nortel is doubling the carrying capacity of optical transmissions every nine months—making Moore's Law (transistor density doubling every eighteen months) seem old-fashioned by comparison.

What kind of company can handle this relentless and accelerating throb of technology? There are competitors all over the place, venture-funded start-ups of every imaginable and unimaginable stripe coming at Nortel from all sides. Add that to the almost Alice-in-Wonderland fact that the fundamental technology Nortel sells one day is virtually obsolete 270 days later. Prices are falling as capacities are rising. And demand for more and more bandwidth shows no signs of stopping. This is no place for a genteel competitor. This is a prescription for cutthroat competition, driven engineers, and surefooted vision at the top.

And the perfect sport for such a company is car racing. But not just any kind of car racing; it has to be the most competitive, technologically challenging, and heart-stopping kind of racing around. So, not surprisingly, Nortel sponsors a Formula 1 racing team—BMW Williams. Auto racing is aggressive, appeals to rich and poor, and combines grease and noise with death-defying feats of bravery and staggering payoffs for those who risk it all. Try stopping from 120 miles per hour and downshifting into a corner on the tail of another car that is going just as fast in front.

In contrast, Cisco sponsors golf. The 2000 Pebble Beach U.S. Open was a major Cisco event. Golf is a safe sport. Tennis, which Chambers plays, is a refined sport. NetAid, the company's attempt to use the Web to raise charity money, is a safe effort.

Cisco lives life safely. Nortel fancies that it lives it on the edge. Can this dinosaur of a telecommunications giant really think that it can wrestle the Internet equipment mantle from Cisco in the next few years? This is audacious thinking for a company that has been losing market share to its Silicon Valley competitor steadily in routers and switches—which is where all the money is in the IP world.

The real difference between the two companies is in something so fundamental, and so basic, that it is easy to overlook it. Cisco has built a sales force that knows how to sell to corporate America, to the business world. Golf fits that middle-class suburban world. Nortel has a sales force that knows how to sell to carriers and telcos. It is a very different universe. If it were John Roth out on the front lines, this engineer-turned-salesman would know how to convince the customer that he really did have the products to solve his problems and could make him feel good, and safe, and secure in buying from Nortel. But it is not John Roth on the sales call. It is a team of engineers, telling an engineer's story, with all of their emphasis on speeds and feeds and technical details. Nortel has the better technical story, with a vast pool of talent and years of engineering expertise. But it hasn't figured out the sales part of the equation because that is not what the organization truly values yet.

Cisco, on the other hand, does. This is a company that has a team of smoother salesmen, Willie Lomans in their early years, a vast army of sales executives and account executives who know that it isn't the technical details that will win the sale, but the tickets to the ball game, and the handholding, and the gospel, the story, the sermon of John Chambers. Just be like us. Sign up with us and join the cult. We'll make you look good, and you'll be part of the big IP family. Those who believe that technology is important will scoff, and those who buy Cisco gear will never admit that it is the warm and fuzzy feeling that tipped the scales.

But in the end, there's little doubt who will win the sale. Over the long term, Nortel may be able to beat back Cisco as the market shifts to service providers and consumers from enterprises and businesses. It may be able to marshal its engineering expertise and its managerial technology vision to get out in front of the market and cut Cisco off at the pass. But it is not going to make a dent in its brash young Silicon Valley competitor's side until it realizes the secret that IBM understood so many years ago. Selling technology to business is much less about the technology, much more about understanding the business.

And while the two company leaders are so very different, they represent the two schools of technology business: engineering and sales. One is an aristocrat of the New World economy, a master salesman whose company has never seen even a blip in its revenues or earnings, whose execution in both the router and switch markets has been flawless, and whose sermon has been masterfully crafted to appeal to the emotions and fears of business managers while ringing up sales for Cisco. The other is led by a shirtsleeves engineer, a man with a deep and passionate fascination for technology itself, who got the IP religion only a few years ago and who is hamstrung by a giant bureaucracy created for the previous telecommunications world. Who has his hand on the tiller? Who has the right stuff? If both, whose ship will navigate the new seas of the Internet Age most effectively? Fiber optics is very different from routing. Could the tables be about to turn on Cisco? Or is IP going to conquer all and make fiber optics seems like a niche transmission market in service to the real sweet spot of the Information Age: the place where intelligence is added to the network?

When asked about Cisco, John Roth is both gracious and blunt. "I admire Cisco's marketing machine. It is a fabulous marketing machine, and they have a dynamite sales force. They're a very impressive company—very in tune with the customer. But starting from small networks, they don't have much capability in terms of end-to-end. And trying to move from building a network for an enterprise customer to building a network for a service provider is quite a different task. It's an orders-of-magnitude difference in complexity. They're doing extremely well with ISPs, which are growing rapidly in complexity. So they're following the traffic, and I see them diversifying. But they're trying to get into optics now, so they're getting away from the things they understand.

"They're moving off of their turf and onto mine."

PART THREE

FAULT
LINES

CHAPTER 7

THE HOLLOW
CORPORATION

THE SUN IS STREAMING ONTO THE POOL OUTSIDE THE HOTEL conference room's floor-to-ceiling windows. It's a glorious day in early June 2000 along the southern coast of Spain. The meeting is being held in the village of Los Monteros, which sits just this side of Marbella, a tony resort town, where the affluent drive German cars and live in homes ensconced behind thick stucco walls and ribbons of iron bars. On this particular day Los Monteros is awash in bougainvillea, fuchsias, and a lush profusion of exotic semitropical plants.

The occasion is the annual gathering of Avis's information technology troops from around the world. Several hundred strong, they've come to this jasmine-scented corner of the world to try to figure out how they are going to rebuild their creaky, twenty-year-old software reservations system called Wizard. In its day, Wizard was one of the most innovative mainframe reservations networks in the world. Today, however, smack dab in the middle of the Internet revolution, it's been reduced to a relic from a different, more stable time. Like all companies today, Avis knows it must take advantage of the Web, move into hyperchange mode, survive through constant reinvention. But in a world of unlimited choices, fields of choices that bloom and wither in the blink of an eye, how do you know when the time is right to act, to make the move that could sink a multibillion-dollar corporation with the ease of a gust of wind upending a lemonade stand?

The meeting, which runs for several days, begins, like so many corporate meetings, with internal warfare. Just getting Avis's many different operations to simply talk to one another and to communicate with headquarters is a major effort. Each division, each department, has its own flag planted firmly in a square of turf to be defended to the death.

Several days of battles and rapprochement follow, as teams from all corners of the world debate the next stage of technology for the venerable car rental company. It quickly becomes clear that there will be no easy decisions. Many of the people in the room have spent their entire careers supporting, patching, and maintaining the existing Wizard system. The rise of the Web is all very well, but it has yet to prove itself robust and dependable enough to support a worldwide system such as Wizard.

Finally, by the last day of the conference, the crowd is bleary-eyed and certain of only one thing: Remaking Avis into an Internet Age enterprise will not be easy. The host, CIO of the rental car company, is a young and hip rising star. For the past few months he has been deeply involved in launching an Internet site where the company can sell—direct to consumers—rental cars that are due for replacement. For the final day he has scheduled a series of speakers whose charter is to stimulate the troops and send them back to their posts with fresh ideas ringing in their ears. Anticipating a rousing presentation, he makes the final speaker a representative from Cisco, the company that has mastered the Internet and whose example is like a yellow brick road for all—even a venerable car rental company—to follow.

To tell its tale Cisco sends a ponytailed forty-something, a California caricature, flown in directly from Silicon Valley to deliver the message. Before getting up to speak, he sits cross-legged on the floor, to one side of the podium, fiddling with the slides. He needn't have bothered. His "the Internet will change everything and you'd better get ready" speech is getting a bit tired by now. Everyone's heard it before, including Avis's weary IT people. He throws in some interesting factoids—in five years the Internet reached 50 million users, a total that took radio almost forty years to achieve—but they get lost in the puffery about how Cisco is the master of the universe and business model for the future. Still, he trudges on through the standard corporate boilerplate: Cisco, the poster child for the electronic revolution, holds the key to streamlining business processes, increasing customer satisfaction, improving profitability through the use of the Internet. Just do what we do in your business.

Nowhere is there much sensitivity to the differences between a router company and one that rents cars. The audience, a sophisticated crowd of information technology specialists, gets restless. As his centerpiece, the speaker describes Cisco's own deployment of an online customer-care system. He explains how it took the company three years and at least that many iterations of the software to make the program work and achieve remarkable success. According to the speaker, the new system produced savings of nearly $500 million a year. Most impressive of all was that customer contacts over the Internet more than tripled in the three years, while overall customer satisfaction increased as well.

Next comes a series of metrics that demonstrates just how powerful Internet commerce has been for Cisco: More than 70 percent of the company's bookings were coming via the Web. With Cisco bursting through the $20 billion run rate, this is a big deal and is re-creating the company as it grows.

Following the presentation, during the question-and-answer period, one fellow stands up and asks how Avis, with all its IT personnel gathered in the room, a couple of hundred people at most, can hope to pull off the feat that it took 20,000 Cisco employees (no, the Cisco man interrupts, nearly 30,000 now because we're growing so fast)—IT and networking specialists all of them—three years to get right.

"Outsource everything!" he declares as though he had just discovered the secret to the universe. Get others to do it for you. You don't need a core of competency. You don't need people who understand the technology upon which your company stands. That's Old World thinking. That's yesterday. Today, the hollow corporation reigns supreme.

His outsourcing answer didn't resonate with the Avis group, which had just spent three days excoriating some suppliers and bemoaning the shortage of skilled employees and consultants all over the world. The man from Cisco lost the crowd, and folks started filing for the doors. He was like a cipher, a stand-in for the ponytailed netheads who made Cisco in its early incarnation, but without the depth. Once Cisco was the center of the IP universe. It had a technological core that was something to behold, a soul that was filled with the combined genius of networking geeks, IP zombies, and computer wizards. But that was then.

STANFORD UNIVERSITY IN the 1960s and '70s was a fertile place for computer research. It was where Douglas Englebart did much of his work on the mouse. It was where, on an adjoining corporate campus, Xerox housed its Palo Alto Research Center—PARC—whose machines introduced true graphical user interfaces and applications, as well as local area networking, to the world. In the mid-1970s, the Home Brew Club—the passionate group of computer enthusiasts formed in the very early days of PCs—held its meetings in the auditorium at the Stanford Linear Accelerator. The world's first weather overlay computers—used for years on TV news shows—were made by a company called Cromemco, a play on Crother Memorial Hall, the Stanford engineering building. Across campus another group of students and professors was creating a new type of powerful workstation called the Stanford University Network, which would become the core of Sun Microsystems.

Also at Stanford at that time was an unlikely couple, Len Bosack and Sandy Lerner. The world would never be the same after their paths crossed.

Outwardly, Len, the head of computing services at Stanford's computer sciences department, was the consummate geek—neat as a pin, quiet to the point of taciturnity. Inside, however, raged a brilliant programmer who could pull all-nighters with the best of them. His computer sciences department was one of the most computer-literate places on earth. He was, in short, a master of the programming universe. Sandy, on the other hand, was a flamboyant, outgoing, business school MBA candidate who became intrigued with the productivity and work-group opportunities that computers and networks might produce in the workplace. After graduate school, she took a job as head of computer services at the business school, where she had to work with all the other campus computer departments, including Len's. They met, fell in love, married, and started dreaming about how to make the various computer systems spread around the Stanford campus talk to one another more intimately.

They found the answer in a product built by Bill Yeager, a kindred spirit in computer operations at the Stanford Department of Medicine. Yeager's creation was a router, built around a minicomputer, that linked Stanford's medical department computer system with those of Len's computer sciences department and Sandy's business school. The router reduced the cacophony of multiple systems to a single shared language—IP—and allowed files and messages to be passed across technology walls. As Len, the hard-core programmer, further refined it, the router became capable of interlinking any local IP network.

Interestingly, the initial conceptual ideas for the router were born along with the Internet and came from one of America's most creative, and undersung, early computer scientists: Wes Clark. Clark had been the original lead programmer for the very first interactive computer—the 1940s and '50s Project Whirlwind at MIT. Whirlwind was an air traffic/early warning system that provided live tracking data for all aviation activity in New England and Canada. In those days of the Cold War, it had been developed to provide early warning of the approach of Russian missiles from the Arctic Circle. It was the first computer that allowed operators to interact with the blips and trajectories on their screens, simultaneously track hostile and friendly objects, and support a light pen as an input device.

Clark, however, became fascinated not with giant machines like this one (Whirlwind, once built, was as big as a building and consumed as much energy to operate as a locomotive), but with small ones. Along with the two founders of DEC, he designed and programmed a pair of transistor-based machines, TX-0 and TX-2, based on Whirlwind, that formed the initial DEC computers. But Clark, an idealist and something of a dreamer, had no interest in joining their mercantile effort once the lab's powers rejected the transistor computers. Instead he launched into a program to create very inexpensive "kit" computers for experimental biologists. Some three hundred scientists built the small, $2,000 LINCs (Laboratory Instrumentation Computers) by the end of the 1960s, when funding ran out. While Clark might not have made much impact on the general public, he was well known among the computer scientists who gathered at ARPA during the same period to build the first wide-area networking system, ARPANet. The biggest problem was getting the various custom computers at different academic sites to talk with one another. It was Wes Clark, steeped in the low-cost ethos of cheap computing, who suggested building a series of small computers that could be situated at each site in front of the expensive computers of the institutions. These machines—called IMPs, for Internet Message Processors—handled all the protocol conversion and traffic routing for messages sent via the Net. With these first routers, the Internet was born.

The word *router* didn't come into common use until the second generation IMPs started to appear, and the chief makers of these were the unlikely trio at Stanford. This became the foundation on which Sandy and Len, in 1983, founded a new company, which they called cisco systems (with the *c* and the *s* lowercased). The name was said to come from the last letters of San Francisco or, alternatively, from the name of the ranch town in the Sierra foothills—Cisco—where Sandy was raised by her aunts on a family ranch.

The router was the perfect device for its time. Not only did it let different flavors of computers talk, but it also helped manage external—remote, or wide-area—telecommunications connections so that satellite offices could be connected to the networks via dial-up lines and modems. The couple started out building routers in their living room. These new boxes connected Stanford's networking systems, making campuswide e-mail a reality for the first time. The protocol was TCP/IP; the backbone, the Internet (then known mainly as ARPANet and used primarily for academic and scientific discourse and discussion).

From day one, cisco was the most macho of Silicon Valley nethead programming shops. It had two key components: 110-hour workweeks by Len Bosack and his colleagues, who defined geek chic for the time, and unrelenting, unceasing growth in demand for the product that Sandy tried to fill. Routers put the intelligence into the Net, any net. They are the directors of the whole thing. Networks were exploding everywhere. By 1986 the two founders were clearing some $3 million a year on sales of about $10 million. Pricing was fluid, and depended on whim, but many customers were desperate.

By 1987, when the U.S. government opened the gates of the Internet to all, cisco's market for routers became almost limitless. But in order to exploit the company's true potential, the founders needed an infusion of capital and business smarts. Although the company was generating buckets of money, Bosack and Lerner were stretched too thin; they needed professional managerial help and a more businesslike structure. They didn't need cash. They needed a partner who could help them become world class.

The couple went out on the venture capital financing circuit. Sandy, the outgoing member of the team, did most of the pitch. Len, the quiet programmer, provided the technological depth. They were looking for someone to share their vision and help lead cisco toward an eventual IPO. They were also looking for a potential way out. It was possible that they didn't want to spend the rest of their lives at the company.

Not one of the first dozens of presentations made an impression. This, after all, was 1987, and high tech was almost exclusively a male shop. There were no women venture capital partners yet; the business consisted of old, wise, rich electronics company founders, almost all engineers, and a handful of anointed young men from Stanford and the Ivy League, mostly double e's (shorthand for engineering degree, usually a BSEE) with MBAs, who were apprentices in the trade, acolytes in the new form of investment banking as it was practiced in Silicon Valley. Women, well, they were the waitresses in the diners down the road or the glossy wives of financiers or the oh-so-serious English majors whose eyes glazed over when talk turned to electronics. In addition, Sandy Lerner, no wallflower, was—and is—an exciting mix of incendiary characteristics: voluble, sexy, outrageous, well spoken, and highly intelligent, with a shrewd and savvy business mind. This big, bossy, and larger-than-life character dominates every room she enters.

Needless to say, at the time, Sandy's performance did not play well in the pampered, hushed, well-heeled, and exceedingly gentlemanly world of West Coast venture capitalism. The founders grew despondent until the day they met the man who would change their lives and the future of the company they had created together.

Don Valentine is a short, wiry, tough guy and a former Marine—skeptical, pugnacious almost—whose personality was formed in the blast furnaces at National Semiconductor Company during the formative years of Silicon Valley and on the battlefields of Korea. National Semi was one of the meteors of the 1960s' stock market after a group of young hotshot engineers left Fairchild (which itself had been formed by a band of young hotshots—the traitorous eight—who left Shockley Semiconductor) and landed financing from early venture capitalist Peter Sprague, a member of the Sprague Electronics family, which had been a dominant force in tube-based electronics a generation earlier. Valentine was a young manufacturing line engineer who followed the lead man, legendary Charley Sporck, to the new company. National Semiconductor was one of the first of the mass-market semiconductor companies, and it perfected the ability to manufacture its products so efficiently that it could profit handsomely even with the precipitously dropping prices that characterized the new transistor and integrated circuit world of the 1960s and '70s. This set the stage for what would come to be known as the semiconductor pricing curve. From 1967 through the 1970s, Sporck and his team figured out how to start the company, manufacture integrated circuits, go public, and get profitable—laying the groundwork for Bob Noyce and his partners at Intel, as well as scores of other companies to follow. National Semi also had a volatile stock price and weathered several gluts in the semiconductor market—especially the digital watch and calculator phenomena, both of which nearly finished off both Intel and National Semi when production ramped up so fast that prices plunged to fire-sale levels in a matter of months. It was the perfect training ground for a venture investor.

National Semi stock made Don Valentine wealthy enough to become an investor in other companies. By the mid-1970s, he had become part of what was an unwritten, word-of-mouth circuit of well-heeled private investors, venture capitalists, and former executives of electronics firms who financed all kinds of Silicon Valley entrepreneurs. At that point Valentine got a phone call from a young guy who had been given his name by Regis McKenna, a local Silicon Valley advertising and PR whiz. However, when Valentine met the kid and his partner, he was put off by their appearance and demeanor. They didn't look like serious businessmen to this former Marine. They didn't look like wise investments. The leader of the two, the one who did most of the talking, was a barefoot, foul-smelling, twenty-year-old vegetarian with dark, piercing eyes and shaggy black hair. To Valentine's eternal regret, he sent Steve Jobs, Steve Wozniak, and their questionable idea for a company called Apple to a buddy of his who had just retired from Intel. Mike Markkula put up $250,000, became partners with the scruffy pair, and went on to be the long-time chairman of Apple, with a one-third stake in the company that ballooned at one point to more than a billion dollars.

In the small, tight, mega-rich world of venture financing in the 1970s and '80s, that story was impossible for Valentine to live down. He became known as the man who missed the opportunity of a lifetime, who lost a chance to get in on one of the most legendary business successes of the last quarter century. It was also the reason he was far down on the list of people cisco's founders approached. When Sandy Lerner and Len Bosack came to Don Valentine's Menlo Park offices, he saw something that all the other VCs had missed, a jewel of an idea whose brilliance was undeniable: the product that could quarterback and direct network traffic, both locally and around the world. This time, the eccentricities of the company founders would not cloud his vision. After all, he had had ten years to think about his missed opportunity, ten years to watch the Apple saga unfold. He wouldn't make the same mistake twice.

As a result, Valentine made Lerner and Bosack an offer they couldn't refuse. His venture firm, Sequoia Associates, would give the two founders $2.5 million in exchange for one third of the company. But to hedge his bets, Valentine extracted from Lerner and Bosack the right to choose the management team at the fledgling company and an ironclad agreement to be able to buy the founders out if they didn't do what he told them was good for the company. He also capitalized the first C, and from that point on the company became Cisco Systems Incorporated.

Don Valentine is a calculating man. He considers very carefully both what he says and what he does. He knew from the beginning that Cisco's future depended on easing out the voluble founders, especially Sandy, and their core coterie of too smart and too uncontrollable Stanford programmers. Geniuses, yes. Team players, not a chance. The challenge, however, was to avoid alienating these key players until suitable replacements were available. Therefore, choosing the right person to bring order to a fast-growing but dysfunctional anomaly of a company like Cisco was not going to be easy. Valentine started off on the wrong foot. He filled the job of president without consulting either founder. It may have been contractually legal, but it set off a two-year battle between the founders and the venture capitalists that could ultimately end in only one way.

The man Valentine picked in 1988 was John Morgridge, a fifty-four-year-old veteran of Honeywell and Stratus. Coming to Cisco from Grid Computer, he jumped off a big failure in the high-tech game right in front of the axe. An early maker of technologically advanced, expensive, stylish, heavy (ten pounds plus) portable PCs in the mid-1980s, Texas-based Grid never could get its act together. One of the company's big problems was its product reliability, arguably directly the fault of Morgridge, who was the company's president and chief operating officer. Elegant yes, but not rugged enough, Grid never could get marketplace traction because the market for gold-plated laptops for well-heeled road warriors never amounted to as many units as necessary to sustain the company. The remnants of the crashed-and-burned start-up had just been sold off to Tandy, and the executive figured he was about to get the heave-ho. But the failure didn't bother Valentine; he had had his share of setbacks and openly admitted them. High tech was filled with brilliant failures. What mattered to Valentine was that Morgridge had learned from his experiences at Grid.

As the two men talked over a period of weeks, they developed a bond founded on a shared view of business and a similar outlook on life. Morgridge, a short, wiry guy with a bawdy sense of humor, was very much in the Valentine mold. Like the VC, he was notoriously parsimonious and unpretentious, and he was also an ex-military man. Just the person to rein in the Cisco founders, keep expenses to a minimum, hire a strong executive team, and keep the router rocket ship on course.

Morgridge did his job. He got the finances in order, built a sales force, and tried to manage the demand. The former Air Force officer even managed to bridge the gap between the geeks—the original founders and their friends—on the one side and the more polished and professional team he hired on the other side. In the early days, Morgridge and Sandy got along too. Each, in a different way, was very much an original, and each respected the no-nonsense toughness in the other. It was soon apparent, however, that this arrangement would not last. Sandy was not the kind of person who could play the soldier to Morgridge's general—especially in a company she helped found.

Eighteen months after the new president's arrival, Cisco was preparing to file registration papers to go public and was on track to sell $100 million of products in the fiscal year. Although the date picked for the IPO was February 16, 1990, not February 14, it was always referred to as Valentine's Day within the company, a little insider joke that did not amuse Sandy. By then, her efforts to swallow her gall weren't fooling anyone. Cisco was coming apart due to internecine warfare, even as its market continued to soar.

The IPO went well. Cisco shares opened at $18 and closed that day at $22.50. Suddenly Sandy and Len, the two lovers from Stanford, were worth hundreds of millions of dollars. The newfound wealth, however, did not ease the serious tensions growing within the executive suite. On the contrary, it seemed to energize Sandy, feeding into her belief that she knew what was best for Cisco, the company she nurtured like her very own child. She developed a deep distrust of Don Valentine, who, she believed, was managing the company behind her back. The Valentine's Day link to the IPO only added more salt to the wound. In addition, she came to question Morgridge's ability to lead a high-tech company. After all, he wasn't a nethead, wasn't even an engineer; and, among the elite computer geeks in the inner circle at Cisco, that meant he just "didn't get it." Besides, she now had enough money to tell anyone—even the CEO of the company—to go to hell, and she frequently did. Sensing that Cisco was becoming increasingly dysfunctional, Morgridge took the unusual step of hiring a company psychologist, to whom employees were encouraged to unload pent-up emotional baggage. Sandy availed herself of the opportunity. Every day. And did so loudly enough that everyone in the company could overhear her gripe sessions.

Sandy, left in her position as customer advocate and vice president of customer relations, fumed, and Len, who was chief scientist and married to her, went along. The first person who understood the crusade of "IP everywhere," the imperative that was going to ignite Cisco's afterburners and invigorate global trade and opportunity, was Sandy Lerner. She had been selling the benefits of being able to connect lots of computers over network wires and telephone lines since the company was started. Now, with the opening of the Internet to the public in 1987, Cisco was finding a whole new dimension of business feeding demand. Routers were streaking off the shelves, and the company was

booming; but the founders, the husband and wife who had conceived Cisco, were being shunted aside. Sandy's resentment of
Morgridge's team of new executives grew with the company's
revenues. In her role as the customer's advocate, she was making
what were increasingly considered unrealistic and insulting demands on everyone else in the company. Fix this. Do that. It was
customer advocacy by fiat, and when a manager didn't dance fast
enough for her liking, she berated him as incompetent to the
whole company—and also shared that opinion with the customer who had complained in the first place.

Less than six months after the IPO, the executive team told
Morgridge they would resign en masse unless Sandy was re-
lieved of her day-to-day duties. It was the end of the first fiscal
year (which for Cisco runs from August 1 to the end of July)
and of the founders' era. On August 28, 1990, Sandy and Len
left Cisco. Six months later they sold all their founders' shares
back to the company for the tidy sum of $170 million—roughly
two-thirds of the equity in the company. Although gone, the
founders left behind an indelible impression. Sandy's over-the-
top customer advocacy was now built into "Cisco's DNA," as
the first and current human resources manager, Barbara Beck,
recalls. "From day one we cared more about customers than
anything. We were fanatical. Always have been." And the elite
core of netheads that had been assembled by Len Bosack were
the heart of Cisco's customer support system, the priestdom of
these hand-tooled and specialized minicomputer-like routers
that the company was selling. While some of the earliest technical team members followed Len out the door, most did not. And
it wasn't long before the company was attracting the best and
the brightest engineers from all over the country, not just from
Stanford. Institutions and big companies were all struggling to
link up their networks and to make them work most efficiently.
Cisco had the right product for the time. It was the place to be.

A few months after the departure of Lerner and Bosack,
Morgridge hired his chief lieutenant and heir apparent: John

Thomas Chambers. Like Morgridge before him, Chambers had been tested by failure, the disintegration of the once great Wang Labs. Furthermore, he was cut from the same physical mold as Valentine and Morgridge—small, thin, and energetic—although he was a bit smoother, more country club, less blue collar. Most important, though, just like Morgridge, he wasn't an engineer. Before he came to Cisco, Chambers knew little about networking, which initially didn't endear him to the company's elite programmers. His gentle personality and native smarts, however, enabled him to win over the programming troops. He might not have understood just how the products worked, but he could damn well sell them. And sell them he would have to, because Cisco, at the time, was still a small player in a land of giants.

The bigger company was 3Com, which was founded by Xerox exiles who specialized in Ethernet networking equipment. In 1987 3Com also bought Bridge, the early networking pioneer that built "bridges" to link "hubs" (concentrations of network users) together. The combination of 3Com's network card and network operating system business with Bridge's connecting products for local-area networks created what should have been a juggernaut. It was not. The two companies could never mesh. From the very beginning, the acquisition was sabotaged by inept management that only exacerbated internal squabbling and eventually led to walkouts. More fundamentally, however, 3Com realized far too late, and without enough fire and vigor, that it was the router—the place where intelligence is added to the network by directing packets of data to their destinations—that was the only defensible business battleground in the IP networking game. Putting intelligence into a network is the one place where high prices can be defended—anything else in the network data transmission game is essentially a commodity and as such will tend to cutthroat pricing and falling margins. Routers, with their complex software and multiprotocol translation capabilities, are the quarterback of networking. Control the router that controls the packets, and you control the network . . . and the money. This is what

Cisco and John Chambers have always understood, while the competition—both actual and wanna-be—has too often become enamored of high-speed transmission bells and whistles. The battle would not be fought over hubs, Ethernet interface cards, and bridges, all of which ultimately became commodities. The battle was in delivering intelligence to the networks, sorting and dispatching packets, and Cisco got there first.

There were other giants as well. Networking became a fast-growing opportunity for a series of successful new companies. Cabletron built a very profitable hubs business. Synoptics developed the 10BaseT plug-and-play Ethernet cabling scheme that uses basic phone jacks and took Ethernet from an arcane sideshow to a widely deployed standard. Wellfleet, headquartered outside Boston, came after the router market as well, but the company hedged its bets—and dissipated its focus—by also churning out hubs and bridges. Cisco, under the conservative and cautious John Morgridge, stuck with routers.

Ironically, the split with the founders had another profoundly positive impact on both Cisco and Don Valentine. It made them both richer still. Getting back two-thirds of the company equity set Cisco up to make an unprecedented run of acquisitions, which proved to be one of the most powerful weapons that company management would exploit in creating its New Economy business model. Acquisitions were something John Chambers could do.

UNDER MORGRIDGE AND CHAMBERS, tightfistedness became a corporate trait. There were few perks for the executives. No one flew first class. Morgridge was a stickler for using senior discounts and flying coach. But at the same time, the company became renowned for its customer service. As some of the elite left in the wake of the founders' departure, Morgridge, John Chambers, and Vice President of Business Strategy Ed Kozol (who does have an engineering background) made sure to hire technical salespeople who could help configure routers and solve customer problems. The plan: Make everyone in the company able to help a customer solve a problem. And do it all online. This was Cisco's rallying cry from the very beginning.

As the company with the key product required to gain access to the Internet, Cisco was quick to seize the potential of the online channel as a friction-free way to make sales and handle support. By the early 1990s the company was handling more than half of all service and support calls over the Internet, and many router sales were handled entirely online. This makes the company's trumpeting about how 70 percent of all transactions come in online somewhat disingenuous. Cisco has *always* done most of its business on the Internet. By 1992, Cisco reached $300 million in sales, and its stock was continuing to move up. There was only one thing missing: a path for growing the company beyond routers alone.

It was in early 1993 that Chambers and the other top executives started studying the networking marketplace and looking for the products to fuel the next stage of growth at the company. At this point Cisco sold routers primarily to large companies and institutions, which had aggressively adopted the PC revolution and, right after it, the networking infrastructure to feed traffic into the router. But the architecture of the first generation of networking was inherently limited and somewhat inflexible. Individual workstations or servers would be connected to the network through a hub, which in turn up-linked all the nodes on the hub to a router, all of the many users sharing a single 10-megabit-per-second Ethernet connection to the router. The routers acted as gathering points for several hubs and interacted with other routers in a loose free-for-all of interconnections, also called a "meshed" network. As more users waded onto the network, the effective throughput available to any one user dropped out on the edge. Those 10 megabits of available Ethernet bandwidth were being parceled out to many; and with no ability to manage or assemble the different users and their requests into a priority queue of any kind, corporate networks quickly became sluggish.

The answer, in this Silicon Age, was the development of hardware-based Ethernet (or, more generically, IP) switches. A switch makes an unshared connection between two points (or nodes) on the network. These devices allowed a single end device, whether server or PC, to get a full 10 megabits of Ethernet dedicated to it, all the way through to the router. This meant that power users and, more often, power devices serving many users, could opt out of the shared system of basic networking for a higher throughput, better access to the server, and a smoother experience with the network. But there was a threat to Cisco inherent in the rise of the switch culture. Originally, LANs were linked together by hubs that fed into routers, with a large number of routers directing the traffic around to pockets of users. With switches, many users could be linked together directly to a few bigger routers. This was a threat to Cisco's core business. In 1993, when Boeing, one of Cisco's biggest customers, told Chambers that it was considering shifting a $10 million router order to Crescendo, a fresh upstart selling networks built around switches, Cisco's early leaders cashed in a few of the shares that they had bought back from the founders and bought Crescendo for $97 million.

The acquisition stunned Wall Street and dragged Cisco's stock down. Crescendo had sales of barely $10 million—the purchase price was ten times sales for a new garage company in the odd and esoteric marketplace of networking, which had little glamour and was highly mysterious. But customers responded to the alliance favorably. They liked being able to buy the combination of switches and routers from one vendor, and they bought them in droves. Adding switches was a way to boost network performance relatively easily, and they worked hand-in-glove with routers. Switches could be deployed on network branches where traffic was bogging down, while existing hubs and wiring schemes could remain intact for less-used pathways. By the end of the next fiscal year, Cisco's sales had tripled to a billion dollars, and by the late 1990s switches were well on their way to overtaking routers in terms of revenue.

The acquisition marked several key lessons that would be crucial to Cisco in making its acquisitive ways pay off in coming years. Chambers and the CEO of Crescendo, Mario Mazzola, agreed that no one would be fired without both men's agreement. It was the beginning of the fabled Cisco method of acquisition, which was born more from experience at it—at last count the company has acquired some seventy-five companies during Chambers's time at the company—than any kind of magic touch. In fact, only a handful of those acquisitions have been successful in terms of generating direct revenues and products. Most have sunk into the fabric of Cisco, and the youthful enthusiasm that was bought has been subsumed into the organization. But there were two important elements that the Crescendo acquisition highlighted. First, it was located in Silicon Valley, making it much easier for the two companies to work together. Second, and of paramount importance, the acquisition immediately added products to the Cisco sales arsenal and was driven by customers, not by technology. If a big customer wanted to buy something, Chambers was determined that Cisco would sell it. This, more than any lip service to bigger paradigms and revolutions, is really what the Cisco acquisition game is all about. Getting what the customer wants to buy.

Crescendo set the stage for a series of acquisitions over the next few years. As the switching market started to develop, Cisco bought a number of other small switch companies and quickly consolidated its marketplace lead. By 1996 Crescendo's product line was generating nearly $500 million of Cisco's $2 billion in revenue. A string of small companies like Kalpana (with high-speed switches and remote-access links), Lightstream (ATM switches), Grand Junction (higher-speed Ethernet, 100-megabit-per-second switches), and several others started to give Cisco pieces around the edges of several emerging markets. But there was one crucial missing factor: size and market heft. Only in routers, and now in switches, was Cisco number one or two in the market.

In 1995 the time had come for John Morgridge to step down in favor of his handpicked successor. There had been grumbling about Chambers's lack of technical experience, but the success of the Crescendo deal, which he had spearheaded, bought him credibility inside and outside the company. Switches had been a bet-the-company deal, and it came through magnificently for Cisco and for Chambers.

As Chambers took over the company and Morgridge became the chairman, their combined lack of technological knowledge led to a big, and controversial, acquisition that would have a profound effect on the character of the company and its future.

FOR MOST OF its life, Cisco had been on an IP crusade. All the early technical staff of the company and most of the salespeople sold routers and understood routers and the way that Ethernet and all IP networks handled and managed packets of data. Cisco had concentrated on selling both the switching equipment that companies needed to give increasing data capacity to workers and servers and to the routers that formed the meshwork backbone of both corporate networks and the Internet. The enterprise, or business, sector had become the company's most important financial market, and the geeks and netheads in the core of the Internet (which at that time was just getting the boost it needed from Netscape and the frenzy of its 1995 IPO) all agreed on one thing: The best way to move data was with packets and routers.

But the telco world, which had developed ATM (asynchronous transfer mode), disagreed. ATM divided data up into fixed-size cells that could be transmitted very rapidly. While there was lots of religious language from each side of the debate about the demerits of the other, all the griping hid a bigger issue. ATM was booming as the telecom market prepared to beef up voice circuits with ATM equipment, which just happened to have been designed to fit right into the equipment bays and slots of the incumbent phone companies. What Chambers realized was that staying away from ATM because it wasn't IP was a death sentence for Cisco. To Chambers, the issue was simple: Customers were placing big orders for ATM equipment (and its lower-speed predecessor, Frame Relay) to beef up their connections between sites, as well as to take advantage of bulk data purchasing opportunities directly from the carriers. If Cisco was going to grow, it had to make sure that it offered all the products companies might want to buy—or it was going to cede its role as the supplier of everything that a corporation, institution, Internet service provider, or even carrier needed. This had become the central tenet of Chambers's strategy for the future of Cisco. No longer content to toil away selling routers and switches to people using networks in their businesses, Chambers now wanted to sell data solutions, from soup to nuts—wanted to be the preeminent supplier of all the gear any data-sophisticated customer would need to tame the Internet. He had learned this lesson during his years with IBM: Sell everything the customers need to buy to equip their networks. Be the one-stop corporate customer's partner in networking, just as IBM played the same role vis-à-vis computing.

To do this meant forgetting about technology orthodoxies, ignoring cries from the IP bigots, and getting a foot into the big ATM switch and gear markets. Three potential acquisitions could instantly have given Cisco credibility and a major market share in the ATM space: Fore, Cascade, and Stratacom. The first was dismissed for cost and location reasons. Headquartered in Pennsylvania and with a rate of growth that was eclipsing even Cisco's, Fore looked like too rich a prospect. Cascade was in fact the most likely, even though the company was located in Massachusetts. Cisco had already acquired an ownership stake in the company when it made an early-stage investment; in fact, Chambers and Cascade's president, Dan Smith, had a handshake arrangement for a sale. But Cascade specialized in very big ATM switches that were especially well suited to carriers—and that wasn't quite the right fit for Cisco, which had negligible carrier business and a marketplace emphasis that was laser-concentrated on the enterprise customer. At the eleventh hour, the deal fell apart, but without Smith's being informed. The combination of physical location, an emphasis on carriers rather than on enterprises, and a mismatch in culture caused Chambers to walk away, a move that Dan Smith remembers with bitterness. Now co-founder of Sycamore, a major optical networking company, he still says he "can't trust Cisco."

That left Stratacom. The company was headquartered in Silicon Valley and had one other big thing going for it: Its product line was aimed squarely at the big enterprise customers and the service providers selling to them, rather than the carriers. Stratacom had specialized in the earlier generation of Frame Relay switches and was about to expand its ATM presence in a big way. Chambers and his acquisitions boss, Mike Volpi, figured that if Cisco combined its LAN switches and routers for the campus or facility architecture with Stratacom's ATM technology designed for the wide-area telecommunications transportation market, it could outfox the competition and offer enterprise customers the right collection of equipment both for today and, as data needs soared, for tomorrow. Chambers met with the president of Stratacom and, in what is also a Cisco hallmark, offered $4.5 billion for the company almost from the very start of discussions, a vast premium over the company's then market value. Two weeks later, on the day that the deal was finalized, Cisco sold all its stock in Cascade. Press reports were the first time that Dan Smith heard about his partner buying his major competitor or his own deal with Cisco being over.

ACQUIRING STRATACOM MADE Cisco bigger, ultimately by several billion dollars a year in revenues. But it also brought the company into a new playing field: the big telecom networks. ATM and Frame Relay were a telco standard, and Stratacom was providing the gear to let corporations hook themselves up to the telco networks. It opened doors for Chambers. It helped develop the soup-to-nuts package he was selling in the executive suite. Now Cisco had a backbone network beachhead and was selling gear from the long-haul to the desktop.

As Internet use started to go through the roof in 1997, Cisco kept buying company after company, creating a kind of institutionalized culture of acquisition, which proved disruptive on a project-team level. Instead of designing products to a single unified vision and blueprint, Cisco's chief engineering task was to make all the newly acquired products work together. Doing so required unwieldy workarounds and incredibly arcane and confusing software interfaces. Dozens of little pockets of energy formed around groups of engineers from acquired companies. Some worked out: Crescendo, Kalpana, Grand Junction. Many didn't: Lightstream, Ardent, Precept. But the company kept buying. And because it had all that founders' stock in its coffers, it could keep doing so.

For instance, in 1999, Cisco bought Cerent for $6 billion in stock. Cerent's play was to allow data traffic to get hijacked onto the older SONET networks. No other company was on the market with sophisticated products for this very specialized market, and Cerent picked up a number of early sales. The big competitor, however, was Nortel, whose products were already dominant in long-haul and metro networks—in the latter holding a 70 percent market share already. Lucent was a nonplayer in this market until in early 2000 it bought Chromatis, a newer start-up than Cerent. This start-up has an even more compelling story to tell the existing SONET industry regarding flexibility and the ability to cram more data into existing SONET networks, and its innovations might make Cerent seem an interim-stage product. Could incipient irrelevance be one of the dark clouds on the fast acquisition path? Buy too soon, and be passed by a later start-up with a better proposition.

There were reverberations about the high price Cisco paid for Cerent—a new-generation SONET company dreamed up and crafted for purchase by a smart Johnny Appleseed of a venture capitalist, Vinod Khosla, whose promiscuous financing has created a number of competitive start-ups. Cerent had just shipped its first products. How could that company have so much value? There were rumors of troubles in the Monterey deal, another acquisition that was in the optical area—optical cross-connects or switches similar to Lucent's, but with optical and electronic cores—because it had been sued by Alcatel for intellectual property theft. Worse, in a mid-year earnings call, John Chambers admitted that while he was hoping to be able to announce Monterey sales by the end of 2000, it now didn't look realistic until sometime the following year. Monterey finally announced a field test, but it is well behind Lucent in developing lambda routers.

To help it find its footing in the world of light, the company broke an inviolate John Chambers rule in late 1999: Only buy companies that are local. It bought a portion of Pirelli, the Italian tiremaker, which had one of the most advanced optics groups in the world. The company held some of the seminal patents in the dense wave division multiplexing market, and it also gave Cisco a foothold in the components that make up a fiber-optic network. The Pirelli acquisition hasn't gone smoothly either. Products were not competitive in the long-haul business, and in a market that doubled in size for the year, the Pirelli market share dropped from nearly 5 percent in early 1999 to less than 1 percent by the beginning of 2000. More recently, Cisco has sold off some of the Pirelli businesses and appears to be attempting to stanch the flow of red ink in this operation.

Finally, in the midst of all of this, Cisco bought a small Swedish firm, Qeyton, that sells gear similar to Pirelli's. However, Qeyton specializes in a different part of the equation: the last-mile connections between big customers—read enterprises—and the carrier networks. At a price of $800 million, this one might be the real steal if the company can get its products focused into the Cisco selling machine and become the way to bring fiber capacity to end-users. However, Qeyton has yet to ship and will have its hands full competing with Nortel and smaller companies such as ONI (a young, tough start-up that is already selling systems that use DWDM to link end-users and the long-distance carrier networks), Ciena, and others. Again, this might be the mark of a culture of acquisition at all costs. Cisco may well have bought the wrong company and, without internal development troops to create its own homegrown products, could have taken a major misstep in a market that is morphing as fast as the regional and metropolitan optical universe.

While making these acquisitions, Chambers created a magnificent marketing and positioning campaign that interwove the themes of Internet efficiency and the virtue of acquisitiveness: speed, time to market, squeezing every efficiency out of the Net. The game was to dance ahead of the marketplace by listening very carefully to what customers were buying—and then to buy either the competition or *its* competition and create an interconnected combination of equipment that gets the business.

Just buy another company. Just go get it. It was a strategy ideally suited to Chambers, his background, and the landscape, the environment he was working within. He didn't have the hubris to think he could see the future. He wasn't an engineer. What he could do was talk with customers. And he could buy companies with the bulging wallet that the founders had unwittingly given him. He would buy lots of hives of entrepreneurial excellence. The process of identifying the right candidates would become the entire organization's task. A few key executives would ride herd over particular sectors of business, but sales and acquisitions would be everyone's job. (Today, as the company is growing in head count, add "finding new employees" to the list.) Hire the very best people possible and turn them loose. Evaluations and bonuses were paid on improving customer satisfaction—make that the core driver of everything. Trust that the right new products would bubble up to the top, and don't aim R&D for the breakthroughs. Figure that customers will tell you about those in plenty of time for you to respond—such as buying a promising start-up in the field once it has proved out the technology and is poised to go to market. Add Cisco's sales might to the newly acquired company's product. Make the chief engineering task the integration of new products into the family tree of software, not the creation of new kinds of breakthrough products that anticipate the market. Talk endlessly about the value of the best-of-breed strategy that acquisitions can support—downplay the lack of any kind of advanced engineering vision because that becomes clear only as events unfold and new companies are bought. Sell the big picture to customers, and freeze them in their buying decisions by always copying the new products that other companies are announcing.

It was the John Chambers mantra of management. Unfortunately the Stratacom acquisition was not a success. Even though the company was located nearby, cultures clashed repeatedly. Stratacom was big enough to be able to challenge Cisco in every internal area, and the duplication of teams led to internal warfare. Furthermore, Frame Relay and ATM did turn out to be dead ends for the most part. Worse, the deal seemed like a sellout to the original "IP everywhere" crowd. The old-timers didn't think buying into a bad technology in order to shore up a sales portfolio was the right way to go. But arguably—*economically*, rather than *technologically*—it was. More important, the acquisition of Stratacom represented the stodgification of Cisco. Now there were systems and procedures. It didn't feel like a cutting-edge kind of place anymore—no more "us against the world" of the telcos, no more "power to the people" and up from the wiring rooms and the trenches. People started drifting away; brilliant, talented people headed out for the venture shops and other start-ups and dot-coms. Cisco, which had been nearly as gold-plated on a résumé as Stanford, now had to become even more interested in defending what it had than in forging into new territory.

Under Chambers, Cisco was changing. Acquisitions on every front were going to be the company's R&D now. The smart teams of guys in every product organization would look out for new hot boxes in their sector that customers wanted to buy, and *boom!* the company would send in a SWAT team to take over all the details of the acquisition. Since Cisco came with lots of money and a culture determined to make a deal, it was hard to resist the offer. The sales pitch was simple: "We're the best in the world. You're world class too. We want to work with you so bad we'll pay you more money than you ever imagined. Isn't that great?"

The deal was completed with lightning speed. It usually started with tentative contacts, usually initiated by Cisco itself, but not exclusively, and then moved on to one-on-one time for the chief executives of the two companies to get to know one another, usually over dinner at Chambers's house. At the heart of it all, the key team members made a fundamental evaluation of whether the two firms were a "good fit" and had a similar view of the future. Translation: The new company's management didn't despise Cisco, eat with their fingers, or think they would one day overthrow the router and put Cisco out of business.

If all went well, an offer would be made. Almost always high, more than fair. A premium. In this one area, Cisco was able to be magnanimous with its stock and its money. This made everyone happy. A booth was set up in the entryway of the new company. Within thirty days, everyone in the new company had been moved over to the central Cisco human resources system; health care and pensions had been adjusted; minor problems had been solved. It was left to the engineers to make sure the new products were compatible with Cisco equipment, update the software, and get the products into the pipeline. It almost always meant that Cisco acquired not just intellectual capital—the smart new employees Chambers likes to claim are the real secret of good acquisitions—but also soon-to-generate-cash products. This acquisitions fever reduced the time for both research and product development and brought a steady flow of cash into Cisco. In the meantime, the "Cisco Kids," as they came to be called in hallway vernacular, simply by virtue of the extraordinary Cisco sales force, could count on sales three or four times larger than any previous projections made when they were a struggling independent with products on the horizon.

Chambers's business acquisitions strategy beat the competition into submission as demand continued to skyrocket and the Internet turned into a five-year phenomenon. Competitors stumbled, tripped all over themselves, and left the playing field, admitting defeat and ceding all the revenues of the meteoric routing sector to Cisco. 3Com should have been a player; but instead of coming straight after the corporate space and duking it out in the only profitable part of networking's first decade, the company's management tried to avoid Cisco and eke out profits on every other sector of networking it could find. Bay, the product of an uneasy east-west marriage between Wellfleet and Synoptics, never united to ignite its business in a way consistent enough to mount a credible enterprise alternative to Cisco— until it was bought by Nortel, which had its own blind spot from years of selling mainly to big phone company carriers. Cabletron bet on the wrong side of the equation—hubs—for far too long, always felt more comfortable with the netheads than with corporate data departments, flaunted its anti-establishment management style, and missed the routing game as well as the corporate tornado of data gear needed as the Internet vortex spun up to speed. Lucent, buoyed and supported by its tight relationship with AT&T, finally got religion in the late '90s and bought odd companies until finally landing Ascend, the one networking business that had beaten Cisco in an emerging networking sector—the Internet service provider and new carrier markets. The telco giant, however, never focused its attention on enterprise customers, where the money and innovation really were, and recently spun off its struggling enterprise operations.

King's X to Cisco.

Throughout the years, there have been dozens of small acquisitions in every corner of the enterprise, carrier, service provider, and consumer space. There were acquisitions to fill out the cable-access-line and the core carrier market. There were wireless and voice-over-the-Internet buys, deals for software and hardware and alliances and everything else. Chambers has no technology bigotry about him. He's delightfully promiscuous as long as he can sell the product to customers. The only other rule is to get into the market early enough or in a big enough way to have a reasonable shot at market dominance—or, at worst, the number two position—and to never give up on a sale.

But the easy pickings aren't so easy any longer. Arrowpoint is a classic example of this. The company specializes in a kind of "content switch." These switches are intelligent boxes that can direct Web page requests to servers that are located closer to the end-user, or that are idle, or that are particularly well suited to the exact kind of content that the requestor is trying to receive. These will be an important component in building Web server clusters and hosting centers in the future. But it is also a market with total revenues of less than $500 million, and Arrowpoint wasn't the leader. How could that possibly justify a price of nearly $6 billion? The simple answer is that in Old World accounting, where a company's price has to be figured against the books of the acquiring company as cash in subsequent quarters, it couldn't. But in the New World "pooling of interests" method of accounting, where the price disappears into something called "goodwill," it is like funny money. Spending $6 billion on Cerent or on Arrowpoint was a penalty-free, purely paper transaction for Cisco. In the quarter before Cisco bought Arrowpoint, the tiny target company had revenues of about $10 million. That made the purchase price 150 times trailing earnings. This is an astonishing multiple and cannot be justified on anything other than religious grounds. Perhaps if Arrowpoint dominated this market sector, and if the growth were going to be stratospheric, it could be justified. But this is an emerging sector where Arrowpoint was third.

In a company without a technology heart, this is a mark of desperation, an effort by the brain trust at Cisco to keep pumping up the sales numbers with more and more products, whatever the cost. With stock as the currency, there's no penalty for paying inflated sums for any company. These principles powered the Cisco R&D-by-acquisition strategy. It fits elegantly into a sales-driven schema, and it worked perfectly as long as demand continued unabated, as long as every customer was continually buying more stuff, never retrenching. Signs of overbuilt capacity slowed the telecom market late in 2000, as several new carriers started to suggest they would miss their numbers. Cisco, an aggressive extender of credit as well as an investor in many companies, could be rocked by failures. But it is hard to see a slowdown in the demand for bandwidth, as more and more users get their hands on high-speed digital lines and start to experience true interactivity, as the fiber-optic and "Ethernet everywhere" opportunities rewrite the landscape again. And if there is a slowing, it will be in the service provider and new carrier space. But Cisco makes its money from enterprises and businesses. No evidence of slowing there yet.

This world according to John Chambers elegantly likened his vision of Cisco as a company to the emerging structure of the Internet: a world of links and interconnected Web sites. It wasn't a big leap to see a similarity between an influx of brilliant pockets of talent and an Intranet with lots of great Web sites. This was the way Cisco saw itself: acquisitions, pools of feverish activity, connected to a whole through the burgeoning spaghetti mass of Cisco's IOS software. All of it held together tenuously under the big tent of Cisco's relentless sales force. See an emerging market sector? Just buy a company that has a foothold in that area, and let the links and connections that the Internet can foster work for Cisco as well. It was the Internet, with its crazy quilt of meshed and interconnected relationships, stretched into a business model. And as long as demand continued to expand, as long as competitors left the most lucrative portion of the market to Cisco, as long as there was no pain in paying wildly high prices for unproven products and companies, and as long as investors wanted to believe, really wanted to believe in the sermons that John Chambers gave them, it all worked.

The fact that the company's products fueled the Internet made it perfect to reinvent the corporation as an Internet-powered one. Integrating the company's burgeoning business systems across and through the Internet itself, both as a management tool for quick response and as an example of Internet synergy and business use at its best, was an ideal story, even if it was almost transparently self-serving to anyone who took the time to actually analyze the gospel of its chief priest and holy man. The press picked up on the tale; and as the demand for Internet access and the use of the Internet for all kinds of transactions continued to grow exponentially into the late 1990s, Cisco created a virtuous cycle that fed itself. Not only was it selling boatloads of routers and switches to everyone who wanted to get on the Internet bandwagon, but it was also showing the world how to use the Internet as a business tool. This was synergy at its best. In the stampede down the path of the New World Internet, in the tulip mania of dot-com enthusiasm, Cisco was the bellwether, the navigator for the whole crazy flotilla of venture-backed enterprises and the fear-driven enterprise rush to embrace the madness fast, faster, fastest. All of it fed the surge of Cisco and the success the company kept posting quarter in and quarter out.

Cisco and John Chambers became emblematic of the friction-free economy—the Internet Age itself. The company ethos was rooted in a never-ending upward-spiral stock market and the ability to use an almost inextinguishable source of stock. It was a business model of total expediency. If a paying customer wants it, we'll get it. And it was a business process built around partnering and linking rather than making anything in-house. What made this model unique was that there was no belief that the company would add its value in more technology or engineering. Cisco's big value was in offering the one-stop shop. The Cisco of John Chambers is selling pickaxes and jeans and supplies to the miners of the IP mother lode. No. *Thinking up* the pickaxes and shovels but getting others to make them. This was Information Age, Intellect Age at its purest. All the items are stamped with the name Cisco, they are certified to work together, and they are expensive. Few are made in Cisco factories; in fact, most never touch Cisco except in taking the initial order, and providing the final destination for the payment. There is little added-value engineering, no new initiative independent of customer requests, and a weak tradition of engineering-centric design. Everything that Cisco sells is made to work together after the fact, not from the ground up. In a sense, Cisco is the Wal-Mart of networking. The company uses the tools of modern technology—computers, networks, supply chains—to deliver a whole panoply of networking products that it simply *sells*. It hardly *makes* anything.

In a New World view, this is a mark of greatness.

But it also risks losing the very core competencies that once made the company great. If suppliers do all the value-added engineering, what is to stop them from coming after Cisco? This is exactly what the hordes of chip makers now supplying Cisco products can do. And after years of supplier and out-sourced dependency, Cisco no longer has the in-house skills to fight back.

Offer nothing new, package everything beautifully, and make it easy for the customer to buy it from you. This is the Achilles' heel of the company from a traditional point of view, where value is added by a company that deserves to get your money. It explains the enormous push the company has made into services, consulting, and networking. The only value that Cisco can offer is the ability to help a company tie all its networks together. This is a unique skill that Cisco has to offer. But is it enough? This Cisco is a sales and support organization for the hundreds of products it is feverishly buying. Call it acquisition fever. It is not delivering a tightly crafted family of products designed to fit together. Except after the fact. As long as the flood tide is rising, no problem. But at some point all great companies have to create something that the customer didn't know he needed, before he asks for it.

There is no master plan. That is the master plan. Is this a new business model? Is this the conglomerate model remastered for the Hollow Corporation of the new millennium? In this New World, if speed to get products in front of customers is more important than engineering value, Cisco will win. If demand never flags, Cisco will win. If customers keep paying a premium for the Cisco brand and the umbrella of software that can make all the pieces work together, Cisco will win. If there is an unending army of outsourcers to let Cisco lay off core procedures and processes to others, Cisco will win. If it buys meteoric companies, it wins. If Cisco customers keep needing to have their hands held and are willing to pay Cisco for the privilege, it wins.

But knock out any of these props in its business model and Cisco may very well lose big.

CHAPTER 8

AN EMPEROR WITHOUT HEIRS

THERE IS ONE GLARING HOLE AT CISCO: SUCCESSION. JOHN Chambers has not designated a clear number two—or even a handful of potential successors. In fact, both his executive vice presidents departed hastily in the waning months of 2000. He has created a company that revolves so totally around him that if he were any less outwardly gentle, kind, and magnanimous, Cisco would be called a cult of personality.

For a long time the presumed heir apparent was Don Listwin, known as "The Hammer" in the corridors of Cisco City. A hard-driving numbers-oriented sales manager, Listwin provided the muscle behind Chambers's nice-guy affability. He had been put in charge of arguably the toughest sector—service providers. He had failed, however, to take control of this market, and John Chambers, the velvet hammer himself, decided it was time for him to go. Chambers knew that the service provider business was a tough one, that Cisco had to fight every inch of the way. The real trouble was that Listwin and his wife—Lorene Arey, head of public relations, or corporate communications—were a little too full of themselves. The first time Arey had quarterbacked a story in the press that identified her husband as the heir apparent, Chambers and the rest of the executive team could forgive it. After all, Listwin, another short and intense executive cut out of the Don Valentine mold, was the company's only executive vice president at the time. Chambers told them that he didn't want it to happen again. But it did. By then, however, there was another executive vice president, Gary Daichendt, chief of worldwide operations.

The final straw was another fawning profile of Cisco that came out in *Fortune* in the spring of 2000. It recounted the same pabulum about Cisco, talking about the brilliant use of information services and the Internet to improve the bottom line and pointing to the genius of the company's acquisition strategy. The gossipy piece described Chambers, the executive who flies around in a corporate Citation jet, as especially close to his parents—just an aw-shucks good ol' boy from West Virginia.

There was nothing even vaguely objectionable about any of that, of course, and overall the story told the same tale that Cisco has carefully crafted for years. What was new, however, and what would ultimately prove the downfall for Listwin and Arey, was that they invited the writer up to dinner at their palatial mansion in the hills above Silicon Valley. There they opened a bottle of Chardonnay, made (by others of course) from grapes they grew on their own land, and presented a picture of a "golden couple." The writer described Listwin as the heir apparent and limned the couple as living the ultimate good life in the heart of twenty-first-century Silicon Valley.

It was a major strategic error, and it infuriated John Chambers. One of the cardinal rules of life at Cisco has always been tightfisted fiscal conservatism. The image of the fabulously wealthy lieutenant and his wife, living like Caesars, rubbed the wrong way. Worse, the couple had allowed the writer to imagine that Listwin was the next Chambers, even though the executive VP was careful to make it clear that he didn't anticipate his boss leaving anytime soon.

It wasn't enough. A few weeks after the article appeared, on the day of the fiscal-year-end earnings call in early August, an unwilling Listwin showed up in front of a hastily convened meeting of his staff. Behind him filed in the company's most senior executives and officers, who stood in a careful row behind him, as if the whole thing had been orchestrated. One person described it as "looking like a Mafia hit team rub-out." The senior guys were there to make sure Listwin told the story exactly as scripted. Listwin announced that he was leaving to head up a new and powerful Internet-based phone company, to be created out of the merger of a couple of phone.com companies that seemed very hastily assembled and not very promising.

And it was done. The once high and mighty Listwin (along with his wife, who left in the same operation) was gone. Chambers announced the departure that day, during the analyst earnings call where he publicly said goodbye to the former executive vice president. And just like that, one of the company's two executive vice presidents . . . vanished. John Chambers had made it clear that he would broach no ego that could challenge his own.

A few months later the company's other executive vice president, Chief Operating Officer Gary Daichendt, abruptly resigned as well. There was not even the pretence of a new job. Just a buried Thursday night news release. Although Daichendt, an old sales force colleague of Chambers's from IBM, had, by all accounts, done a superb job of overseeing Cisco's sales force, he had built almost no visibility outside the corporation and had little involvement in top-level strategy. His departure cleared the most senior ranks of the company at a time when Cisco is being challenged more than ever before.

For a $20 billion company, Cisco's entire management team seems weak on big company experience, which could be a great advantage as well. Someone in the executive ranks must step up to the enormously complex task of making IOS the Windows of the networking age, of charting a course into the wireless and fiber-optic arenas, of preaching the sermon of Cisco as poster child corporation for the Internet Age. Chambers has surrounded himself with very bright, very smart sales-side executives. But none is the kind of senior manager who could replace him were he to become tempted by his flirtation with George W. Bush's election campaign to run for the Senate or the governorship from California, as has been rumored.

The fault lies partly with Chambers, who has been loath to surround himself with contrarian thinkers with talent greater than his own. Partly it is also simply an issue of speed. Cisco has grown so fast and so relentlessly that there are no executives with internal experience turning around a division, or facing a downturn, or beefing up market share in a rigorously competitive market. "Just get on with it" is the management motto. Growth has been unrelenting.

Cisco's executives are great at managing when the tide is rising unceasingly. Few of them have experience in any other kind of environment. They may never need it, either, but broader experience usually translates into wisdom and perspective.

The way Chambers dealt swift retribution to Listwin for crossing him demonstrates a certain intensity—even a ruthlessness—that is usually hidden from outsiders. For all his ease of manner and light touch, Chambers can be tough on the people who report to him. He is a perfectionist with a low tolerance for anything less than startling performance. At every quarterly earnings conference he makes a point of putting one or another of the execs on the spot, publicly demanding that they promise to improve market share.

For all his Dr. Feelgood preaching, Chambers has a weak record when it comes to senior managers who are women. One of the company's more impressive candidates to succeed him a few years ago, Jayshree Ullal, has been on a sabbatical for six months and, when last heard from, was reported to be in India. This powerful and charismatic woman ran Cisco's enterprise business and made it exceptionally valuable, routinely beating estimates handily. However, she never seemed able to break into Chambers's inner circle, which consisted of Don Listwin, Mike Volpi, and Charlie Giancarlo. With the hiring of the smart, slick, very wealthy, and quick-witted Carl Russo as head of Cisco's optical business, and the promotion of James Richardson as head of enterprise networking, Ullal, perhaps sensing diminished opportunities, has disappeared.

Another high-profile woman, Judy Estrin, left the post of chief technology officer after only a year in the job. Estrin had started one of the earliest networking firms, Bridge, which merged with 3Com in the late 1980s. A pioneer in networking, she has a very long history with start-ups but found Cisco stultifying. In order to counteract the impression that Cisco is a macho place, Chambers often points to Sue Bostrum, who runs the company's new and successful consulting operation, and its long-time human resources head, Barbara Beck. However, neither is an officer of the corporation.

In recognition of his weakness on the technology side of the ledger, and in an attempt to bolster his core of senior executives, Chambers recently convinced Ed Kozel, the former chief strategy officer, to return as the chief technology officer for the service provider line of business. Kozel was the architect of the Crescendo and Stratacom deals, and Chambers often talks about how this was the man who made him wire up his new home with network cable, who made him see the light about the vast possibilities of the Internet—especially an Internet with Cisco at its core, an Internet that would do nothing but grow and grow.

What is not lacking among Cisco's executives is experience in the entrepreneurial sector. But it is very different to succeed in a stealth start-up, attacking a corner of an emerging market with no entrenched competitors, than in a $10 billion division where profit-and-loss success doesn't mean simply putting a Cisco nameplate on another hot box. And unlike at GE, where Jack Welch had three world-class contenders for his job, John Chambers has failed to develop even a single successor among the executives who remain. Ironically, it was exactly this lack of succession planning that brought down Wang.

Mike Volpi, chief strategy officer, has never run an operating division with profit-and-loss responsibility. Larry Carter, the CFO, is not CEO material. Carl Russo, who is trying to make the optical business great, is a charismatic guy, whose billion-dollar stake in Cerent lets him be refreshingly ascerbic—but can he run a $5 billion business? Rick Justice, senior vice president of worldwide operations and an increasingly visible officer of the corporation, is an exception to the all-Cisco background; he previously ran a division for H-P.

Down the line there are some big holes. For instance, in wireless, Cisco doesn't have a serious advocate; the same is true in the service provider space. With the departure of Listwin, Kevin Kennedy was promoted to take over the job but has yet to join the enterprise (James Richardson) and small to mid-sized business (Charles Giancarlo) executives as an officer of the corporation. This is probably the toughest job at Cisco, and Kennedy will need all the smarts he brings from seventeen years at Bell Labs to make this a victorious market for the company. One bright spot is Giancarlo, an exceptionally intelligent man with excellent academic credentials who came to Cisco with the acquisition of switch maker Kalpana. Under him, Cisco's small-to-medium business efforts have prospered.

For all intents and purposes, this is John Chambers's show. He plays the starring role with relish, basking in the applause from the only audience that matters—investors. The stock has been a very good friend for most of the company's public history.

Even after the Wall Street blood bath of 2000, the stock price was still eighty times earnings for the previous fiscal year. Its investment growth multiples are legendary: Try forty times its price at IPO—even at its 2000 low. Sixty million shareholders are happy with John Chambers; there's a real wind at his back. But Chambers realizes better than most that he's sailing into uncharted, dangerous waters in which lurk mines that could sink his ship.

The problem of succession is only one challenge facing Cisco. The greater danger—entirely of Cisco's own making—has bedeviled the great companies of the past. This threat transcends the world of business and enters the Darwinian world of natural selection. It is almost a law of nature: A successful creation, entity, person, being, company spawns offspring that will better it. This is a secret of life that is equally as true about business. In the same way that Intel and Microsoft finished off the minicomputer industry with PCs that were cheaper and better and easier to use, Cisco, with its extraordinary success, has given seed to a horde of new challengers—savvy, tenacious upstarts that sprout like weeds and move with breathtaking speed and agility, companies that can sniff out and exploit the weaknesses of giants. Companies that use better technology chops to run rings around the big guys.

Chambers knows intimately the danger of this economic Darwinism. He has always said that the competitors he fears most are the guys who can start with a blank piece of paper. Within this war zone of natural selection are two other principles that Chambers knows as well as he knows the list of names he keeps in his pocket: (1) In a rapidly shifting environment, new combinations of capabilities can quickly become dominant, and (2) there are extraordinary, and unpredictable, mutations of technology that seem to come like clockwork every few years. Cisco is perhaps the best example of the first. When the router was suddenly central, and essential, to the Internet, the company was able to turn the tables on all the original giants of the networking industry and leave them in evolutionary backwaters of their own making. As for the second principle, look no further than to how mainframes mutated into minicomputers, which were eviscerated by PCs. Transistors (mainframes) preceded the integrated circuit (minicomputers) that led to the microprocessor (the PC). Or sliced another way: Cheaper long-distance phone calling in the early '80s led to the cell phone services of the '90s, followed by the Internet of the new millennium, and whoever knows what tomorrow. Creative cannibalism. A frenzy of innovation.

Take all of these principles together, apply them to the ever-expanding New World economy of networking, and it is clear that the anointed leader of the networking pack—Cisco—will be hard pressed to continue its spectacular rise. In fact, it is the law of change, aided and abetted by a swarm of new companies, that is about to shatter the cozy world of the company. It is in the transition from communications networks built on electrons and packets to a Brave New World built on photons where Cisco must do battle. Cisco was built to deliver intelligence in the electronic age of networking. In the coming years, new companies will emerge that will deliver intelligence in the age of light. How this battle will actually play out in the marketplace is currently unclear. But it will be a contest whose outcome will determine the future of Cisco.

True, Cisco's breakneck ride in the communications and financial world to the pinnacle of public acclaim and investor adoration has already been nothing less than marvelous. But the rules of networking and the wonder of a wired world that John Chambers so passionately speaks of will soon change the underlying foundations of the very business in which Cisco excels. In that market transition, Cisco and John Chambers are going to have to reinvent themselves once again.

It is going to be increasingly hard to do this with a $20 billion juggernaut, and here's why.

As the next new new thing of photon-based networking develops, there will be no shortage of well-financed competitors, and they won't be carrying the baggage of the electronic world. Cisco, however, will be forced to do so in order to keep its current customers satisfied. These hordes will train their sights on the grande dame of packet routers and switches, and they will use their light swords and wands to do battle. Imagine the Lilliputians tying down Gulliver.

To be sure, when there were few, if any, legitimate competitors to Cisco's markets, Chambers and his vast crew of salespeople, trainers, and technicians ruled the roost. They could charge what they wanted when demand for their products was red hot. The propitious pricing anomaly of extraordinary demand and inept competition let the company continue to raise prices on routers in the face of declining prices in nearly every other part of the technology landscape.

Cisco is quick to innovate by acquisition, generally buying already-developed products rather than setting off on its own along a technology path. It also has a much bigger inertia to account for (the large installed base being both a source of recurring revenue and a weight around the company's neck) than any of the dozens of garage start-ups. It can be out-innovated and out-maneuvered by a focused start-up.

Even today, hordes are gathering at the gates, the inevitable offspring of this fecund environment, small companies bursting with the brightest minds sprouting in fields Cisco has made fertile, chipping away at one or another section of the fortress. These hordes have thrown out the end-to-end business model that made Cisco oceans of profits and are offering their products at prices John Chambers is not in a position to compete against. They offer customers the network know-how and cobble together the best and the cheapest solutions to deliver bandwidth. Sure they'll work with Cisco gear. Or anyone else's. In this world, brand names don't matter. After all, whether it's water to the kitchen sink or information to the computer, the user doesn't care who makes the plumbing, as long as it works. And the user wants that plumbing at the best possible price. Period.

CHAPTER 9

JUNIPER, REDBACK, AND THE BARBARIANS AT THE GATE

TAM DELL'ORO IS A SMALL, ENERGETIC, AND FEISTY WOMAN with a full head of dark hair and enough charm and smarts to have carved herself out a niche in the market research world, concentrating on network equipment. Her research agency—the Dell'Oro Group—which resides in the tony Silicon Valley enclave of Portola Valley, tracks actual sales of a string of network components, including routers, switches, and data and optical gear.

In a business filled with prognosticators and seers who readily offer up forecasts of the size of segments of the business in years to come, Dell'Oro doesn't do so with much relish.

Having made too many public pratfalls and mistaken predictions in her earlier years, she now focuses on actual shipments, triangulating between unit shipments, publicly reported revenue, and pricing/configuration lists. Her numbers track roughly a quarter behind the calendar year but are about as accurate a gauge of actual shipments, and momentum, as can be found.

For years she has been watching Cisco, first when she was a researcher working for the sales team at Synoptics, the Silicon Valley innovator of phone-jack-based Ethernet—10BaseT, it was called. In those days—the late '80s and early '90s—the networking business was a lot smaller. When her company merged with Wellfleet, a Boston area router maker, in 1995 to form Bay, she was already out on her own. Now, in the summer of 2000, after five years of tracking, she has learned to deeply respect Cisco's power. Surveying the stream of market sectors where Cisco has dominant share, from routers—legacy high-end, 93.7 percent; legacy low-end, 84.6 percent; voice-and-data midrange, 90.6 percent; voice-and-data low-end, 93 percent—to Ethernet switches, with an aggregate 60 percent market share across the board, and on to WAN routers, Dell'Oro has nothing but praise.

"An extraordinary achievement. Unprecedented ability to sell its products and to deliver the products and services that customers need. I have watched it take market share away from every competitor and consolidate its lead in sectors where there used to be much more even competition. They never let up."

This analyst is smart. She knows the game between journalist and pundit requires the ability to provide a quotable sound bite, to point out a new insight. There's a pause as she studies the array of tables spread out before her, twenty, almost thirty pages of close typed numbers: the record of Cisco's marketplace domination over the past few years. "There is one very interesting pair of tables, however," she adds, reaching into the sheaf and extricating a single page. "For several years now Cisco has done nothing but improve its router market shares in every segment.

"Except this one. The wide-area network, core router market. Big Iron. The biggest of the routers, the densest, the machines at the very core of the biggest data networks. Here Cisco's share has dropped from 90 to 75 percent in two years."

What happened?

"Juniper." Her finger runs down the page to Juniper, whose share has leapt up to 22.4 percent in eighteen months. "There are three key, new, fast-growing market segments: core routing, subscriber aggregation, and content switching. Cisco is being challenged in all of them."

IF YOU WANTED to design a company to go after Cisco in a narrow market sector, Juniper Networks is the company you would create. The way the company founders envisioned it, Cisco's primarily software-based routers had about run out of steam, and it was time for hardware, not software, to take over the heavy lifting of routing data packets.

And so Juniper was born in 1996, with the explicit goal of creating a new router platform that could meet the anticipated growth demands of the Internet, one that was particularly optimized for the needs of the service provider market sector.

"Three things were clear to us," says Scott Kriens, the company's chief executive, a guy who is quick to be self-deprecating, although Juniper's sales are up 300 percent year-on-year. Kriens, like his counterpart at Cisco, comes from the sales side—he was head of sales at Stratacom when Cisco acquired it—and doesn't sport an engineering background or a fancy academic pedigree. He has a degree in economics from a blue-collar, commuter school, California State University in Hayward.

But he has something that few of his peers have: Kriens is a keen student of business and economic models, and he has closely studied the historical ebb and flow of successful companies in the high-tech universe, especially the networking world. Instead of "tying together a few hundred thousand mostly corporate employees" to the Net, Kriens says, "the New Net was going to have to connect two or three billion people all over the globe. The scale of the problem—getting high-speed access to many— is multi-thousand-fold different."

The real core of Cisco's business is centered on a giant mass of software that makes its many acquired products capable of interacting with one another. Cisco calls it IOS, or the Internet-working Operating System. But, in the face of a widespread belief in the primacy—no, the inevitability—of open standards and access, especially in networking, Cisco's IOS has been very carefully crafted to be closed, to limit the ability of anyone else to write enhancements to the core products without Cisco's express authorization. At the same time, Cisco's IOS is the de facto industry standard, simply based on the number of pieces of its equipment in the network.

With that in mind, Kriens and his colleagues have set about creating a new operating system, called JUNOS, for the New Net. And it is expected to go head to head with Cisco's new operating system, competing for market share when the older company's version is finished. But Juniper isn't about software alone. It's about hardware, big hardware, the kind of hardware that can stand up to the demand of billions, trillions of fast-moving data packets zipping about the earth. And it works hand-in-glove with the JUNOS software.

In that regard, Juniper is ahead of just about everyone else, although several other big router makers, including Avici, Pluris, and IronBridge, have announced products as well. But Juniper, which was well funded by the most fabled venture capitalists, set about developing its products with a semiconductor chip mindset. The performance levels the new Internet would require dictated a hardware solution focused on IP.

"In order to move that much traffic that fast, you can no longer handle routing in software programs—which, by their nature, are more flexible, but slower, than hardware. This software form of routing could run quite successfully on a small scale," says Kriens, referring to the old New World of corporate LANs and even the earlier days of the Internet. "But now, to handle the next generations of speed and size, routing has to be done in silicon, with large-scale chip architectures and a semiconductor methodology.

"It is a different performance level; it's a different scale and a different application problem. This opportunity is fundamentally different from the past. 3Com, Bay [and its constituents Synoptics and Wellfleet], Cabletron—all of them tried to do exactly the same thing that Cisco did: deliver multiprotocol software-based routers. Cisco simply out-executed them all.

"But in this case we're solving a totally different problem, actually selling to a totally different customer base: the service providers." This isn't the first time a networking company has done this. In the mid-1990s, Ascend Communications focused totally on developing digital connection equipment for Internet service providers so that they could efficiently handle the burgeoning growth of subscribers clamoring for Internet access. It was a very successful strategy and the only time that Cisco was beaten handily in a core networking specialty it had targeted for domination. Ascend's secret was a tight focus on one customer sector—and only one—and relentless breakneck engineering totally dedicated to economically solving a scale problem of large proportions (that had never been encountered before) for that sector of customers. This is exactly the formula that Juniper is following as well.

The biggest, baddest gigabit routers are what Cisco and Juniper sell today. They can move at least 1 gigabit per second, 10^9 bits per second, or 1 billion bits. In fact, Cisco claims that its top-of-the-line model—the Cisco 12012—can run at 2.5 gigabits per second. But Cisco uses a slightly misleading method for measuring the throughput of its routers—a technique that must be a marketing department ploy. The company counts both the bits that come in one side and those that leave the other and adds them together as the aggregate throughput. However, since it is really only the output that counts, the company's claims of throughput are actually half. This means the Cisco 12012 still qualifies as a gigabit machine, but not by much.

Juniper's products, a series of core routers—high-performance routing behemoths designed to forward more packets per second than anything else on earth—are aimed squarely at the service provider sector. They are all built around variations of a core chipset that was designed from the beginning to be a modular and extensible platform.

But more important, there was the Juniper software. This was a classic example of the blank-sheet-of-paper paradigm of technology evolution, the start-up advantage that Chambers is so frank about fearing the most. Starting its development effort in 1996 and tossing aside all the now extraneous features that legacy routers have layered onto their core products, Juniper made JUNOS the software brains of the platform, highly optimized and efficient, streamlined to take advantage of the new hardware. But most of all, it was also Cisco IOS-compatible.

Juniper routers would work with Cisco and other vendors' gear. This kind of interoperability took hundreds of person-years of software programming effort, but it gave Juniper a huge advantage over its two primary Old World competitors. Both Lucent and Nortel were steeped in a kind of Mad Hatter's tea party of proprietary telco interfaces that were fundamental to their legacy business models and dismissive of either the de facto requirements for standards or the dominance of Cisco gear in the IP networking world. The oldsters didn't make this kind of compatibility a priority. As a result, Juniper has been able to sell its products into formerly all-Cisco IP networking environments while the two much bigger companies have found selling routers very hard slogging. But more was at stake. JUNOS was also capable of one crucial set of new features for service providers: the ability to interactively provision bandwidth and routings from a browser interface, remotely. The provisioning issue has become huge as service providers have struggled with the logistics of giving broadband connections to many end-users. Juniper's new generation of routers can provide a much easier—in some ways trivial—method for setting up and adjusting connections and bandwidths to thousands of subscribers.

Juniper's routing systems were also built from the ground up to do much of the packet processing in hardware and to supply rate limiting and priority queuing for packets, as well as cut-through routing for voice over IP and virtual private networks (VPN—private network "channels" carved out across the public Internet). All of these are critical in making IP networks that were formerly highly unpredictable and chaotic, robust enough that companies will feel confident running their mission-critical processes and businesses on the Next Net.

These important features were integral, not bolted onto the Juniper system. Combine them with the crucial hardware chipset that allowed common routing protocols to be handled at wire speeds (the maximum possible electronic speed that can be achieved over the wire itself). Add a fast switching fabric, or cross-connect—a kind of digital patch panel, which are supplied by many vendors for Cisco—to swiftly interconnect all input and output ports. At Juniper, the result was an integrated, well-managed, and extensible family of routers that was better than Cisco's, that threw out all the old legacy features of routers in favor of highly specific hardware that worked with software designed from the ground up just to move packets and to make the management of those packets and the services that went along with them easy for service providers.

JUNOS was a breakthrough of significant proportions. In comparison, Cisco's IOS family of software was antiquated and overburdened. It had to support a multitude of products and lots of legacy features. Everything was always bought off the shelf as part of the expediency model of the Internet economy and in keeping with the Chambers mantra. It was hard to retrofit Cisco's IOS for the avalanche of new, more reliable routing techniques that were being spawned to make IP more robust; and, in fact, by the time Juniper started selling products in 1998

Cisco's IOS was creaking under the assault not only of dozens of bolted-on products, but also of new IP-based services like voice and security that continued to be innovated at a breakneck pace for an ever-increasing number of users. IOS was workable for the corporate networking market of the early 1990s, which was when it was created. But it was far from what was needed for the new world of service providers five years after the Internet had taken the world by storm.

Cisco started rebuilding its IOS. But the company's critical error was its lateness in finally realizing it was going to have to reengineer its fundamental systems; by then, Juniper had already consolidated its beachhead and built a lead. It is a classic problem for the leader in a previous generation. And as a result, Juniper looks poised to further exploit its advantage in the very high-end turf and move down the market to pick up more and more of the routing business that has always been Cisco's monopoly. This is going to be increasingly likely as service providers—the Juniper market—become more important and the enterprise customers who need to buy and install their own data connections with owned-and-operated networks wane.

Kriens is a student of technologies past. "IBM was the leader in all computer markets, using a mainframe to solve all problems, and it worked for a long time. When you get the feedback that your product, unchanged, captures 100 percent of a new market, like IBM and DEC and Intel and Microsoft and Cisco all have, the classic mistake is that the legacy company misreads that to mean that they've solved the problem, instead of seeing what it really means: That they've been placed there because there's a demand for which there is no alternative supply. It is a mistake made over and over."

As Kriens sees it, Cisco just assumed that it could take its standard software and hardware and introduce it to the relatively new and unserved service provider market. He calls it the 5 percent mistake: "Fervently hoping that any new innovation represents no more than a 5 percent deviation from its existing product line. [Market leaders] take the product they have and put it into the market and sell against that opportunity, and it is an immediate unanimous success," says Kriens. "This relaxes their focus or their urgency in building something from scratch for the new problem"—in this case, for a new generation of service providers who want to offer storage and applications themselves, over the network. Juniper, though, saw the problem, saw the opening, and has exploited it. And very well.

Yet demand for Cisco equipment continues to soar. More and more places are being networked. Cisco's local business, the enterprise and campus and home gear, is not part of the Juniper equation.

Juniper has leapt into the service provider market with a product platform built for this sector. It is a high-margin business, with plenty of room for profit. Since 1998 the average price of a core router (set by Cisco, of course) has doubled, to $200,000. This is a very healthy market space, indeed.

Kriens admires Cisco—but warily. "One of the things that we've learned really well from Cisco, and that they've done fantastically well, is to stay focused on the small start-up competition. Most companies that have success immediately begin to believe that their only issue is managing other big competitors and declare themselves no longer to be in that small-company category. Cisco and John Chambers maintain their focus on making sure that nobody smaller than them gets to do to them what they once did."

But Kriens is being generous. Juniper is doing exactly to Cisco what he claims Cisco works so hard to nip in the bud.

If Cisco is to limit the loss of service provider market share, it will require radical new approaches and lots of new engineering. This is not a Cisco core strength. Worse, in a technology market, the most advanced and most cutting-edge technologies usually filter down to influence the rest of the industry, with falling prices. Again, because it is Juniper—not Cisco—that has grabbed the cutting edge, Cisco is working from a weakened position. In effect, Cisco is playing catch-up here to a company that started with a blank sheet of paper and out-innovated the big gorilla. Add that to the beginnings of a new generation of optical equipment that aims to bring to photons the intelligence that Cisco's routers offered to packet networks. Companies like ONI and Ciena are selling next-generation purely optical solutions to routing and switching in regional and metropolitan networks, again built from a clean sheet of paper. These are not the big behemoth competitors like Nortel and Lucent that Cisco can almost certainly out-execute. These are nimble, well-financed companies where engineering is paramount, the passion for the network economy still burns, and manufacturing these state-of-the-art products is a core competency. This is exactly contrary to the Chambers Internet business model sermon. For that reason, these companies are doubly or triply dangerous to Cisco. Has the go-go Internet model of the past few years already run out of the steam that hype could give it?

Is this the beginning of a serious domino effect? If Cisco loses hold of the heart of the routing universe, what else might be at risk? But more important and immediate, can this David of a company that is Juniper take on the Goliath that is Cisco? And can other firms use the same model?

For Kriens, one of Juniper's primary strengths resides in the talent the company has attracted from different segments of the industry.

"Juniper was built with about an equal mix of people from the semiconductor and computing industry on the one hand and people from the networking industry on the other. The computer industry knows how to make large-scale chips and very dense architectures . . . but they don't know the networking applications. The networking industry understands the complex software that can move packets around, but they don't know semiconductors. So Juniper is a mix of talent from multiple industries, which is one of the other classic leading indicators of a new market segment opportunity. Not only is there not a company prior to ours that did what we have undertaken, there's not an industry segment that owns the collection of skills needed to execute it technically. The root of this company was to recognize that and try to build this cross section of talent from multiple industries."

The business role model for Juniper is unabashedly Sun, although Kriens also mentions H-P and Intel. It is a company founded and led by a trio of exceptional scientists: Dennis Ferguson came from MCI, where he designed the telecom company's commercial Internet service architecture, and has a background in router protocols; Bjorn Liencres was a senior architect in Sun's enterprise server division and the creator of several key components of the company's chipsets for multiprocessor servers; and Pradeep Sindhu, from the Computer Lab at Xerox PARC, did fundamental research into multiple processor computer architectures, research that was incorporated in the Sun multiprocessor systems. This is the first leg of the Juniper story: engineering excellence.

But there is also a practical, real-world or economic edge to the engineering model Juniper has built that is fundamentally different from anything that Cisco, chiefly a software company with lots of acquisitions to integrate, has ever achieved. "We've adopted a design methodology that is borrowed from our people who come from Sun. If you look at a Sun server line, they design a microprocessor, and then they build a single-processor version of the server, and then they build a cost-reduced smaller packaged version, and then they build a multiprocessor version, which is the bigger one. So we had this basic chipset and architecture, which launched the M40, and then we built smaller packages of it for different price performance points in the 20, 10, and 5. And then we did a multiprocessor version of it in the M160."

Building, debugging, and finishing these chipsets (constellations of central processors and surrounding adjunct circuits in a tightly designed combination that all populate a circuit board) were huge projects that took time, as long as two and a half years. So in order to leverage the cost of R&D, Juniper had to get as many products as they could out of that design center, a level of technological planning that Cisco, with its unceasing wave of acquisitions, was never faced with executing. In fact, Cisco has increasingly farmed its chip design and development out to its suppliers. Leveraging the designs is common in the computer and semiconductor business. But it was a new, perhaps risky approach for the networking business, which was, until Juniper, all about putting new releases of software out and buying the hardware and the processors off the shelf. Chambers, caught up in the flush of the Internet economy and lacking a pivotal engineering group, created a standards-based networking family by integrating new start-up products using off-the-shelf parts. Much tougher, and much more risky, was to create and engineer an integrated single networking platform, based on advanced hardware (chipsets) and software (network management, services, and provisioning) that required real engineering breakthroughs, but that could then be exploited in many market sectors. Kriens was the kind of businessman to take the risk.

Kriens, forty-three, was raised in northern California and got his college degree in economics in 1979. He was a car buff. He worked in marketing at Burroughs until it was bought by Sperry, and then at Tandem until Compaq bought it. Then he joined Stratacom as vice president of sales and operations.

"For me, personally, the most formative experience in my life was at Stratacom, and particularly of working for Dick Moley [founder and chief executive of Stratacom]. What he taught me was discipline and focus—and not to be swayed by stories in the market and marketers and marketing, as much as by listening to customers and looking at what you believed with common sense to be the issues and the answers. Then not wavering."

Tight focus defines Juniper's target audience. Ask Kriens what percentage of its sales goes to service providers, versus enterprises, and he says, "100 percent. We work hard *not* to sell to the enterprise." Juniper is a company with an extremely rational and well-thought-out hardware structure, a carefully and elegantly written software system, and a clearly definable target audience with a huge potential for expansion. If Juniper can keep delivering the equipment that carriers and service providers need to make ever more efficient and economical use of their networks, the opportunity is vast. The stock remained one of the few P/E highfliers to weather the bloodletting in telecom, dot-com, and networking in the fall of 2000. Kriens has 4.5 percent of the company's stock. That stake was worth about $2 billion at the end of 2000. He has started collecting expensive sports cars.

Juniper is trying to build the highest-performing network devices in the IP world. Period. The target market is made up of the largest network providers, who are processing the highest number of packets. No single enterprise company can process as many packets as even a small service provider with multiple customers. The target is carriers and service providers—no deviation. This is very different from Cisco's core business customer.

"The future of wide-area networking is in service provider markets. If you think about it, it is all a simple transport problem. The same as transporting anything. Very few businesses run their own trucks and own their own airplanes, because FedEx can do it a lot cheaper." Once the package leaves the shipping dock, it's in the hands of the professionals.

In the case of data transport, says Kriens, "once the packet that is generated on the desktop leaves the local community at the shipping dock, whatever the definition of local is—a small business or a large campus, some local community of relatively static users, in fixed locations, in a LAN, or on a wireless net—we take over. The enterprise and location-based networking space is where Cisco rules. Once you leave that local community, that's where the processing of the packets—the software

used to set up traffic control and priority control, policies between users, and the ability to monitor the up-to-the-millisecond
status of the global resources that are accomplishing all this connectivity and delivery—gets layered into the network. This is
what we do.

"Local distribution [of data] is going to be a problem
solved by those who can do it at the lowest cost. But once you
move outside that local area, to a world where there is constant
change, aggregated streams, content priorities, random contention, and constant reconciliation between service providers
and customers, with network outages all going on at once—
that is the world that we have built our hardware and software
systems to serve. And that's what we focus on."

Juniper is proving it's possible to take on Cisco and win.
Can it keep chipping away while acting like a small start-up, or
will Kriens and Juniper lose sight of the market, get big and
slow, and start watching the competition too closely? The chief
exec is quick to make it clear that this isn't a dead-end swamp
of high-end routing that will stay esoteric and tangential forever. He believes his company's routing platform will be
adopted throughout the service provider and content networking world. Judging by the company's believers—UUNet, the
world's largest data-centric shared public network and a part of
MCI, which has become a major Juniper endorser, as well as
the British giant Cable & Wireless, PLC, and start-up carriers
like Broadband Office and IPERGY, as well as big ISP consol-
idator Verio—the customer part of the equation is well in hand.
Factor in the fact that almost every new hot-box maker or
equipment seller in the IP, fiber, and wireless markets resells Juniper routers in order to get away from Cisco's hegemony—
these include Corvus, Ciena, Sycamore, ONI, Nortel, and many
more—and the company is building a very defensible beachhead right down in the middle of Cisco's highly targeted service
provider arena.

"What we do with our systems is to optimize the networking resource, the bandwidth, by giving all the power, the priorities and the distribution of traffic capabilities they need, to the service provider, the network operator," continues Kriens, who gets excited enough to stumble over his words as he describes the networking landscape. "Smaller networks where profits are elusive have even greater and tighter concerns over optimizing their use of capacity, reducing costs and getting maximum utilization out of the network resource. So our products are no less important, perhaps more important, for smaller networks, to give them technology like ours that maximizes their performance and their asset utilization."

It is all about intelligence. At the core of the network, trillions of packets are going to be flooding across the amorphous and quasi-public Internet in the broadband world. Moving, managing, and massaging them is the job of Juniper. "Our market is about $2 billion this year. And it is projected to get to $6 billion next year. In our own space, there's so much headroom that the less time we spend worrying about what other people are doing and the more we remain focused on solving our own and our customers' problems, pure execution, the more successful we'll be."

However, economic Darwinism—the triumph of better economic models, occasioned by new technology, over older-generation solutions—cuts all ways. Recently a new company has come onto the routing stage. Called Procket, the firm includes Tony Li, the wizard of BGP (border gateway protocol—the soul of a router) who helped build the Cisco 12000 and then jumped ship to Juniper to help design the M40.

Now Li has landed at Procket with a new team in stealth mode, but with what appears to be another new routing platform. The advisory, finance, and management teams are gold-plated; indeed, one of the same financiers who backed Juniper four years ago is a major investor. And the makeup of the technical team sounds eerily similar: two techies from Sun with expertise in SPARC microprocessors—Bill Lynch and Sharad Mehrotra—and the networking genius Li. Even more ironically, Cisco was also one of the original backers of Procket—now it will be a direct competitor.

The lesson? No matter how advanced your technology, some hot-box gunslinger is around the next corner ready to try and outgun you. This is another of the fundamental laws of life in the networking universe.

JUNIPER HAS ALREADY drawn a line in the router sand, but there are two other beachheads likely to get just as treacherous for Cisco.

Back in her office, Tam Dell'Oro turns the page. On the back of the same sheet as the core router statistics is another new market that her team has only just started following. In two years it has grown to a $400 million business—not in the same category as the $2 billion core router market, but on a swifter trajectory. This one is called broadband aggregation. "Here's another battlefield in the new Internet. Cisco is playing catch-up. Redback invented the business and is still holding its own against them."

Aggregation matters because it is the most efficient and intelligent place to layer in subscriber management at the granularity that a service provider needs—down to the individual subscriber and to different data streams within the last-mile DSL, cable modem, or dial-up line access. This is where each subscriber's individual service is added to thousands of others, where the packets are shot off to the wide world of the Internet.

A few years ago the media started to talk about DSL lines—the high-speed transport system devised by the Bellheads to maximize the data capacity of existing copper phone lines already installed at every home and office. A very smart networking engineer by the name of Guarav Garg, who had sold a company to Bay Networks a few years earlier, started thinking about what this would mean if it actually came to pass.

It didn't take him long to see that hundreds of high-speed DSL lines, from all sorts of central offices in a metropolitan area, would aggregate to thousands of lines very quickly—all of them capable of demanding and delivering lots of bits all at once, and lots of services as well. It would swamp the connections upstream (closer to the core, or long-haul connections) from the end-users. Then what? How could a carrier or Internet service provider handle that many individual customers, stay on top of it, dole out independent sets of services to each one according to level of service or time of day, provision new services and lines quickly, and make money?

The result Garg and some partners came up with was a new kind of device, another hot box, that combined a switching fabric (to interconnect every line to every bigger capacity pipe) with a chipset and software designed to manage thousands of broadband accounts. This box—called a Redback after the name of Garg's company—was placed in front of a big core router, and it managed all the high-speed connections the service provider was delivering. Cisco reacted in classic fashion: by creating an add-on box for its routers that could perform some basic aggregation. But again, by having to start with an existing product family, the gargantuan of networking was hamstrung, and its solution never matched Redback's blank-sheet-of-paper design.

As the DSL market has continued to grow, the aggregation business has been very good for Redback. Sales are set to nearly quadruple this year at the company that inaugurated the field, and aggregation industry run rate is about $400 million for 2000. Redback still has more than a third of the aggregation market, Nortel almost 30 percent, and Cisco 20 percent. More ominously for Cisco, Redback is attempting to integrate a metro optical-transport company—Siara—into its product offering. Redback's products not only aggregate subscriber data streams, but they now also move and transport traffic around regional and metropolitan areas, bypassing the traditional routed and switched environments that Cisco dominates. In this architecture, the network operator moves all his traffic to one location, where a single big router—usually now a Juniper box—sorts and diverts everything one time.

Redback's original boxes provide the subscriber management systems, and acquiree Siara's the switching and transport components to aggregate broadband data traffic between end-users. "Our products work really well together," adds Kriens.

This was another missed opportunity at Cisco. The behemoth thought aggregation was just a 5 percent deviation from the previous world it dominated and imagined that its existing gear could meet the challenge. But it couldn't. Redback's aggregation products are better, by a significant margin, than Cisco's bolt-on solution. Nortel gained its market share in the sector (the only area where Nortel has been able to hold its own against Cisco) by buying another hot start-up, the high-speed Ethernet switch company Shasta, and selling its product line, which included some advanced blank-sheet engineering work—aggregation features that were built in. However, there have recently been some departures en masse from that group, and it may have trouble keeping up with Redback's torrid pace of innovation.

TOUGH SLEDDING IN broadband aggregation points to another major failure in the Cisco constellation. DSL, a business that has been picking up speed after a slow start, has been something of a failure for Cisco. In order to run high-speed data connections like DSL out to users, access gear is needed at both the customer's end, whether it be in the house, at the office, or on campus, and at the central offices where all the lines converge. Cisco sells products for both ends.

But in the DSL concentration market, it has lost market share steadily since 1998, primarily to Alcatel, the giant French telecommunications operation, but also to Lucent. According to Dell'Oro numbers, Cisco is fifth in this DSLAM (digital subscriber line multiplexer) market space. The DSL market is Alcatel's one jewel, and the firm is also vying for market share leadership in the other part of the equation—customer devices—where Cisco is only in fourth place. In an earnings call earlier this year, Chambers pointedly called out the executive running that business and asked for a promise "that you'll improve our share in that market sector in coming quarters." It hasn't happened yet. The DSL market space has not been a success for Cisco.

The problem is complacency and that end-to-end strategy of Chambers. With singular focus, Alcatel decided to make DSL its own. Cisco, on the other hand, doesn't bring any great value add to the equation. Good enough products, yes. But Alcatel and Lucent also make the chips. Cisco buys them. Basically, Cisco is a screwdriver shop, in some ways more like Dell than the IBM of old—assembling the parts made by others and putting its box around the product. Here, in a price-oriented consumer market, extra value is hard to demonstrate, and cutthroat pricing puts great pressure on the company's historical margins.

While DSL is the broadband telco line connection, there are two other ways to get broadband data to users. Dial-up modems and ISDN connections are still a $4 billion business, and Cisco is solidly in second place behind Lucent, with 25 percent of that market. Interestingly, the Lucent share is almost entirely due to Ascend, which pioneered the digital side of this market sector and was holding off Cisco quite well until its founders decided to throw in with Lucent. Since the Ascend acquisition, Lucent's share has been crumbling; Cisco and several others have improved their share as a result.

Another sector where Cisco shines is in the cable concentration and customer equipment businesses. Here Cisco, with a massive contract with AT&T, has done very well in concentration gear for cable network centers. Cisco has a 60 percent market share in this sector—a business that has grown to be worth about $500 million in the year 2000. Efficient execution and an inside seat at the table have given Cisco powerful success here.

But this may well be a finite business opportunity. AT&T is cutting back sharply on its cable ambitions, and eventually the shared hub architecture of a wiring scheme like cable is going to run out of steam. (Cable shares the network between many homes, while a DSL-based broadband connection gives each subscriber an individual high-speed switched channel. Lots of cable users can slow down throughput while DSL is theoretically unaffected.) With DSL, higher-speed services to individuals can be more easily delivered, providing another point of differentiation for service providers, one that will be exploited once broadband lines are widely installed. Cable has been a well-executed business for Cisco, but does it have legs?

The only other way to get broadband quantities of data back and forth to the New Internet will be through some kind of wireless link. These range from today's text pagers to tomorrow's higher-speed cell phone–based GSM and CDMA systems that will make every cell phone an e-mail portal and browser. Two kinds of services are likely to play a role in this sector going forward: cellular-like data services of many kinds and central-point-to-many-point wireless transmission networks that bring relatively large data channels through the air to buildings or, ultimately, even individual subscribers.

Cisco's wireless efforts have been half-hearted and uncharacteristically ill executed and thought out. Two purchases supposedly make up the basis for the Cisco offering: Aironet, an also-ran wireless LAN supplier for in-building wireless data networks; and Clarity, a point-to-multipoint microwave wireless service. The former was one of many companies building low-data-throughput, radio-based, local-area Ethernet transceivers and hubs. It had little to distinguish it when Cisco bought it and has not done much since. Rumors swirl about Aironet being for sale.

Clarity, on the other hand, actually had some interesting technology and claimed to have beaten the multipath problem that bedevils most wireless systems: High-speed frequencies bounce all around and off buildings and other objects. Synchronizing them between the transmitter and the receiver is no simple task. Clarity was supposedly purchased for this solution, and in the fall of 2000 Cisco finally launched its ISP version of the service—to almost no acclaim or attention.

This product was supposedly targeted at ISPs and other service providers and carriers that wanted to provide a relatively big broadband connection to a particular building that was typically not served by fiber-optic cable. Using a central point and targeted antenna, the product could deliver a 155-megabit-per-second beam to a small satellite dish mounted on the target edifice. The problem is that there are far too many suppliers of this kind of equipment already, and there is little to recommend Cisco's version over all the others except for the brand name. That might be enough in a slightly more mature market or if Chambers had understood the wireless market and could help direct its efforts. In an explosive technology sector like wireless, it is engineering innovation, clear economic advantage, and deep customer understanding that will produce the ultimate winners. Cisco fails on all these metrics so far in the wireless market.

In the end, neither of these acquisitions was more than a dipping of the toe into the wireless market. And both were on the wrong side of the business. The money was in building the infrastructure—the towers and switches and routers—needed to move the torrent of wireless data that will soon be available in most of the cities of the world. Cisco has not moved into the radio space effectively to bid against Nortel and Ericsson.

It used a relationship with Motorola as a crutch to back into wireless in 1998 and 1999, but when it became apparent that the once great American wireless and radio operator had become an ailing business, Chambers and Cisco started cutting ties. A few years ago Chambers liked to talk about "his special relationship" with Chris Galvin—the grandson of Motorola's founder. But the youngest Galvin turned out to be a poor leader, and the company reeled from his mismanagement.

Without Motorola, Cisco was left with just a couple of second-rate technology companies, no ties to the prevailing cellular data standards that were evolving all over the world, and little chance to influence the routing or switching of these new flows of packets that should start coming online in the next few years. This has been a major error in effort, strategy, and tactics at the company. To correct it, Cisco has struck a new alliance with Nokia—the Finnish company supplies the wireless knowledge, Cisco the routers and switches to move data around once it is captured at the cell sites. It might work, and Chambers has started claiming that the company is a part of many of the newly awarded wireless data contracts around the world. However, given Cisco's near monopoly of routers, Chambers's claim may be a smart way to spin what looks like a business opportunity that the Silicon Valley giant has so far squandered.

All of this was weighing on John Chambers's mind as he surveyed his empire earlier this year.

Cisco had won the cable business, but it was finite—possibly very finite. DSL had been a disaster for the company from the start, and nothing he had done had changed it.

Juniper was coming after Cisco at the core of its business, attacking at the center of the crown jewels; and the biggest, newest customers were heading for the competition's products.

Redback had started another wildfire, with a whole new business region, and was holding its own as Cisco struggled to rejigger its equipment to address the aggregation space, only to find itself several turns behind. Before Cisco even had a chance to catch up on the aggregation front, Redback bought a metro optical transport company and threatened to rewrite the business equation in aggregation services by adding pure optical transport.

WITH NEW COMPANIES attacking sectors of its business, Chambers turned to Cisco's acquisitions team and tried to buy an early stage contender in a new market before the sector had really jelled. It was time to buy a layer 4–7 switching company. Layer 4–7 switches were the latest thing in the world of the Next Net, and the next frontier for service providers. These are smart combinations of gear, services, and high-speed switching and routing fabrics that run server farms feeding up massive Internet streams or hosting lots of different traffic streams. These are like the doorman and concierge service at a great hotel, welcoming guests and dispatching whatever they require to them. These layer 4–7 systems are used to balance, smooth out, and distribute data as a result of an avalanche of requests that can slow to a trickle a few moments later. They are used to manage the servers of a data storage vendor over the Web or those of an application services vendor who is selling software by the hour. They are essentially smart management and data-manipulation systems for a local server farm, big data site, or carrier network operations center. These switches work with caches and numerous statistical algorithms to maximize performance across a range of local and remote devices. At their core they read the data and make decisions about how best to deliver it based on what kind of information is contained in the stream.

It is a local sell. It fits the world where Cisco has been most successful: An enterprise IT manager needs to maximize assets. So does a new service provider or a new carrier. Setting up this kind of fine-grained capability at the edge of many networks is justifiable. Cisco already had a position in the market, which it had quickly cobbled together when it started to hear requests for proposals from customers. The initial answer was to sell an upgrade board. And being that it was Cisco's upgrade board, it was quite successful, reaching $40 million in sales by the middle of 2000. This was an appliance-like product that let local server farms be tied together and managed; and while others offered appliances as well, Cisco easily stormed the market.

But the real action in the layer 4–7 switching business was in another sector, which was growing much faster and which required a much higher level of engineering integration. This was the purpose-built space: front-end systems for large throughput data centers and farms that took the form of both appliances and more complex engineered systems. And here there were three good-sized competitors duking it out: Arrowpoint, Foundry, and Alteon.

Each had been fighting since the market emerged, and the business was fast approaching $500 million, on a sixfold growth rate—steep even for Silicon Valley with its nosebleed numbers. The Cisco acquisition team sprang into action. Here was a wildfire Chambers wasn't about to let get away from him without a fight, Juniper and Redback be damned.

The downside of Cisco's highly vaunted acquisition march was that by mid-2000 Cisco couldn't start seducing a company without raising the price rapidly and getting a much worse deal than anyone else might have negotiated. The tradition was to make a preemptive bid rich enough that there was no doubting the appeal, and all that stock from the founders let the company act like a drunken sailor when it came to spending for new companies. Get the other company to respond quickly, when the size of the offer was still breathtaking, before wind of it got out. Then swiftly announce it, preempt second-guessing, and close it all in thirty days.

The team crowded around and tried to decide which of the three companies was the right candidate.

The acquisition, made May 5, 2000, was startling. Arrowpoint, a company in Massachusetts, far from Cisco headquarters in San Jose, that was struggling to hold on to third place in the nascent market, was the target. The offer: $5.7 billion in Cisco stock. In the previous quarter the company had sold some $10 million worth of products.

But the price and far-off location aside, there was something else wrong with the acquisition. Cisco bought the wrong company. It didn't have a choice. The first target had been Alteon, the actual market leader, an innovator and a force to be reckoned with. And Alteon was in San Jose. However, the Alteon deal was dead before it could get placed on the table. First, the folks there were a little too blue collar for the bluebloods of Cisco. Second, Alteon still had its techie founding team, and they would only kowtow to technical heads greater than their own. Cisco didn't have those guys. The preliminary discussions were filled with animosity, and Cisco moved on.

A few months later Alteon offered itself up to the only other buyer who made sense. Getting a bit of a discount for being second to the altar, Nortel bought the company for $5 billion. Alteon's run rate was about $150 million; Arrowpoint's $40 million. It set the stage for a real marketplace struggle between the two big companies and a true test of just how effectively each of them can deliver on the promise of the future they are trying to win.

In the wake of these two astronomical acquisitions, Wall Street started voicing doubts about the long-term sustainability of the acquisitive market strategy in the face of such elevated price tags. Another problem is the self-fulfilling value proposition of high-valued stock buying overvalued start-ups, somehow intrinsically validating each other's price in a loop. How can one of these new and evolving technology companies justify that price? Billions in revenues? Unlikely. In the Cisco formulation, there's simply no time to waste—buy now at whatever price. But look at it coldly. Cisco's recent optical acquisitions (in the past twelve months) have cost something in the neighborhood of $10 billion (give or take a billion or so). So far, revenues for all these companies and products combined are nearing $1 billion. No matter how you slice or try to justify it, that's a pretty risky idea for most prudent investors. But then they aren't quite as caught up in the circular hype of the Internet bubble.

"IT IS A crazy market," Tam Dell'Oro concludes. "Maybe the infidels will overthrow the emperor. But the crazy thing is that Cisco's other, core, businesses show no signs of letting up. In fact, in the last year or so, Cisco has increased its market share from 44 percent in 1998 to 56 percent of the high-speed switch business by 2000—in that same period, the size of the market has doubled from $6 billion to $13 billion.

"This is a money machine."

The opportunity in the networking space that Cisco already occupies is almost breathtaking. Everywhere that companies have already installed networks, they are upgrading the lines and linkages to deliver a full 10 megabits of switched capacity to every end-user. This is the victory of IP, in the form of Ethernet. Having already won the corporate data-networking game, Ethernet and its 10-megabit, 100-megabit, now 1-gigabit standards-based speeds are about to become the data dial tone for the broadband age.

This full Ethernet dial tone will be enough for most conceivable personal needs. Every new business wires for this from day one. All of it requires high-speed Ethernet switches and good routers. Much of the competition has fallen away. Cisco is able to carry all of its other businesses with the profits it gets from this burgeoning and nearly limitless expansion of the basic networking infrastructure of the business world. This is what fuels the company's extraordinary growth, the string of successful quarters, the beating of analyst estimates each quarter by one penny, and the momentum of this company. Its core business continues to explode at a geometric pace.

As long as that continues, and there is no reason to believe it won't, Cisco can keep posting spectacular financial results.

The problem is somewhere else. It is something shared by many technology companies. It has tripped up IBM and DEC, Apple and Microsoft. Eventually even the most profitable legacy business needs new markets to win—and profits from the Old World can hide failures in the New World for only so long.

Cisco's problem is in the light world, where a completely new universe is being created to deliver that Ethernet dial tone—or IP webtone—entirely with fiber optics. And while it will interoperate with the Old World of electronic routing and packet intelligence, this next universe will be based on a whole new set of assumptions and innovations, companies and customers, disruptive technologies and technical fault lines.

In this, the world of the new new new thing, Cisco is carrying all the baggage of the past. That is rarely a prescription for success. Forget the Internet as the driving force of this next generation—it is no revolutionary New World with brand-new business models and a new kind of human being aborning. That was part of the religion of the Internet, the sermon of John Chambers, the dogma of the blind followers in the early days of the Next Net. This was the hot air that filled the bubble of the Internet economy. Those days are over.

The real radical and evolutionary disconnect is in the move from packets to photons and the capacity explosion that accompanies it. This is a technology and engineering rebellion that will have a profound impact on all of us.

Unfortunately for John Chambers, this is exactly where Cisco is weakest.

PART FOUR

INTO
THE
VOID

CHAPTER 10

THE MIGHTY FALL

FOR QUITE A WHILE, THE WORLD HAD OVERVALUED THE telecommunications sector of the stock market. Then one day it all changed.

July 20, 2000, was the day the market turned against the telecom and networking companies and the formerly untouchable Internet infrastructure business started to crumble. That was the day that Lucent announced its third-quarter earnings and disappointed Wall Street once again. Worse, Rich McGinn's guidance for the fourth quarter and the following fiscal year downgraded expectations in what was now the third straight profit and revenue disappointment at Lucent.

McGinn also confirmed what had been circulated among traders and Wall Street for months—Lucent was going to spin off its microelectronics business, its semiconductor fabrication unit, and call it Agere Systems. This was the strongest single part of the company with sales revenue rising at 37 percent. The reason? The communications and opto-electronics parts and semiconductor components businesses were in a boom of demand and consequently were being very favorably valued by the investment community. McGinn reasoned that by spinning off this top-performing sector of Lucent's business and giving existing shareholders stakes in the new company, he would answer grousings about the company's slipping share price by putting some new stock in their pocket.

It didn't work. Lucent stock dropped precipitously, losing one-third of its value within days. It was McGinn's second spin-off. The first, announced some three months earlier, had involved Lucent's enterprise networking business. That company—now called Avaya—was being prepared for a September IPO, and it was the remnant of the end-user customer business that AT&T, through Lucent, once commanded. Now a pale shadow of its former self, the enterprise networking division had been trounced by Cisco; and instead of figuring out how to fight in that space, Lucent had thrown in the towel. McGinn wasn't the first to abandon the business networking market to Cisco— 3Com, another networking company that had been in decline for years, had beaten him to it earlier in the year after years of incompetent management.

To the financial markets, Lucent's second spin-off in a year seemed like a strange way to win the battle for the telecommunications networks of tomorrow. Admittedly, focusing everything it had on the service provider space might have been a good strategy for Lucent; but stripped of the ability to make its own chips and integrated circuits and of its ability to sell into the extraordinarily profitable enterprise and business marketplace, there was not much left in the end-to-end entity that Lucent had been created to exploit a scant four years before. With only the service provider market to keep it afloat, Lucent was betting everything on one pony—a new and emerging market as well, with uncertain financial or technological prospects where it had a decidedly checkered history of success.

The problem, as the analysts and investors saw it, was that Lucent still hadn't delivered the 10-gigabit fiber interface. Nortel had introduced one nearly 18 months before, and that had turned out to be exceptionally successful for the Canadian company. Among those who tracked such things, the 10-gigabit fiber interface was the new new thing, the protocol that would change the Internet forever—the place where packets of data, bursts of electricity, energy, and intelligence gathered up into Internet Protocol traffic, meet the blinding light of the fiber world. This was going to be the portal for two worlds to meet.

At its core data networking has always been an electronic phenomenon. Bits of data, written as zeros and ones, are sent as pulses of electricity over wires. Gathered into packages— packets—they have addresses read by routers and switches and are shunted all over the world. Wherever they meet fiber threads, glass wires, they are converted into pulses of laser light. The faster the lasers can take in the electronic bits and accelerate them into the luminous world of photons, the larger the interface and the bigger the bandwidth of the connection. Currently, the fastest of these bridges, or portals, operates at OC-192, or about 10 billion pulses per second. Only a couple of years ago the sagest of Bellhead telco pundits and planners thought that OC-48, or 2.5 billion pulses per second, would be enough to carry the datacom industry for a number of years. However, with the Internet growing at an accelerating pace—the exponential pace of Metcalfe's Law— they were wrong.

Lucent, and the management and science team assembled by McGinn, had held off investing enough resources in the higher-speed interface, figuring that they could milk the standard interfaces that they had introduced only a couple of years earlier. With the caution of years spent in the voice circuit world, the Bellheads had planned for a five-year product cycle and were blindsided when a year after introducing the Lucent 2.5-gigabit-per-second fiber systems, Nortel trumped them with 10 gigabits. Even worse was ahead: Nortel had started to demonstrate an 80-gigabit system—80 billion bits of data over a single wavelength, on a single fiber.

The carnage had started to show up in the beginning of Lucent's fiscal year, which runs from October 1. In the fall of 1999, right before the Y2K frenzy, slipping revenue levels started to become apparent. The results for Q1 displeased Wall Street, and in a matter of a few days in late January, the stock fell from nearly $80 a share to $60. But McGinn convinced the board that he just needed a few more quarters to execute his turnaround strategy: Carve up Lucent into its constituent blocks, distribute stakes in the new spin-offs to shareholders, and keep the core fiber-optic and service provider business intact. It made some sense; after all, most of the company felt more at home with carriers and service providers than with enterprise and business customers. Enterprise was a messy and complicated business, whereas the service provider space was a much better fit. This was true for both the cerebral McGinn and the Lucent Bell Labs crowd.

There was just one big problem: By missing the transition to the 10-gigabit wave, Lucent looked like a dowager aunt at the Predator's Ball. Service providers wanted the hottest of hot boxes, as did the newest generation of competitive carriers like Qwest and Global One that were building out greenfield—new, from the ground up, unencumbered by legacy equipment, built in a "green field"—data communications networks. The only ones willing to wait for Lucent to get up to speed were the old-line carriers, which certainly were upgrading their networks, but only as they were pushed into it by new carrier and service provider competition. Lucent looked like a dullard, out of touch, even though it was at Bell Labs where many of the discoveries that created semi-conductor lasers had been made and where data transmission over fiber had been pioneered.

Missing this market transition was a gigantic miscalculation for Lucent and McGinn. Instead of being on the cutting edge, competing with the kinds of products and R&D toys Nortel was trotting out, Lucent could only watch. As a company, it was exceptionally dependent on slow and cautious telco customers. If it was to have a chance for a place at the new new table, it would have to hit nothing but home runs. No doubles, no fungoes, no almost-over-the-wall fly balls to deep, deep center field, the kind of shots lesser companies emerging in the marketplace were afforded by patient investors and venture capitalists.

Despite knowing what it needed to do, Lucent continued to whiff at the plate. Revenue growth for the third quarter, from April to June 2000, was far below Cisco's and Nortel's numbers, and this spooked the markets again. In order to stanch the wound, McGinn fired the head of fiber and split the business into two units—long distance and metro. For the metro unit, he hired Bob Barron, the former president of Chromatis, a company that Lucent had acquired a few months earlier. Although Chromatis, bought for $4.5 billion in May 2000, had no product for sale in the market, it had developed a promising way to pack existing SONET networks with more data. Turning the crown jewels of Lucent's future over to a new acquiree might be a bit precipitous, but the reasoning McGinn used seemed to make sense: Lucent had to hijack new and fresh thinking if it was going to recapture its leadership position in the fiber world. At the same time, he gave the long-distance fiber unit to another relative newcomer, Jeong Kim, who had been acquired when Lucent bought an ATM start-up called Yurie Systems a year earlier. All of a sudden, Bell Labs had new leaders in its core fiber-optic business who had little sense of the past—a situation that probably was exactly the right thing to do.

It all might have worked. The noble history of Bell Labs, the smart and Wall Street–savvy McGinn slicing out chunks of the company and extracting value from them for the core shareholders, the fresh executives, the mad rush to get into the technical leadership role again with products like the Lambda-Router—all of it made sense. Certainly revenue growth was disappointing—but it was still above 15 percent. The net income loss for the third quarter of 2000 was troubling, since what had been a 23 cents per share gain a year earlier had now evaporated and was a 9 cent per share loss—but losses weren't bad in developing markets. There was still room to hope that the dot-com free fall that had started in March, which showed no signs of relenting, would still spare the communications and networking infrastructure makers.

Then, in October, McGinn had to admit to the board at Lucent that the next earnings call was going to be worse than the last one and that he needed to guide the market analysts downward in their expectations for the coming quarters. It was the last straw. Meeting over a weekend, the board asked for his resignation. In his place they reelected Lucent's original chief executive, the former head of Cummins Engine, Henry Schacht. The stock plummeted in a free fall, dropping below $20. The once highly regarded Lucent had hit some kind of bottom and, for now, is seemingly out of sync with the market game. With resources as extensive as Lucent's, though, the company is still a major contender. However, having spun off both its communications chip business and its enterprise computing unit, the current Lucent is a pale shadow of the glorious vertically integrated communications behemoth it once was. Whoever follows McGinn will have to reinvent this company for a very different world.

But there was still one big optical company that seemed to have the story right. Nortel, with its chief executive John Roth, was talking about the Internet Revolution, running a lot of image advertising on television, and asking its rhetorical question "What do you want the Internet to be?" Best of all,

Nortel had reported superb numbers throughout the period of Lucent's descent into oblivion. The big Canadian company blew through already-elevated expectations for its second quarter (reported in June 2000), especially in its fiber-optic business. Sales were up 80 percent in the optical arena, further highlighting the troubles that Lucent was struggling to solve. With anemic growth in Lucent's optical space and booming growth on the part of Nortel, it looked as if Lucent was going to miss out on what the investing public saw as the next gold-plated opportunity post-dot-com: building the infrastructure to deliver broadband data access to the world.

The results sent Nortel's stock soaring, and from the middle of July through September, it rose from $50 to $80 a share. With media, analyst, and chat room buzz all about the new fiber-optic markets that were going to open up, Nortel had become a market darling. Indeed, its results in July were so good that Nortel's stock took off while even the most golden of the market's networking stocks—Cisco—floundered. Cisco's stock had started heading downward after the announcement of its purchase of Arrowpoint.

The market was crazed for any company with the words *fiber optics* in its business plan, but "content-switching"? What was that? It didn't have the kind of cachet that light beams conjured, and it wasn't really clear why it was going to be so very important that it was worth another $5 billion of Cisco's stock. Could a business model based on acquisition long be maintained in the face of such ridiculous valuations? Other questions started surfacing about Cisco. How long could these superheated acquisitions go on? Was there something a bit dicey about Cisco's financing the purchases of its equipment—vendor financing it was called? What happened if there was a downturn, as was starting to look possible? Would Cisco's self-financing arm be highly exposed? And the old rumblings about the purchase accounting sleight of hand that high tech employed continued to get play too. Was the Cisco surge at an end?

Nortel's stock had actually started its rise a few months before, buttressed, ironically, by John Chambers, who said in a couple of forums that he was growing less concerned with Lucent and that Nortel was his biggest competitor and a serious, and legitimate, threat for Cisco. For more than a year, since Nortel bought Bay in 1998, John Roth had been preaching that Nortel had made a "right-hand turn" and was no longer thinking like an Old World telecommunications company. He was proud of that memo he sent out that called for the turn and told the troops that Nortel would deliver "webtone—the high-performance Internet—everywhere." He took every opportunity to describe the great Canadian telecommunications equipment maker in terms of Cisco. The Nortel name and its message seemed to be everywhere during the big sporting events of the summer, especially the Olympics from Sydney, claiming ownership of the Internet. Even in Cisco's backyard, Nortel managed to finagle the contract to "wire" the new San Francisco baseball stadium, the ultimate in high-tech ballparks.

With the number one position in fiber-optic gear of all kinds—from SONET equipment for regional communications networks and local metropolitan on and off ramps for getting traffic from SONET rings to local companies and end-users, as well as a near monopoly in long-distance terrestrial data transportation—the company was not only delivering the right results but also talking the right game. For years Wall Street had been looking for a competitor who could trip up Cisco. Lucent was the first candidate. But now, as the optical arena got more and more valuable, it looked as if the prime competitor was going to turn out to be Nortel. Today's market was all about the information transport game, and the company from the Great White North appeared to be primed to be the key player.

But before Nortel could begin raking it all in, there were considerations to be made, issues to deal with. The one key factor limiting the onslaught of the bandwidth extravaganza that the fiber pundits and prognosticators were convinced was just around the next corner was not technology so much as economics. Fiber was a tried and tested means of gathering—aggregating—lots of packets and shooting them off across the nation. Thus the initial blush of sales for fiber came in the core of the very biggest networks, where money to pay for orders was not hard to come by. But other than expensive SONET rings, fiber had not proven usable in metropolitan networks or with end-users. Lasers were too expensive and finicky and required too much tweaking to be cost-effective in highly congested local environments.

At the same time, there was a developing broadband business in supplying the final mile—either with DSL lines or cable modems to deliver broadband connections to end-users. And while these markets were still in the early-stage growth phase, they existed and appeared pregnant with potential. The problem was in between. The techniques for getting traffic from central offices and collection points to big junctions and jumping-off spots for the big carrier networks was in its infancy. The smart money was betting that fiber would be involved. But the technology of slicing light wavelengths in a fine enough way to make fiber capacities efficient and economic for feeder networks and data tributaries out to individual companies and surfers was still in significant flux. Numerous DWDM start-ups were building systems of equipment that could fill partial wavelengths and dynamically reorient the content of lambdas and light waves on the fly on the basis of demand. But this was not simple work—and the delivery of broadband services like DSL was spotty at best. And worse, horror stories started piling up about poor DSL throughput and availability. While there was a great deal of demand, the marketplace seemed to have trouble delivering paying service.

However, in the frenzy of the dot-com era, investors bid high every company that might bring to market some solution for connecting the long-haul carrier world to the end-user-who-just-wants-broadband. While investors bid up a number of challengers to Nortel's domination, the reality was that the grande dame of fiber continued to consolidate and lengthen its lead by selling to its traditional telcom customers. All of these monopoly carriers not only had the money to pay for more equipment, but they were also desperately looking for solutions that would let them cram more data into their wires and switches. Nortel's product portfolio was broad, and it fit right into the carriers' purchasing plans.

However, this couldn't last under the withering assault of dozens of new, innovative, and well-financed start-ups. Nortel had to create new-generation products if it was going to keep its hands around the market for the metropolitan fiber equipment that it had pioneered. For years regional voice traffic had been carried by expensive and very slow and difficult-to-configure SONET rings of fiber, fed by highly conditioned, voice-friendly ATM and Frame Relay–based data traffic—the kind of data traffic that a telco could love. These SONET rings were installed at the cost of at least a million dollars a mile—in New York City, $150 million a mile—and they were highly inflexible to boot. For the "Baby Bells," the cost of these inflexible data networks was justifiable; and since they were the monopoly, it didn't matter to them if it took a few months to get you your services.

The first generation of SONET and ATM gear, where Nortel excelled, was far too expensive, however, for the new generation of carriers and service providers who were clamoring for more data capacity. It was natural, then, that there would be a lot of talk about 10-gigabit optical wavelengths and dense wave division multiplexing and IP directly over fiber. This was what misled the investment world into thinking that the outrageous rocket science of fiber optics was about to be applied to the mid-mile problem of linking the astounding transportation capacities of long-haul telco networks—measured in terabits already today, or trillions of bits per second, with peta, yotta, and zettabit gushers to come—with the final mile of the end-users who were ultimately going to pay for all this.

But the truth—the reality—was that the first generation of this equipment was too limited in functionality and too expensive.

With fiber technologies erupting all over the place, it was still unclear midway through 2000 what products would ultimately win in the metro network—the block-by-block network of wires and fiber that makes up the last mile and neighborhood web of a full-blown world of networking. The metro then links into regional networks, which in turn have networking peering points (physical locations where many networking users hand off traffic to each other) and points-of-presence with long-haul carrier networks. This meant that while there was a great deal of talk about the coming optical revolution, service providers were sitting on their hands; and the market had yet to come alive.

A number of companies emerged claiming that they could either solve the metro network bottleneck or address the long-haul portion of the fiber network market with innovative technology that could get rid of one or another expensive part of today's networks. Nortel, by virtue of its optical dominance and SONET equipment, was one of the first to deliver products in both the long-distance and the regional-market sectors. But this kind of early position can be a bad thing in a fast-moving market. The company ended up with a first generation of gear in a business that rapidly adopted whatever the latest and fastest and hottest of boxes was. In both key areas, Nortel soon had full-blown competitors coming up from the blank sheet of paper.

In the long-distance market, the companies were Corvus and Sycamore, while in the metro arena they were Ciena and ONI. The oldest was Ciena, which was focused on the metro marketplace where once Lucent and Nortel had all the business to themselves. Founded in 1992, Ciena had quarterly revenues of about $500 million by late 2000. Its products made use of DWDM technology to move data around in metro and regional networks. However, more recently, a second-generation metro DWDM company has appeared. Called ONI, this company has developed a more flexible and competitive set of equipment to solve the same metro networking problem. But what they both demonstrate is just how competitive every corner of the optical marketplace is.

In the long-distance market, two key companies have arisen to challenge Nortel's dominance: Sycamore and Corvus. Sycamore was created by two of the founders of Cascade (sold to Ascend many years ago after being snubbed by Cisco) and focuses on moving data around in backbone carrier networks. Corvus, a spin-off from Ciena, was started by one of the founders of that company who was convinced that he had invented innovative techniques for getting data to move long distances without amplification. What all this activity meant was that Nortel, which had a year earlier seemed to completely own the fiber business, suddenly looked like maybe it wasn't quite so dominant or in control. Could the fiber front-runner be caught by the newbies?

No one doubted fiber's ultimate importance, but two other factors started to appear on the radar screen that, combined with everything else, suddenly made investors get nervous. The first was a worldwide shortage of fiber-optic components—the specialized high-performance lasers and integrated circuits that were essential to making fiber gear and filling orders. Nortel was the first to mention supply limitations as a possible problem at its summer earnings call; Cisco soon followed. But neither had an answer.

Second, JDS Uniphase, an Ottawa fiber-components company created by former Nortel employees, used its high-flying stock to make a stunning $41 billion acquisition of another major fiber component supplier: SDL. The result was a near monopoly on lasers and components from one supplier; and in an era of exploding demand and difficulties in delivering products, it set the stage for skyrocketing prices and marketplace complication. Nortel answered by leaking word that it was in discussions with Corning about selling its components business . . . but they fizzled out.

Nonetheless, Nortel had carefully created a portfolio of products that stretched from regional gathering points to the core of the backbone network itself. John Roth described how "the network is getting bigger and bigger. At one point it was a challenge to fill 10 gigabits between any two cities. . . . We're now at the point where it is easy to fill 10 gigabits. In fact, we can fill several multiples of 10 between any two cities in North America. So junctions that made sense in the old days don't anymore. Especially because wherever you hit an interchange, the traffic now slows. You want to go in the express lane; you want to go nonstop directly."

Nortel had the technology to create that express lane, and its business was booming in that regard. But Roth and his people weren't covering all the bases. On the IP side of the game, Nortel seemed to be missing the boat no matter what it said in public. The company announced that it would not come out with a long-awaited Big Iron series of routers based on Bay technologies. Instead it would continue to sell Juniper's top-of-the-line gear. After months of promising the imminent release of these units, it was an embarrassing lapse. Worse, in many market sectors where Bay had previously battled to sizable market share against Cisco, those shares were in decline under the Nortel management—if not in full rout. John Roth, who aggressively promoted his company's IP religion, wasn't actually delivering on the sermon. IP networking market share was slipping, and any slowdown on the fiber side was going to be dangerous for a company that was no longer being judged by the metrics of slow, predictable growth but had become a growth and go-go company by its own estimation.

Roth had two answers.

One was to dabble in network services that Nortel can deliver to its customers—things like customer contact software or call center management systems. Cisco, of course, is already doing these too and is aggressively targeting the legacy voice business with IP. But Nortel does have a second card up its sleeve.

"Where we think the biggest opportunity lies is in the wireless Internet revolution that is getting under way this year," says Roth. "We are starting to deploy data services at 64-kilobit levels for the Palm and other devices. This is a major revolution. If the pace of the Internet is quick, and the pace of cellular was quick, what will the combination be like?"

Nortel crunched some numbers, tried to quantify the business and the growth of wireless. The Yankee Group predicts 50 million regular Internet users, on wireless, by 2003. By 2002 there will be more cell phones in the world than wired phones; within five years, more wireless data traffic than wireless voice traffic. If predictions hold, the demand for wireless gear would be enormous, worth hundreds of billions of dollars in the next five years.

"What this means is that wireless and wired voice and data must be delivered on a single infrastructure to have any hope of coping with all of this. And it must come with integrated networks," Roth insists, referring to the need to hand off data calls between handhelds, cell phones, and land lines all the time. "These are big steps. Only a company like Nortel can deliver on these kinds of products that are integrated, operate across transport and technology boundaries, and can scale up to handle the world's biggest data rivers and down to the individual on a cell phone."

Roth comes by his exuberance about wireless naturally, since he was originally a radio engineer. But is this just another wave of technology that the engineers will love and the consumers will eschew? After all, even in the best-case scenarios for the new generation of wireless networks—3G—throughput speeds will be unlikely to rise much above current dial up speeds. Fine for e-mail, but by no means broadband. It is very possible that the big wireless data revolution may take much longer than the pundits forecast to get in gear. And then Nortel will be left with only the fiber business to prop it up, since the IP sector has yet to be anything other than a disappointment.

The wireless world has not only its Pollyannas, but also its doubters. The cell phone was such an extraordinary success because it duplicated the existing voice world but made complete mobility possible as well. The impending wireless data universe doesn't do any of this. Slow speeds and small screens and tiny keyboards are all worse than the existing experience most users have when they search the Web from their desktop machines. Add high prices and the questionable value of mobile Web surfing, and it may be slower to catch on than many think, especially as the economy seems to be cooling. Remote e-mail is a powerful application, but there are already cheaper ways to get it—enhanced paging or voice-enabled Web sites that read it to you on a cell phone are the low-cost alternative to high-priced PDAs.

It's true that Nortel is far ahead in wireless. But Chambers and all his legions of fellow crusaders have IP. And IP always wins—or so it seems. IP is simple. IP is democratic. IP requires little in the way of specialized equipment. IP supports multiple speeds on different "hops" during the same Web page request. It allows all devices to contribute to data transport, to work together. It automatically reorients and reconfigures around failures. It is cheap. It is widely understood. It is supported by thousands of companies. While the future will almost certainly ride on light or in the wireless Ether, the present is built on packets that are fundamentally electronic. There is no end in sight for this. Even worse for those in the light world who want to imagine they can tackle and best Cisco, the future of data in the light universe is going to combine the intelligence, flexibility, and open-ended nature of IP with the speed of lambdas of light. But it is certain that the important part of the equation won't be the going fast, but the adding of intelligence. And there Cisco rules. Just look at what happened in early August 2000, when Cisco stepped up to the plate and announced another terrific quarter. Sales were up by 60 percent year-on-year. Earnings beat consensus estimates by exactly a penny—for the fourteenth consecutive quarter. It was an incredible performance in a market that had already turned against the dot-coms and was starting to question the telecom infrastructure sector's health.

But the real news was elsewhere. First, Cisco reported that enterprise sales were exceptionally strong. Surprising even the company itself, sales to corporations were up nearly 50 percent year-over-year and 30 percent sequentially. This was the second straight quarter of accelerating enterprise sales, which, combined with growing strength in government and global sales, were fueling Cisco's strong numbers. Chambers seemed surprised by these results—pleasantly surprised. At the same time he had to admit that sales to the service provider and consumer sectors had not risen as quickly as he had anticipated.

The enterprise networking arena had been given up for dead by most of Cisco's competitors, and even Chambers thought it had matured by 1999. The constant drumbeat of attention to the world of fiber optics and the service provider area (especially with the emergence of the ASP, or application service provider concept—delivering software programs on a per use basis over the Internet) had made the media focus all of its attention there. As a result even Chambers had turned to the new and emerging businesses in his portfolio—Cerent especially, with its Old World carrier emphasis on squeezing performance and cramming data into old SONET rings—and had started to think of the enterprise as a candidate for the corporate scrapyard. But a funny thing happened on the way to the crusher: As the noise of broadband settled across the nation and as the Internet truly started changing company behavior, big businesses were the first to upgrade their existing networking infrastructures to get higher data throughput for their users. The winner? Cisco.

But in the earnings call there was little mention of the enterprise sector, just short speeches by Carl Russo about the optical business and by Mike Volpi, who tried to make some sense out of Cisco's disjointed acquisition plans in the wireless space. As he worked his way through the two-hour event, Chambers also emphasized the new and made a number of self-congratulatory comments about Cerent, which was on the verge of achieving quarterly sales of $250 million, enough to support an annual run rate of $1 billion. This became the cry of the earnings call: an optical business doing a billion dollars a year already. Although Cerent's performance was certainly impressive, when compared to Nortel's annual sales of nearly $5 billion in the same SONET sector, it wasn't exactly going to make the Canadians shiver in their timbers.

But for all the talk about Cerent and its good sales into the carrier market, where Cisco had rarely made much headway in the past, Chambers raised more questions than he answered about the fiber-optics business. He admitted that supplier shortages had been a major negative and had lengthened lead times to an unacceptable twelve-week gulf for several popular products.

There was more. Cisco's other key optical networking product, bought on the same day in 1999 as Cerent, was an optical cross-connect switch created by a Texas-based company called Monterey. The value of optical cross-connects was that they could be used to "switch" light wavelengths around inside a big network without ever having to convert them to electronic signals. Chambers had to admit that the switch was delayed and wouldn't be generating revenue for another year.

The analysts, fixated like all the rest of the market on short-term gains and the latest, newest, next great thing, leapt on the delay in the Monterey product line and were all over Chambers for it in the Q&A that followed the call. But they missed what really mattered. None of them dug in and asked anything about the enterprise networking market growth. It was the second quarter in a row that Cisco and John Chambers had talked about the resurgence of the business, enterprise, and commercial networking markets, but no one seemed to care.

The results were nothing out of the ordinary for Cisco, and the market reacted mildly. The stock held its own, but in the month of August it was Cisco's stock that was wallowing while Nortel's kept up its steep ramp. Fiber optics had become the momentum player's cry, and Nortel looked like the golden child for the new millennium. It was a heady time for Nortel, and the company spared no expense in getting its message out to the world. Maybe Cisco had finally met its match.

But then a few big network operators—MCI first, then Sprint, Global Crossing, IXC, even AT&T—all reported weaker-than-expected sales. Wall Street, which seemed to be looking for reasons to sell tech and Internet stocks in the wake of what now appeared to be a permanent bloodletting on the dot-com front, didn't like the sound of this. There was talk of a slowdown in capital investments for new networking gear, talk about a surfeit of capacity in the long haul, about the gulf between the end-users and the big carriers.

The real problem, though, was at AT&T. When AT&T admitted that its big bold move into consolidating as many cable subscribers as possible wasn't going very well, the market started a rout in earnest. Sales and income were weak, and the business plan to buy up lots of cable systems in order to deliver broadband services to subscribers was proving much more expensive than at first hoped. It turned out that much of the wiring of older cable systems had never been upgraded, steeply increasing the costs for the strategy. The answer Ma Bell's management came up with was a punt, not a bold offensive move. It too was going to cleave itself apart and spin off a series of separate companies in IPOs. As the United States geared up for the presidential election of November 2000, the stock market, and especially the tech-heavy Nasdaq, took a pounding. No one was spared.

Had the Internet Revolution run out of steam? The dot-coms had, and one of the biggest bubbles ever created in the financial markets was wiped out.

From the market peak on March 10, 2000, to Election Day that November, the Internet market lost $250 billion in paper value. Stocks like eBay dropped from a high of $80 to $3 a share. Everything was revalued—always downward. And many were out of business. Big and small Internet companies alike started to pull the plug as their once-profligate venture capital backers realized that the trajectory to profits was far too long to make sense. And now, in September, the telecom network providers and even the infrastructure companies started to feel the heat.

A few days earlier, Lucent provided mediocre fourth-quarter earnings and McGinn was history. Now it was Nortel's turn at bat. In its third quarter, revenue had grown 42 percent year-on-year, and optical sales were up nearly 90 percent. On the surface, decent numbers; but what caught the attention of investors was the sequential quarterly growth—it wasn't up but was flat. The cause was a shortage of components that rendered Nortel unable to fulfill some customer orders. It spooked the already-twitchy market. The stock dropped $20 in a single day.

Now even fiber optics wasn't a sure thing anymore. There was no safe haven in the stock market. Nortel, a giant, well-managed company, had been unable to guide the analysts early in the quarter and appeared to have been caught unaware by the slowing of the growth pace in the fall quarter. It wasn't that the company was doing anything wrong—it was just that any mistake in judgment was going to be heavily penalized. This was no longer the Nortel of yesteryear, with highly predictable dividends and 10 percent growth per annum. Now a 64 percent rise in earnings per share wasn't enough. Nortel had talked its way into the high-growth Internet, and it had to deliver on that promise. When it didn't, the bottom fell out of the stock.

Unfortunately, the company had also made a major mistake that contributed to its failings, which few recognized. Although it had bought Bay Networks several years earlier in order to bring in IP knowledge and tried to integrate networking thinking throughout the company, it had failed to understand, or to attack, the one market that Cisco had never made any secret about: the enterprise networking game. Nortel, for all John Roth's insight and engineering acumen, fundamentally didn't understand how to sell to businesses. Nortel was great at selling to carriers and to service providers and to wireless geeks and to netheads. But what Nortel never figured out was how to sell to business people. And, more particularly, how to sell Internet and networking gear to businesses.

This is a sales challenge that has less to do with "feeds and speeds," in nethead vernacular, than it does with understanding what the customer's business needs really are. Selling into this crowd required an entirely different kind of sales engineer— one who could empathize with a white-collar manager whose real concern was getting more widgets shipped every day, not somebody whose business was about transporting bits of data. There was a fundamental gulf inside Nortel that couldn't be easily bridged. IBM and Cisco knew how to sell to businesses. Nortel and Lucent knew how to sell to carrier geeks, Bellheads, and their brethren the netheads. But that wasn't where the money was . . . yet.

The result was that when Nortel hit a speed bump in the fiber-optic business, it didn't have the IP business to smooth things out. Worse, because it was struggling with fielding an effective sales force to the businesses adopting the Internet at breakneck pace, it was also missing out on the insight that that kind of contact, across thousands of customers, could produce. Nortel talked a great game about its acquisition of Bay and its adoption of the Internet speed of change and all that. But the bottom line belied the confidence that John Roth exuded.

Nortel's share of product markets was slipping wherever Cisco and Bay had competed in the past. Nortel's share in routers and switches was down to dwindling single digits, while Cisco's was breaking through to 90 percent in several key legacy router segments. These were billion-dollar market sectors, doubling in size between 1998 and 1999 to $3 billion and now on run rates to reach $5 billion in 2000. Nortel, for all its fiber-optic strength and its opportunity in wireless, had a giant hole in its side in the one data-networking segment that was accelerating at unheard-of rates: the IP networking universe.

THE INTERNET HAD given. It could also take away. And now there was only one unscathed player—one titan—on the field left unbloodied. Of course it was the youngest and the least experienced of them all, and, to an old-style investor, the most troublesome. It had no background in telephony yet was talking about taking on the voice world with voice calls and services over IP networks. It was audaciously moving into the rocket-science field of fiber optics by brashly buying companies and claiming it could sell their gear through its world-class sales organization. It had a corner on the enterprise data communications market that seemed to drive its profits but was having some trouble trying to transition from its traditional customers to a whole new breed of service providers and New World carriers that were looking to utilize the coming bandwidth overload by providing services across the public network that used to be bought and run locally.

Cisco, the emblem of the Internet, the company whose business and the Internet were inextricably linked, had one simple truth: IP networking will win. It combined that with one simple mantra: Be just like us. Adopting the Web will free you and your legacy company . . . never mind the fine print and the difficulties that many legacy companies will face in transitioning to the Web. Never mind the distinct possibility of extinction or the fact that taking the wrong path to the wrong vision of Internet commerce could lead to an untimely demise. With its extraordinary sales, its consistent message, its legions of new employees singing the company song, a country filled with Internet and dot-com apologists and early, frenetic, proselytizers for the new new thing pursued with unthinking abandon, Cisco was the bellwether of the age.

"Be just like us."

This is the gospel, the good book of this movement. It is what gives the company its cultist undertones. Thousands of like-minded employees, all of whom espouse the simple formula: Follow our example, and you too can reach the city on the hill. Use our gear, sell over the Internet, rethink your business . . . and send us your networking dollars.

It is easy to be seduced with the vision of friction-free new economies, especially when one company, with an unbroken string of profitable quarters, keeps raking up extraordinary gains in the face of an unslaking, ever-accelerating demand. And the story is so deeply intertwined with the company's persona and image, its genetic code, that there is no telling any longer where the Internet tale stops and the Cisco vision begins.

The fundamental elements of connectivity, linkage, and networking that the Internet has made common are being applied to Cisco by its preacher-leader. John Chambers has a vision of business leadership driven by an Internet architecture, with the quick hits, the short attention spans, the links and partnerships and sponsorships that underpin that world. He's a master at communicating it, and his message is one that many unthinkingly follow, especially those who've not weathered a downturn yet. Acquisitions are the R&D of the times. Carry a big wallet. Sell the whole solution. Don't be dogmatic; acquire and integrate and provide what customers ask to buy. Use the Internet for its operating and fulfillment efficiencies. Promote the company's own systems to prove value. Encourage a bedrock belief that outsourcing can solve most problems. Outsource everything possible. Keep finding and funding new acquisitions at an accelerating pace, in order to fuel the sales funnel and to bring in new R&D to the company. Knit it all together with internal engineering teams, but don't expect breakthrough engineering to come from inside.

Field a superb sales force, because this is really the value add that Cisco and John Chambers provide. Make customers' networks work. Period.

The result is a hollowed-out company with a superb and driven sales force selling the broadest collection of data communications gear at high margins. But there are too many core centers of excellence, no single technical direction except for the reverberations from its original IP DNA and the need to keep legacy Cisco gear compatible. There are lots of satellite groups filled with young turks and clusters of entrepreneurs trying to find the path forward. And there are a few smart marketers and Web artisans running their sectors highly efficiently using New Economy streamlining, a handful of strategic thinkers with little operational experience executing a fast and furious purchasing spree, and a giant sales force that is always on the lookout for the next acquisition. But there is no compelling technical leadership—in fact, there is a vacuum at the top technology tier.

And there are those relentless, spectacular profits and earnings that show no sign of diminishing.

The conventional wisdom says that a company has to add some value to the supply chain, somewhere. Cisco doesn't do much internal R&D; it outsources almost all of its manufacturing, supplying only product engineering, marketing, administration and accounting, and a sales force to sell the whole kit and caboodle. Is this sustainable? So far it has been. Cisco is far and away the market leader in table after table of IP industry sales reports—especially in routers and Ethernet switches of all kinds. Is it because it dances very well? Is very lucky? Has it been blessed with inept competitors?

All of that, and more. Cisco is a company that has a wonderful virtuous cycle at work. Competition has fallen away; the demand for communications gear continues to grow both in real dollar value and in terms of how critical these information systems are to many businesses and individuals. Only one company has the breadth of products, the experience, and the solidity to ensure that it all works together. Only Cisco is a safe choice in the universe of data communications.

Can it last? The Web ought to ultimately provide an extraordinary place for commerce, conversation, and entertainment. Thus far it is truly unknowable where the changes it is bringing will end. With the end of the market's infatuation with the dot-com era, one phase has passed, and now the telecom and equipment vendors have been hit hard as well. But the inexorable growth in the need for communication services has only just begun. New businesses are about to erupt that will sweep away the current pricing and delivery mechanisms of much of the market and will shift the landscape once again. Some of these are Telseon, Yipes, Extreme, and Luminous. All of these companies are building the equivalent of extended LAN networks out into the metro regions. The idea is to supply simple, Ethernet-based dial tone at ridiculously low prices. It is like Occam's razor—the simplest solution is almost sure to be the one that triumphs. Use the same protocols that have proven so effective in the LAN, and apply them to the mid-market, the metro and regional networks. Then hand everything off to high-speed glass to get shot around the world.

Call it the 10-gigabit gambit. This is where the proverbial line in the sand has been drawn.

On one side you have Cisco, with its routers and switches employed by heavy users of a networking language called Ethernet, bundled together in the loose mesh network jumble of IP.

On the other you have Nortel, with a series of proprietary transmission schemes doctored and tailored to get data up and onto light waves, the fastest thing anyone has yet discovered— but which require carefully fine-tuned and expensive equipment all along the path.

Ten-gigabit Ethernet over fiber is the next thing beyond rocket science. No longer are IP and the router at the center of the leading edge in the network explosion. The future is light.

But what still counts is where the intelligence is added to the network. Routers. Intelligent switches. Aggregation and subscriber management systems. And the dirty little secret of networking is that the biggest opportunity to sell networking gear is still to companies of all sizes, all over the world. This is where the margins are. Only one company has made this sector its overwhelming focus. Sure, keeping up with the service providers is good business in terms of staying on the cutting edge and hearing what the new hot boxes are. But the bread-and-butter for Cisco is selling to companies and upgrading the existing networks of its enterprise customers. Mining its existing customer base is extraordinarily profitable.

For Cisco, and John Chambers, the problem is that the company has grown too large, with too unbroken a string of improving results, to stay satisfied in the warm and comfy pool of IP that it grew up in. To keep growing at its torrid pace, it has to find new markets to conquer. And at the same time, there is a new revolution going on in the supply side—the Ethernet dial tone networkers—that will flatten the networks, reduce prices and complexity, and finally make it easier for many companies to simply buy network services, rather than buy the gear, hire the staff, and supervise their owned-and-operated networks 24/7. In this New World, no one cares what equipment is used, and margins will fall. It is a market that Cisco can sell to, but it won't generate many profits or those big fat profits. On the other hand, the only choice is to leap into the fiber-optic fray and the wireless wars, no matter how much engineering is needed, because that is the only place in coming years where margins will be big and profits assured.

Looking across what must appear to Chambers and his colleagues to be a chasm in the fiber universe is that 10-gigabit standard. To a company without an R&D soul it must appear to be a forbidding leap across to a place that requires outrageous engineering on the fringes of the hardest problems of science ever tackled. There are lots of young turks at Cisco. Will one of them step up to the challenge?

And even more daunting, there is already one company that is dominating the 10-gigabit photon business on the other side of that chasm: Nortel Networks. The company is well entrenched with a big lead.

But that is only half of Cisco's problem. Ten gigabits of data, the place where fiber strands can take over transmission of data, is also going to be extremely important because it just happens to be the same speed as the current top end of Ethernet-capable equipment: 10-gigabit Ethernet. This is behind the newest emergent networking architecture: Replace the carefully planned-out traditional telecom architectures that the lumbering RBOCs and the bigger competitive local-exchange carriers have built out already with high-speed Ethernet networks that operate not just in a local campus or building—but regionally.

These new high-speed Ethernet service providers are already popping up all over the place, delivering cheap Ethernet-based bandwidth over fiber interconnections. They are buying gear from anyone offering the latest hot box, undercutting the incumbent carriers by thousands of dollars a month, and re-selling Ethernet as cheaply as possible, over as wide an area as possible. We are about to enter the age of Ethernet dial tone. These New Age carriers have no allegiance to the past, a vision of delivering standards-based, plain vanilla Ethernet wherever customers want, and the ability to dial up and down bandwidth as the user needs. The cost for all of this is an order of magnitude less than for existing lower-speed services provided by the incumbent and larger carriers. Based in Ethernet means there is an entire mature (at least for the technology market) industry already building products for the standards, so the high-speed Ethernet business will start off with cut-rate pricing and lots of competition. And it will rapidly devolve to commodity pricing and thin margins.

Ethernet webtone is a gigantic opportunity to sell lots more Cisco gear. But the risk is not only that the margins will get squeezed and the business turn into a free-for-all where all of

Chambers's carefully crafted story has no resonance, but also, and perhaps more important, that the company will no longer control the customer. If ten thousand network providers can rise up to deliver broadband in every neighborhood, why would corporations continue to build, maintain, and upgrade their own internal networks? The reason that there aren't dozens of competing network and data services companies already is that you still have to be rich to create a broadband backbone network today. ATM data junctions, with up to 155 megabits of throughput per second, cost in the neighborhood of $65,000 per month in big American cities in the fall of 2000. Gigabit Ethernet has eight times as much data capacity and is *starting* to be offered right now at under about $10,000 a month. Bulk data capacity prices rarely rise over time. Or take it to a more granular level. A single T-1 line, which might be enough for a company of ten or so, is equivalent to about 1.2 megabits per second, or about 25 phone lines. Cost? Around $600 per month. Ten-megabit Ethernet dial tone—10 megabits of data, or eight times as much capacity—is already being offered in San Francisco and New York for around $1,000 a month. The economics of deploying these simpler, more tolerant and flexible networking systems could unleash hundreds of new network providers and add lots of software services bought across this newly high-speed broadband Internet on a per user basis. In this highly likely scenario, Cisco's world would tilt, even as it had nothing but opportunity all around.

THE PROBLEM IS all about that hollowed-out core of a company and an Elmer Gantry at its head who can talk about the city on the hill, but who can't tell you where exactly it will be pitched without consulting his customers. Cisco doesn't see the future through technology; it sees the future through its customers. This kind of reactive leadership works fine when none of the competitors have any idea where the market is going either and the best you can do is listen to customers—this characterized the early days of the Internet and data networking. It also will work very well when a market sector has matured enough to be stable, which is where the IP game is today and explains why Cisco's enterprise numbers continue to roar ahead. But what happens when it hits entirely new technology, where it has no innate knowledge and skills like those Cisco's early router denizens brought to the networking game? What happens with fiber optics in the metro network, or wireless data everywhere?

At Nortel, there is no doubt what happens. John Roth, engineer extraordinaire, rolls up his sleeves, puts up his technology periscope, sets a course, and gets all the thousands of other car aficionados who make up his company to give everything they have to fulfill that technical vision and its best-case guess of how the economics will work out.

But John Chambers doesn't have that technology vision. He has to bet it all on his customers. And they can't see the future in the tea leaves of the present. Cisco will keep exploiting its dominance in the universe of IP, and it will keep selling more and more gear, to more companies, who will use it to supply service and networking and solutions to yet more companies. But ultimately the intelligence that Cisco gives to packets will happen in light, and some post-rocket scientist will win a Nobel Prize for the effort.

It won't be in a Cisco lab. If Chambers can, he'll buy the company before anyone else. But at a company with a weak senior management team, a leader who appears increasingly isolated at the top, and no evidence of a truly coherent technology vision, that doesn't seem likely.

At the moment of its greatest triumphs in the data-networking space, when its engine is running on all cylinders, Cisco appears about to run out of long-term gas.

On one hand, Cisco is trying to claw its way into the fiber world, with a business structure and soul that are not well suited to marshaling the kind of integrated science and technology initiatives that could make the company competitive and world class. Bet right, as it has done with the acquisition of Cerent—even though that acquisition is a SONET play and by definition backward facing—and niches could open up for it. But bet wrong, and the market is unforgiving. Buying research departments all over the world and trying to integrate them is a tough road without a visionary technologist who gets it right at the helm.

On the other hand, Cisco is also sitting atop a revolution from beneath that will make its products even more important and pivotal, while changing the company and the marketplace indelibly. If Cisco's Web vision is fulfilled—the decentralized, robust, and vibrant Next Net religion of John Chambers—the customers that the company has so successfully served will no longer buy their own data connection equipment or handle their own networks or bother to know what is under the hood. All of this has been essential to Cisco's success in the past five years. The network priestdom will be shattered, and Cisco's crucial account control will be loosened. In a world where bandwidth is a commodity, purchased as needed from a plethora of service providers, Cisco's new best customers will have to be the carriers and whole new generations of service providers who are rushing to deploy IP-based Ethernet webtone—not the business customers who have always been the firm's bread and butter.

Could Cisco ride out rough weather in the market? Was it already being pressured? Was the future arriving already? The market was waiting with bated breath as Cisco prepared to announce its quarterly earnings on the afternoon before Election Day, 2000. Was it the end of the Internet Revolution? Had the greatest proponent of the New World sailed into a storm too? John Chambers had come a long way from West Virginia. How much farther was kingdom come?

CHAPTER 11

BREAKING AWAY

IT WAS THE FIRST MONDAY IN NOVEMBER 2000, TIME FOR Cisco's first-quarter earnings call between company management and the investment crowd. Not since 1993 and the acquisition of Crescendo—the initial acquiree bought to provide the cornerstone of the LAN switching business—had Cisco been under such fire. In the wake of that long-ago acquisition, Wall Street had downgraded Cisco stock—the only time in its ten-year publicly traded career that had happened. Now it looked as if a downgrade might be imminent again.

An article in the *Wall Street Journal* a few days earlier had questioned the company's growth rate, openly speculating on whether any company of this size could continue to expand at its historical rates. The problem was the string of soft earnings reports from blue-chip New World carriers like Sprint, WorldCom, IXC, and Global Crossing, as well as the continuing carnage among both dot-coms and the other big telecommunications equipment vendors. How could Cisco be immune to slowing sales? The junk bond market, crucial to the buildout of expensive data networks for unprofitable new telecom carriers, had dried up. Speculation was rampant that perhaps the big data infrastructure was already overbuilt and that capital spending by the biggest carriers was going to slow to a trickle. In the knee-jerk, undifferentiated herd mentality that passes for insight among many analysts and investors, this would be very bad for Cisco. After all, in the past year, the conventional wisdom had decided that the future for networks was in the carrier and service provider space—this was where the telecommunications profits in the past had all been mined, and so it seemed only natural that the new Internet-based networks would quickly become the domain of the big suppliers who knew how to sell to carriers and service providers. Since most companies bought voice services by the minute, it seemed only reasonable to imagine a world where most companies bought Internet bandwidth—IP dial tone—the same way. This meant that the future was going to be with the wholesalers and common carriers, not the enterprise companies that had fueled the Internet Revolution by upgrading and expanding their own internal nets.

Cisco had brought much of this change in emphasis on itself when, two years earlier, John Chambers started talking about moving into the carrier equipment market and tackling the giant telecommunications equipment vendors directly. For Cisco to continue to thrive, it needed to get into this arena. At first the idea was to build big switches and routers that could work at the very core of carrier networks, putting Cisco in competition with Nortel and Lucent and Alcatel and Siemens for the biggest iron in telecommunications. But from the very beginning, there was also a bit of the brash young upstart about Cisco's pronouncements, and Chambers's contention that IP networks could deliver not only data but also voice, and eventually video, better than reengineered telco networks raised eyebrows. His vision was to create a complete line of Cisco gear that could deliver these services to enterprise customers in coming years. It was generally discounted by the competition, who already had perfectly good (and very expensive) voice circuits in place and had standardized on a series of telco protocols in ATM and SONET (also very expensive) that were overbuilt for video and data as well. This Old World gear fit very nicely into the carefully planned future that the big carriers and RBOC telcos depended on for their utility-like business models.

As the big battleships of Nortel and Lucent slowly turned to encompass the new IP world, it was easy for the marketplace, and the chattering classes, to start framing the future telecommunications battle as one where the upstart IP victor—Cisco—was now moving onto their turf. The implication in all of this was that Cisco was now facing serious, well-financed competition as it tried to build out its franchise from the enterprise to the carriers and that the big telecommunications vendors were going to eat its lunch when it tried to venture out onto this much bigger playing field. As Juniper and Redback started to eat away at portions of the Cisco business, primarily in the service provider and carrier markets, the drumbeat of carrier-centric thinking grew louder. In this worldview, Cisco was at a serious competitive disadvantage.

At the same time, early in 2000, a new idea surfaced and was immediately adopted by many of the most influential network thinkers. It essentially was an extension of the broadband data revolution: If a great deal of data capacity was widely available in the network, wouldn't it make more sense to rent software applications and data storage facilities across the network? In a certain sense it was the old timesharing idea, re-created for the Internet Age. A software service provider could use economies of scale to reduce prices and deliver sophisticated applications over the Net. Companies would no longer buy software; they would only rent it as needed. Data storage, the price of which was already plummeting, would be provided as a kind of "hard drive webtone"; companies or individuals could pay for what they needed, and as their storage needs expanded, it would be easy to turn up the dial for more. As always, the acronyms quickly followed: Providers of software over the Net became known as "application service providers," or ASPs; data storage that was not local, but accessible over a network, became part of "storage area networks," or SANs. Since the carriers were promoting their vision of massive capacity everywhere, the ideas caught on; and influential thinkers and writers started describing a world where all network services were outsourced and where the locus of power shifted from the companies that were generating the data traffic that flowed over the Web to those who supplied the wires, conduits, and junctions to move it around.

The combination of this newly emergent view of the network and the inroads being made by competitors specifically aimed at Cisco's service provider market made some investors start to wonder about the company's unbroken string of successful quarters. Was it over? And not just for the Internet bubble, which clearly was being completely revalued from top to bottom, but for Cisco itself? If the Internet was going to turn into a service-provider and carrier-ruled environment, wasn't Cisco going to be trashed by the bigger corporations that knew how to play that game very well? When both Lucent and Nortel stumbled in mid-2000, it was easy to imagine that Cisco would be the next to crash.

But there was just one problem with the conventional wisdom. Corporate employees were demanding faster and faster access and bigger and bigger bandwidth faster than service providers could supply it. The Internet Revolution really was a real revolution, and the old rules of three- to five-year telecom network planning didn't work anymore. Demand was leapfrogging but not in any predictable pattern as it had in the prior voice universe (build a subdivision, and every house needs a phone) but chaotically, all over the place and all the time (who knew which house would have a band of Napster devotees or launch an online porn server that ran 24/7?). New, greenfield data-centric carriers were arising with pricing that made it impossible to eke out profits from expensive voice circuits rejiggered for data. And corporations, instead of waiting for the RBOCs and big carriers to get service out to them, the way they had in the recent past, were scared that if they didn't grab the Internet ring, they would be left behind. So they built out their internal networks at a pell-mell pace and went shopping for providers who could deliver at the new "Internet time" pace. The result was an unforeseen boom in enterprise and mid- to small-business networking gear and bandwidth—simply to keep up with the emergence of e-commerce and e-mail—that realigned the corporate data environment.

And by the time this situation had become apparent, only the one company left standing and addressing this enterprise market could truly take advantage of the opportunity.

Nonetheless, the pundits still seemed ignorant of what was happening, as Cisco prepared for its first-quarter earnings call on November 6, 2000. For years Cisco had been very carefully massaging, managing, and manipulating the investment community and the press to ensure that there were never any earnings surprises and to explain its complex and technically challenging business to a basically uncomprehending public. After all, while voice services and telco telecommunications had a hundred years of history, and corporate data networks had been widely used since the heyday of timesharing in the 1960s, IP had burst onto the scene only in the previous ten years; and it was really the explosive growth of the populist Internet during the preceding five that put it on the map. As a result, Chambers was always very careful to play down Cisco's extraordinary success at combating its big foes and to avoid any appearance of overconfidence in his earnings calls. John Chambers is a gracious and well-mannered gentleman, and gloating or name-calling is not in his makeup. He always avoided any direct reference to competition and was generous about the opportunities for all players in the market. At the same time, he had developed a style for the earnings calls over the years that included frank discussion of opportunities and challenges that he thought the company was facing. He also always included one or two of his executive team, who made presentations about particular "wild card" topics during each call. And he was always joined at the hip to Larry Carter, the company's conservative CFO, who could be counted on to pour oil on the waters with his carefully managed balance sheets, no matter what short-term concerns were voiced by the analysts and journalists.

It used to be that earnings calls for publicly traded companies were listened to by anywhere from a few dozen to a few hundred analysts and interested parties. They are usually dry affairs, filled with long recitations of hard-to-unravel acronyms and numbers like DSOs (days sales outstanding, a measure of how slow customers are to pay) and inventory turns (how often inventory turns over). The calls aren't actually required by law, but most companies hold them. Getting the phone number to listen in used to require some diligence, and not that many reporters had enough interest to bother, so there was usually little attention. The calls no longer resembled the cigar-filled rooms of the heyday of Wall Street capitalism, but they were still a very restricted affair and generally never included probing questions. The analysts, with their brokerage houses, had the benefit of firsthand information in advance of market opening the following day. Anything substantive was delivered to each trading company's best clients so they could have access to it exclusively ahead of the next morning's market opening.

In recent years the earnings calls of the largest corporations have become much more open to investors and others and any news is carefully released democratically and immediately reported by wire services. As the Web's spigot of information only gets larger, more and more investors use the Internet for trading, and the SEC now requires simultaneous dissemination of all market-moving data. As a result, more and more are listening in. Given the questions being voiced around Wall Street and the recent disappointments at both Lucent and Nortel, it was hardly surprising when Larry Carter, in his initial comments, welcomed the "over 20,000 interested investors and other parties attending this call using the Internet, probably over a Cisco router." But it was an extraordinary measure of the success of the Internet and its power to reshape communications and, more important, *information* itself. Twenty thousand people make up quite an audience for a corporate executive. Cisco had moved into the headliner category and could probably sell tickets through Ticketmaster if it held its events in a stadium.

For those who were listening in to hear evidence of Cisco's incipient demise in the face of a changing market and to divine the shifting, swirling winds of technology and finance, it was a very disappointing afternoon. Because not only did Carter announce another quarter of spectacular earnings—revenue up 66 percent from the previous year's quarter, pro forma income up 67 percent—but John Chambers also went on to explain just what it was that had caused this remarkable and sustained growth. Furthermore, in explaining it, he also pointed to exactly what made it such a powerful engine of growth and where the future growth of Cisco was going to come from. But the optimistic message fell on deaf ears. By the end of the call, during the question-and-answer session the company held with the analysts, the frustration with the endless questions about the carrier side of the business finally broke loose as Larry Carter lost his temper with one questioner. Chambers and Carter then tried to preempt the continuing questions about the company's service provider business by offering one of the most extraordinary moments in modern business history.

Chief financial officers and the executives of big companies are schooled in caution. It is always considered better form to downplay future results than to over-promise and be caught short. For years Cisco has promised growth in the 30 to 40 percent range—and even that, by the standards of the Old World, is breakneck. Although 30–40 percent was accurate back in the late 1990s, in 2000 Cisco consistently hit marks that were the envy of almost every company on earth: gross margins of about 60 percent, and revenue and income accelerating quarter on quarter, hitting mid-60 percent rises every quarter for the year. In an effort to quell the voices of concern and to reassure the markets that Cisco's business was healthy, if not exceptional, Carter launched into his usual guidance estimates for the upcoming quarter.

In the middle of the call he dropped what was a bombshell of historic proportions. Cisco Systems, a company that will have projected revenues of about $30 billion in 2001, announced that it was revising its guidance upward for the coming quarter. For the first time ever, a publicly traded company with tens of billions of dollars in sales was telling the world that it would hit a growth rate of more than 50 percent on a quarter-over-quarter basis for both the upcoming quarter and the full year. No company in the technology sector has ever grown at such a breakneck pace. And no company's executives have publicly made themselves liable for such a growth rate.

Only one company has ever delivered results like this: IBM in the late 1960s and early '70s. John Chambers and the 35,000 employees of Cisco were drawing a line in the sand. What did they know?

IT TURNED OUT that the Cisco mantra—"IP rules"—wins.

Optics is going to be big, certainly, and it is the fastest way to transport data. But IP traffic already is big. Better yet, it is growing much faster, from a smaller base. And, more significant,

IP is heading directly for optical networks—smarts meets speed. The true lesson of the Internet Age is not that speed is the most important thing. Chambers was wrong about this, although he clings to it as a crowd-pleasing line. If it was true, Nortel really would have Cisco by the jugular. The most important lesson of the Internet is that the true value, the place where the margins can be made, is in delivering intelligence to the network, adding smarts to either packets or photons. Someday optics will be able to do this. But not yet. Today intelligence, routing, and switching are all done in packets. And Cisco is the king of packets.

The trouble for Nortel and others is that optical-wavelength solutions are too much like rocket science. They make sense in the core of the network, just as jets make sense for moving packages between San Francisco and New York when a whole planeload of them are going to the same basic destination. But for getting the packets distributed to your doorstep, it makes much more sense to use a fleet of small trucks. Think of routers as trucks and fiber optics as jet cargo carriers. Optics don't make sense yet out in the 'burbs. Eventually, when the physics and economics of this rocket-science technology get mastered, the metro and tributary traffic will be largely carried on wavelengths of light. But no matter how traffic is carried, it will be in a format that is some derivation of Ethernet, the original commercial IP flavor of Internet data traffic, because in this form routing and switching can be applied to the data.

This is the secret of Cisco's success. It has held on to the networking core of most of the big companies in the world. It has moved aggressively into the small and mid-sized commercial market as well, growing that business from essentially fifth place a couple of years ago to leadership market share today. And there is no end in sight. Dell'Oro numbers showed Ethernet switch revenues growing faster on a percentage basis in late 2000 than at any time since 1997—and the market size had tripled since then, to $12 billion. Better yet, Cisco, the market share leader, grew its business faster than the market and faster than number two Nortel. This is execution raised to a higher power.

More switches enable every desktop to run at high speed back to whatever edge router, or gathering point, the corporate or local network supplies to link up every user to the Internet. Companies that built shared LANs ten years ago are coming back and beefing up every connection, every router, every switch and hub so as to be ready for the coming wave of broadband. The result is an enormous opportunity for Cisco to mine its installed base in a way that only IBM and Microsoft have ever experienced. IBM did it with hardware, offering its customers the chance to forever upgrade their equipment. Microsoft does it with software, supplying endless upgrades to Windows and productivity applications as new features become possible. But Cisco has done it with hardware *and* software. And now it is poised to add services. This is more than a virtuous business cycle. This is a *righteous* cycle.

It is an extraordinary market, and Cisco is running at an exceptional clip. It has consolidated its hold on the marketplace in almost every category. Flipping through the charts of markets and shares that Dell'Oro supplies, the router and switch game has Cisco in the lead, with a distancing lead, in most categories. The problem for the investment market and those who invested heavily in the fiber-optic universe is that manipulating light is still an infant science, with no telling how it will evolve. And IP is at least an unruly adolescent, with Cisco its master.

This is the fundamental truth of the Internet Age: Bet on cheaper and simpler IP everywhere. But it is not enough to say it—and then be weighed down by a legacy of gear and thinking. This, clearly, is the problem at Nortel. John Roth gets it, and he talks a very good story about grafting IP passions onto a core company that grew up in the voice legacy days. But it hasn't worked out. The Bay acquisition has not delivered the products or the revenues or the market share that Roth thought he could generate when he was singing its merits to investors a couple of years ago. It is exactly this disappointment that has tarnished the company's stock price.

Much of the rise in Nortel's stock prior to its reversal of optical fortunes in late 2000 was based on Roth's relentless talk about integrating IP with legacy phone gear. For the analysts and investing community, it sounded as if Cisco, which was obviously slicing off the body parts of others in the enterprise networking market, finally had a great competitor. Roth and his public relations machine made as much noise as possible about the new Nortel—with its Bay infusion of IP DNA; its booming SONET business, as legacy carriers beefed up and exploited existing capacity to the full in the metro or regional network; and its optical long-haul business that seemed to have endless growth ahead of it—and the perception of Nortel's value soared. Add spectacular engineering work in Nortel's optical labs that really did push the technology envelope far out into the future, and Nortel seemed destined for greatness. After all, it had the experience and the wisdom and the deep pockets to be the worthy competitor for Cisco.

But the reality didn't match the hype. It had to be galling for Chambers, who thought of Nortel as a carpetbagger from the Old World trying to make hay out of the chaff Cisco left behind on the floor. During the November 6 earnings call, Chambers was careful to describe "three key elements in our success: a booming market; great execution on the part of our people; and missteps and mistakes made by our competitors." It was as close as he would come to naming Nortel and Lucent that day.

But he is right. The only issue might be the order. Luck and disastrous decisions by the competition—especially the tin ear the voice legacy companies seem to have for the rebirth and new wave of acceleration in the enterprise market—have been much more important to Cisco than its near-perfect, by-the-book, Internet-influenced execution. After all, being efficient as a company isn't exactly a new theme in business history. It makes a great story for Chambers to tell, since it buttresses the company's cultlike business model, but it isn't the secret sauce. What has made Cisco so astonishingly successful is first and foremost the failure of its competitors.

A close look through the same sheaf of tables that Cisco dominates shows Nortel in decline in almost every sector of the IP networking space. It is as though the good Canadians have been the guys who couldn't shoot straight. Nortel is growing its presence and its market shares in carrier-type business sectors, where it has taken up the leadership role formerly held by Lucent. SONET equipment, edge and core switches, long-haul terrestrial wave division multiplexing—all have been strong areas of growth for Nortel. But its IP businesses have declined. In overall switch sales Nortel has plummeted to 7 percent market share—a 50 percent drop in its share of the market *since* acquiring Bay. During the same period Cisco has grown its share of this market by 50 percent, from 40 percent at the time of Nortel's Bay acquisition to around 60 percent of worldwide switch revenue today. Move to routers and the story is the same, although worse for Nortel. In legacy routers Nortel has seen market share slip from as high as 17 percent in high-end (high-margin) routers to under 5 percent since the Bay acquisition. In a new category that Cisco dominates—voice and data routers, today a nearly $4 billion market that has grown from zero three years ago—Nortel either doesn't yet have a product or is watching market share tumble.

This is not the mark of a company that has truly committed to IP. Nortel talked the IP talk but wasn't cashing in on the most important marketplace engine yet seen in the computing and networking universe: the buildout of broadband at every enterprise, commercial company, and local government site in the connected world. This is what Cisco has been mining, with exceptional skill and with a laser focus that puts everyone else in the market to shame. Simply put, Nortel isn't walking the walk.

John Roth gets it; but for all the wisdom and senior management savvy of his lieutenants, they haven't made IP their religion. The heir presumptive at Nortel isn't very promising either. Clarence Chandran, the company's chief operating officer, is a wooden but very smooth salesman, without the kind of fire-in-his-eye IP zealotry that is going to be crucial in coming years. Other members of Nortel's senior staff are all from the legacy voice world, except for a few Bay veterans who have yet to depart. As long as optical revenues kept climbing at steep rates, the company's fundamental IP weakness wasn't noticed. Then in the fall of 2000, optical revenue growth at Nortel was flat quarter to quarter, while IP sales declined too, especially in the enterprise zone. Supply constraints—not enough rocket-science laser components—were blamed. But that wasn't the deeper problem. Had Nortel successfully integrated the Bay acquisition and really exploited what it purchased, it would have been able to weather this downturn without pause. But without a booming, growing share of the booming, growing business networking market, Nortel tripped up.

IRONICALLY, IT IS right in the heart of the old telephony business that Nortel and Lucent control their greatest undervalued assets. And it is right here that the next gigantic battle in the enterprise market is going to be staged. For the past year, a majority of Cisco's small-company acquisitions have focused on one particular technology segment of the communications market: voice over IP networks. This is a sector where Cisco is already shipping a billion dollars' worth of product per year, according to Joseph Baylock of Gartner Inc. "Cisco's going after the old enterprise phone market, Lucent's Definity and Nortel's Meridian PBXs and everything else, with both guns blazing.

"And I don't think the guys at Nortel know exactly what to do with their inherent advantage. They have all those phone switches and PBXs in the market. How should they IP-enable them? And if they don't get it exactly right, Cisco is going to eat their lunch."

Baylock's specialty is advising corporations on the pros and cons of telecommunications and networking gear. Cisco is one of the vendors he recommends. "But Cisco has its own problem when facing this market. Where is the weak point that will unravel the legacy voice business—probably a $500 billion a year business all told today including equipment and billed services—and turn it into an IP services market? To do it, Cisco has to get on a fast track to understanding voice customers. Today they have no experience at all with this part of the market. Just saying that all voice will be carried by IP isn't very helpful. Maybe they will buy Avaya, the Lucent enterprise networking spin-off, and instantly have a big installed base of voice customers to service."

Would this help make Cisco a greater company? Stratacom was not an unalloyed success, but it did fill out the product portfolio. And more important, it put Cisco squarely into the carrier game. Cisco has grown up in many ways. It's no longer just an IP company, but is also moving into the wavelength world, both with light and radio, fiber and wireless. But with the arrival of Ethernet everywhere—IP dial tone—which is gaining ground fast, all bets are off as to the ultimate staying power of metropolitan optical solutions based on ATM and SONET. Yes, there will be a need to move big amounts of data around in the light world, both regionally and nationally, but the intelligence will still be in the IP packets. That means more routers, everywhere. The value add will be reading and ranking and directing thousands, if not tens of thousands, of data streams essentially simultaneously. In a world where the computer really does become the network, this combination has to throw the game to the IP players, whose solutions are cheap, simple, and democratic, rather than to the hierarchical telco protocol universe, which is creaking under the assault from the data revolution.

Voice seems certain to move to IP soon. Not surprisingly, this is a massive Cisco effort. Internally, the company uses its own homegrown IP phone system. It is on its fourth version, and its weaknesses are a point of some contention within the company. The same goes for internal call center projects, which are said to be getting John Chambers's personal attention due to a string of failures to deliver and disgruntled customers. Here again Nortel has a powerful piece of the puzzle "but it is almost like they can't figure out what to do with some of the good moves they've made," says Baylock. "[Nortel] bought Clarify, a contact management software company. Call centers, unified messaging systems, and Internet systems—these are the areas that enterprise customers are spending money on, and it is a unique combination of legacy and IP equipment, software, and services. A great business for Nortel. Cisco also grasps it but hasn't quite figured out how to sell the whole package yet." Nortel seems paralyzed, as if the IP part of this doesn't quite fit, even though they have all the customers already. And Lucent and Avaya don't seem to have even figured out what the game is yet, what a great opportunity this could be, and how seriously they are threatened in the core of their traditional voice business.

The one thing that is clear is that getting the world's corporations to move to voice systems delivered over Cisco-supplied IP networking gear all the way down to individual desktops is a massive business opportunity for somebody. Add to it the next play, one that Chambers doesn't hide: Video streaming is an opportunity that will be fed by a broadband data service to every end point. If webcam communication truly gets to every desktop, living room, and car, only a mass of routers and switches in IP networks will be able to handle all the bandwidth required to deliver it easily and economically. Data, voice, video—all hijacked and carried across the IP network from a jack in the wall to the other side of the earth.

This is an avalanche of demand that will drive a buildout of network capacity far greater than anything yet seen. Or imagined.

ABOVE THE SILICON VALLEY, about 200 yards from Highway 280, which slices down the Peninsula from San Francisco, John Chambers lives in a gigantic new home on a small private road. Set just up over the ridge of the hill, it is remarkably quiet for a place that is literally almost a stone's throw from the very busy freeway. The home, which he and his wife, Elaine, moved into late in 1999, has been the setting for several political fund-raisers and is only a couple of blocks from their last, more modest, place.

Looking out across the hills of the California coastal range to the west and equipped with a tennis court—for his particular passion—and a swimming pool, as well as extensive gardens, it is a place befitting the king of Silicon Valley. Like most of the homes of the super-rich, this one has fencing surrounding its two acres—wrought iron, painted black, and with a big automatic gate to keep out the undesirables. But there's one unique thing about Chambers's home, something that is perfectly in keeping with the personality of this prince of American business, even as his company breaks through every conceivable limit. The portal to John Chambers's house is never closed. The gate stays open. He may be the most successful executive in the country, but he isn't hiding behind his gates and keeping the rest of the world out.

It's hard not to wonder what Chambers must be thinking, sitting up in his house above Silicon Valley, as he realizes that he is on one of the great economic rocketships of all time. Just how far could Cisco go? No company of such a size has ever promised growth of 50 percent a year. No company has so thoroughly dominated a market segment since Microsoft's Windows took over the desktop ten years ago. No company has ever executed so flawlessly, delivering an end-to-end variety of good-enough data-networking products tied together by a brand name, a brand name now enhanced, extended, and made mythic by the company in selling its wares. Just be like us. Join our Internet Revolution. We'll show you how. John Chambers is the Pied Piper of Networking as it is applied to the modern enterprise. We'll show you how to be happy. Just buy our networking gear, the services we can help deliver, and our very way of organizing our business in this new Industrial Revolution, the new world of the Internet.

Cisco is sitting on top of the world, with opportunity exploding underneath it, a big and wealthy installed base that is rapidly upgrading every desktop connection to some form of broadband and a crowd of competitors and pundits who think that the new new thing is fiber optics, who are missing the biggest economic engine of modern times: the business buildout of networking broadband to every desktop. This is a company on the edge of greatness. Can it grasp the next rung—the brass ring—and pull itself up to the next level?

Only a couple of things are holding it back. The first, already discussed, is Chambers's failure to designate a successor. The second challenge, an enormous one, facing the company is inherent in the fact that it has doubled in size—from 16,000 to 35,000 employees—in less than two years. Keeping the company focused and on track with such an influx of new personnel is a challenge. At Apple, twenty years earlier, the period when the company mushroomed from 1,000 to 5,000 employees was known as the Bozo Explosion. Administrative inertia bedeviled the company, and ultimately it took a palace coup and new leadership to get the touchy-feely innovator of personal computing back on track. Chambers is fond of talking about how the company gets 30,000 résumés a month and uses the Internet and software to screen them. But at a company that made its mark with a legion of driven, focused, passionate IP netheads who would let nothing get in the way of solving the customer's problems, absorbing this many new people has to take its toll.

Change is necessary in the New World, according to the good book of John Chambers. But can Cisco instill the Tao of John

Chambers and John Morgridge and Sandy Lerner and Don Valentine and Len Bosack in each and every one of these new hires? Other than succession, keeping the company's extraordinary dedication to the customer alive as it hires thousands of new people every year might just be the biggest challenge on John Chambers's shortlist.

"Is it a twenty- or eighty-year company?" Baylock muses. "To get to the latter Cisco has to grow up and change the way it sees acquisitions. In order to have a shot at being a company for the ages, Cisco has to think outside its box. Throw out everything it holds dear. Contemplate a merger. There's not going to be room for lots of server and networking companies in the long-term future. I think that the future will see a blurring of the line between the two, and the winning company will be one that combines servers and networking gear into a single coherent product line."

A merger, not another acquisition. A whole new experience for the Cisco Kids. Done right, not only will it lead to long-term success, but maybe in the process they'll find the successor to John Chambers as well.

The most remarkable New World merger for Cisco would involve Sun. The two companies that started at Stanford at about the same time would, if reunited, become the dominant force in the Internet by a long shot. But Sun CEO Scott McNealy is a loose cannon, not the kind of buttoned-up and cautious person that John Chambers likes to surround himself with. Sun's renegade, programmer-gonzo culture would also be quite a shock for Cisco's good netizen Republicans of today, no longer the hardcore software geekdom of its founding days. Hewlett-Packard in many ways could be a best-case match, since it is very strong in the communications backbone as systems provider to many network carriers, as well as a significant supplier of servers to corporations. Carly Fiorina would make an interesting choice as a successor to Chambers—although she is another non-engineer—and the cadres of senior division managers at HP could fill in many of the holes at the younger company. But do they really have IP religion? Would they be willing to let the upstart rule them? And how painful would this merger be?

HP adheres closely to the Chambers idea about corporate integrity, an increasingly important part of the Cisco myth. Chambers talks about being a good corporate citizen and competing fairly. These are values that the company shares with Hewlett-Packard, and for years Chambers used to joke that he told the former head of the company—Lew Platt—that we "want to be just like HP when we grow up." This merger of two Silicon Valley heavyweights could, just could, create an eighty-year company of broad reach.

A longshot merger partner would be EMC Corporation, although in a world of utility-like web dial tone, combining networking cycles (Cisco) with servers and storage gigabytes (which EMC supplies) could well be a killer combination. There is the geography issue—New England versus Silicon Valley—and another strong ego in EMC's chief executive Mike Ruettgers, an engineer by training, who would have to be accommodated. But listening to EMC's hard-driving leader describe the virtuous cycle of bandwidth, networking, and storage that this company is exploiting, you hear strong parallels to Chambers's gospel. EMC's recent financial results are also very similar to Cisco's.

One thing is certain, however. At the moment there is no end in sight for the accelerating growth of Cisco's business IP networking products. And until a worthy competitor really comes after the cult of Cisco and offers a dramatically better price-performance alternative, Cisco will be king of the IP hill. "Someone who doesn't charge corporate customers as much as Cisco can get in the door to make a bid," concludes Baylock. "There's enough room out there for others to get a shot. And there are so few alternatives that corporate buyers would welcome a healthy alternative."

Unfortunately, most of those who have shown up can't deliver the goods. And Cisco continues to break away.

CHAPTER 12

AN EMPTY FIELD IN COYOTE VALLEY

ON A CRISP, CLEAR TUESDAY MORNING IN NOVEMBER 2000, A crowd of gray-haired Silicon Valley investors gathers in the deserted parking lots at Paramount's Great America theme park and heads in for the annual Cisco shareholders' meeting. Outside an auditorium usually used to screen a recent Paramount movie hit, the 500 or so of the faithful shareholders who bother, or can afford the time off, to attend are greeted with groaning boards of catering company breakfast croissants, rolls, orange juice, coffee, and tea. It is a prosperous group, as well it should be. Cisco has made anyone fortunate enough to have bought the stock before this year a lot of money. Inside the hall, New Age instrumental jazz fills the ears, and onstage Cisco's executives and the show's set-up crew get ready for the highly choreographed program about to start. Later there will be much badinage about the pedestrian product demonstrations that punctuate Chambers's speech. But judging by how carefully everything has been arranged onstage and the army of technicians swarming over the set, there is only mock doubt about the readiness of the demos.

Out in the audience, among the faithful, John Chambers is shaking hands and touching people on their shoulders, thanking all who can hear for their support and asking for their comments. He's moving up the main aisle of the place, as self-assured as Maury Povich, and talking with all the folks who want to chat with him. He is doing this on his own; he simply plunges into the crowd, stopping at each row, shaking hands, graciously accepting compliments. "Great job, John." "Keep up the great work." "My votes are with you." He is at ease in this; his fluid, unstudied, truly interested persona is at work in all its glory. You can almost imagine a spotlight on him. Certainly the crowd buzzed and murmured and all eyes in the place turned to watch as the star of American middle-aged New World corporate culture came up into the audience before his meeting to enjoy the acclaim and the appreciation, to be energized by this love.

Then one fifty-something fellow breaks from the crowd and thrusts an annual report in front of the chief executive. John T. Chambers, at the pinnacle of his career, with a vast and accelerating market ahead of him, signs his autograph. That begins a trickle. More and more white-haired ladies and gentlemen get up out of their seats, waving their annual reports, politely waiting their turn as John Chambers carefully inscribes each one with his name. Soon he is besieged by investor groupies, all wanting something to show that he had touched them. That they had been here. This day.

In that moment John Chambers is no longer the human being, the aw-shucks common man; now he's become the marquee name, the movie star, the celebrity. Increasingly as the crush of the crowd grows around him, instead of continuing to embrace the warm glow of this moment of unscripted spontaneity and warmth, he starts to wear a bewildered look. Besieged by a crowd that has suddenly turned demanding, he seems ill at ease. Seconds later he is rescued by his handler, a sharp-looking blonde, who leads him onstage to the table set up on one side of the proscenium. With that, Larry Carter opens the meeting, and swiftly, with no discussion, the company's own slate of board members is ratified, as is the choice of an accounting firm. Several board members are sitting down in front of the crowd, including a new one, Jerry Yang of Yahoo!, who now joins his favorite venture capitalist Don Valentine of Sequoia Associates, Cisco's vice chairman. (Sequoia backed and created Yahoo! too.) John Morgridge, Cisco's chairman, is there too, representing the largest single shareholder, with 85 million shares—on this day, they are worth about $3.4 billion. Also in the crowd are corporate officer Mike Volpi and another executive who looks like his clone, Rick Justice, head of worldwide field operations. And just that quickly, after a pause while a handful of votes are gathered from around the auditorium, the motions are passed.

With gusto, and apparent relish, John Chambers launches into his stump speech. It starts with the accelerating productivity gains that have come since the early '90s—"growth from 1 to 2 percent, to 5 or 6 percent this year. This is the influence of e-commerce and the Internet as a means of communication. But we are only in the very early innings of this baseball game." Figuring out the winners entails a few basic rules. "It'll simply be the fastest beats the slowest. Not the big beats the small, or the small beats the big. It will be all about speed, all about branding, all about partnering."

Then he moves on to the real theme of his talk this morning: the competitive landscape. "Our competitors in the early '90s, when Cisco really began to use IP as a separate factor for competitive advantage, did not respond. By 1996 we were saving more in our own use of this technology than our nearest competitor was spending on R&D. We were able to put all of that back into our products.

"We set a goal a couple of years ago of $50 billion of revenue in five years. When we said it, we thought we might have stretched ourselves too far. I think there's a good chance that we can reach that goal, if we execute properly, in four years. And there's an outside chance it'll come in three. I'd like to say it is due to inspired leadership—but it is really being in the right market at the right time."

Chambers is pacing back and forth on the stage, wearing his standard blue suit and ever-present black loafers. He's warming up to his topic, and he's building up his points. "In terms of a Q1 update, we were extremely pleased with the balance across the board. It is much more than balance. It is the integration of the balance. From a balanced perspective, we had all five of our major theaters—Asia Pacific, Japan, the USA, the rest of the Americas, Europe—all grow sequentially, quarter to quarter by double digits, and year over year by over 50 percent. What that very simply says, different from a year ago, is that people all around the world are now getting it. You're seeing this IP revolution gain speed now on a global basis.

"Now what is critical is literally delivering a network of networks where it isn't just service providers, or enterprise, or commercial, but a combination of networks that only Cisco can uniquely provide. This allows companies to meet their networking goals and allows us to differentiate ourselves. I've talked to probably 75 percent of the global Fortune 500 business leaders over the last eighteen months. Cisco is in the unique position of not only being the Internet experts. Many companies looking to buy technology from us are also asking, 'How did you do it yourself Cisco, and can you help us?' Our relationship with our customers has never been stronger."

Chambers is zeroing in on the most powerful and potent part of Cisco's business: Its ability to mine the installed base of companies all over the world that are either upgrading their networking equipment or deploying it for the first time. His experience overseas and his willingness to invest heavily in global infrastructure before the market gelled are now going to pay off. But so are the efficiencies the company has created by using its Internet, or New World, business model.

"What is really exciting to me in all of this is how we, more than any other company in the world, have used this technology and the Internet ourselves in order to gain substantial and sustainable competitive advantage in terms of productivity and profitability. We were the ones who told the world four years ago that projections for e-commerce weren't off by 50 or 100 percent, but that they were off by five- or ten- or possibly twenty-fold. And our projections may yet end up being too conservative.

"While e-commerce got people excited, it was really our customer support that put us ahead of the curve. Here we had over a 200 percent growth in productivity. Savings of over $500 million a year. Add that to our ability to have over thirty plants around the world, own only a couple of them, yet be able to run this company with one virtual close. All of this is part of what makes us more effective than any of our competitors. This is half the reason that our gross margins are fifteen points higher than any of our traditional competitors. We know exactly where we are during the quarter, every day. Not two or three weeks later."

Much of this is familiar, but this time he is couching everything he says in terms of the competition. Chambers is striding back and forth onstage, giving his best in front of these very supportive shareholders. He next moves on to the giant new market that Cisco is determined to win. "A couple of years ago we told 275 of the world's largest voice carriers that their business was going to disappear.

"But projecting this wasn't as important as understanding how to move to the next wave. Those companies who were successful would move up the IP data infrastructure and they would add to their revenues faster than voice revenues dropped off. The same is true of the equipment manufacturers. There will not be major voice-only manufacturers. Whether it is circuit-based or PBX, if you don't move to a data architecture, with voice running on it, you run into the challenge that many of our large competitors found out very abruptly—that when their traditional revenues fell off, it was data that would carry them going forward.

"Voice was the primary communications revenue stream for over one hundred years. Voice is commoditizing. Data transport, including voice and video, will be very, very lucrative if done right for the next three to five years. But if competition continues to be encouraged by our government, you will see data transport continue to commoditize. I will give you the data lines so I can give you IP telephony, entertainment, sporting events, computer games. These are waves of new opportunity, then commoditization. From an enterprise perspective, customers are beginning to opt for call centers, applications hosting, unified messaging. But over time, customers will move literally to subscription services both to consumers, small to medium-sized business, or to the enterprise. The point is that the first wave took one hundred years. The second wave five years. The third one will probably be over in three years. And you get the feeling of how drastically business must change to stay ahead.

"When you see transitions at this speed, it is a chance to gain market share at a tremendous pace."

This has long been one of his secrets. Go after markets that are in disarray, spend like a drunken sailor to consolidate business and sales coverage, and then get returns in spades when the market comes back to life. This is based on a simple bet: IP will win, everywhere. So far, it has. There's little evidence that anything has changed in that sense yet. But now, instead of talking about New World networks or end-to-end networks, his conversation is becoming peppered with a new phrase. One that is uniquely Cisco's to deliver: the network of networks. As he spins it, this seems to require a lot of Cisco equipment and the cooperation of service providers who'll also buy lots of Cisco equipment in order to deliver optimal services to Cisco-powered corporate clients.

"Cisco has been the clear leader in the enterprise market with an end-to-end architecture. And now in the newest wave we're going to go after the service provider arena with essentially the same type of pattern. Instead of thinking of service providers as only needing one product, such as routers, or just optical or just broadband, there has to be a network architecture quality about it. Pure transport will commoditize. If you don't provide any intelligence, the IP capability, and the content capability, it will be very hard to compete. We're going after delivering the end-to-end solution, and we are sure it will occur in this market just like it did in the enterprise market.

"Not only are we able to provide that end-to-end architecture among service providers, we are also able to bring our enterprise and our commercial customers to that market. I'm talking about networks of networks."

So here it is. The idea behind much of his next-wave thinking is that Cisco can dictate what features the service providers have to deliver because so many of the world's companies have standardized on Cisco gear. This is a powerful argument, the same one that drove the so-called plug-compatible market in mainframes—everything had to work with IBM gear. The difference in the IP networking universe is that IP is a standards-based protocol, and anyone can make equipment that works to it. Chambers and Cisco have spent years trying to sell the market on the benefits of all-Cisco equipment. It hasn't worked on a technical side, since netheads know that it simply isn't true. There is very little benefit to having all Cisco gear. But from a business supplier point of view, there is great peace of mind to be gained from using one set of equipment that does work. Forget the higher costs. Forget the middle-of-the-road performance. This has been a powerful selling proposition.

Now, in moving into the service provider arena, Cisco is planning to use this customer base as a cudgel to beat the carriers into submission. This approach is very similar to what got Microsoft into hot water with the Justice Department and its antitrust zealots: tying dominance in one marketplace sector with the ability to dictate the use of its own products in another. This is treacherous territory, and Cisco has spent heavily in Washington to convince the government that it isn't a dangerous monopoly that has to be curbed. The Bush administration—a thankful one at that—seems likely to be much less antitrust-friendly than its Clinton cousins.

However, as his pace quickens, and he starts heading to his conclusions, John Chambers isn't stopping for any philosophical musings about the nature of fair competition and the rights and responsibilities of Cisco toward the carrier market. He's focused on his competition—and making sure that he has a leg up on them no matter how tomorrow unfolds. "Whether customers build their networks themselves, pay for it themselves, or whether they outsource it to a service provider to do it, or outsource it consciously to the overall Internet—no matter what, do they want a vendor that has read about it? Or a vendor that has done it already themselves?

"Nortel and Juniper are good companies, but companies focused primarily in one product area, Nortel in optical and Old World voice equipment and a little bit of wireless; Juniper in IP. We've gained more market share from Nortel than probably any other company in the last year. In the optical area we have grown very fast, 40 percent sequentially quarter to quarter even though others claim slowdown in that space. They were not a player in the other segments—they were a tough router and switch competitor a few years ago when they bought Bay Networks. They were advanced in the voice over IP direction back then, but now we have over 50 percent market share there. We've been more effective against Nortel than any other company in the industry.

"The industry that Cisco is in is going to grow 30 to 60 percent per year in my opinion for the next three to five years. How well we execute, or our competitors do, will determine if we are in that bracket, below it, or above. When our stock price peaked at $82 a share earlier this year, the consensus analyst projection for our revenue growth was 33 percent. We're growing 66 percent on the top line right now, and we've promised to continue doing that for the foreseeable future, and our stock is at $50. Explain that.

"It really comes down to this: Do you agree with our strategy? Have we got the market judged properly? Are our competitors truly confined to either one line of business—strong in service providers, but weak in enterprises—or only one or two product areas or geographies? If we execute properly, and our competitors continue their current strategies and implementations, I don't see any limit to our potential. Our relationships with our enterprise customers have never been stronger. The missteps that the large players like Lucent and Nortel have made over the past four months have given us a chance to really break away."

One other company made a breakaway in the technology world. It was IBM in the 1960s, when the world adopted computers for accounting and inventory control; the brand that dominated the market, with 80 percent market share, was Big Blue's. But even in its glory days, the company's growth never rose above 32 percent year to year. The breakaway that Chambers is discussing is almost breathtaking. Last year Cisco sold about $20 billion worth of gear. At its current run rate, it will break $30 billion this year, reach $45 billion next year, and, if sustained, surpass $100 billion in four years. That would be twenty years after it was founded. It took IBM *forty* years to reach market dominance in computers.

Can Cisco handle this growth? Can John Chambers find, develop, and grow managers who can take on massive business divisions and keep them nimble and competitive, rather than have them grow stodgy and hidebound? For all his talk about the power of the Internet to remake Cisco, he also has admitted recently that the company is experiencing supplier problems. Isn't reduced control over its own products the Achilles' heel of an outsourced model? Worse, if suppliers have all the expertise involved in making a product, the buyer is in danger of being hollowed out, losing the core skills in those areas where it leans too heavily on the supplier. The result? Becoming too dependent on a handful of key suppliers, who can ultimately decide to enter the same markets themselves *with* all the know-how and market knowledge you've now transferred to them. And, finally, how long can any company keep acquiring new products, rather than building internal core competencies that can anticipate future customer needs before the customer starts asking?

"At the beginning of the last year we called this the second Industrial Revolution. We pointed out the e-commerce opportunity, followed by a new wave of applications. We talked about the change of revenue that we thought would occur. E-commerce was an example that was just starting because of the networking opportunity. We said that it would change the economies of companies and countries. As it turned out, it happened even more rapidly than we expected. Even though our projections were extremely aggressive, it was a market that grew at over 50 to 100 percent in terms of productivity. Cisco was very uniquely positioned—partly because of luck, partly because of execution, and partly because of things that our competitors did, or did not, do.

"It went from us trying to create a need for networking gear, which was how we characterize our first decade as a company, to customers saying we need to deploy this around the world, right away. We are ready; can you show us how? If we execute right, we have the chance to move into that customer's most important areas, to be trusted in the very core of almost every business on earth, in the very core of what they do and how they contact and manage their own customers.

"If you look at our position and think about our customer balance across service providers, enterprise, and commercial, with none of our competitors strong in any but one of those sectors—while we're very strong in all three. And you think about it in terms of our geographic balance across all major geographies. And you think about our not being dependent on one or two tight areas in optical, or one or two products in IP, or one thing in wireless, but literally across all lines of business—twelve products with a billion-dollar run rate—you begin to see the uniqueness that Cisco has in this marketplace.

"What we believe will occur is that if we execute right, in the enterprise, we are going to be the end-to-end provider of networks, and the best partner for our customers. We are close to achieving the same type of opportunity and market share in the commercial market. And two years ago when we said we were going into the service provider market, almost no one took us seriously. But look at the most recent market-share numbers for total telecommunications equipment, which includes voice and data."

He puts up a slide showing the estimated overall telecom equipment market shares of the three biggest players. The numbers represent the combined total of all equipment and all gear and services. On it Cisco is third to Nortel and Lucent. But not by very much. It's 13.8 percent to 11.4 percent to 11.3 percent. Cisco doesn't compete in voice, only data. And Cisco is growing much faster than either of the others.

"What I'm sharing with you is that if we execute properly we have a chance for a real breakaway. What we generally see occurring is the network of networks. And it doesn't really matter if it is service provider or enterprise or commercial that grows the fastest. Whichever way it goes, we win. If the majority of enterprise customers look like they're going to outsource to service providers, which is how it looked a year or two ago, we are growing rapidly in service provider marketplaces. Or if they decide only to outsource portions of their networks, and keep the rest in-house, as has been happening recently, we have the gear to deliver that too.

"There will be a network of networks. And as a business user or a company you don't care which combination of your own network, Cisco network, and service provider and carrier network you use. You just want it to all work.

"We are the only company that can help make these networks of networks truly happen. And we will. Thank you very much."

The applause is deep. The audience stands, and dozens of shareholders besiege the stage. At first he tries to answer questions and sign autographs standing, but it doesn't work. A few minutes later he is sitting on the edge of the stage's apron, surrounded by thirty or forty people. All are shouting at him, many are thrusting annual reports into his hands, a few are trying to whisper in his ear or pass him their business cards. He's trying to manage all the clamor and all the people tugging at him and pulling at his jacket, but it is impossible. There is too much commotion, and the scene looks more like bedlam than joyous celebration.

From far up in the back of the auditorium, he has never looked so all alone.

Is HE THE Pollyanna of high tech? The last man left praising the Internet Revolution while all the companies he competes with, sells to, and inspires lie in ruins at his feet? Is Cisco recession-proof? In the six weeks between the annual meeting and the end of the Internet Year 2000, all the Chambers optimism can't help change the market's perceptions. In the final week of the year, Merrill Lynch downgrades the stock. Not because of anything Cisco is doing, but because "there is a great deal of uncertainty and spending pull back *among service providers and carriers*" [emphasis added].

Cisco's stock drops to a new all-time low in the mid-30s. The company says there is no change in its guidance for upcoming quarters, and it has seen no sign of a slowdown in orders. No one can believe it. If the service provider sector is growing weak, Cisco will be hurt.

No one seems to remember that this is not Cisco's big market. Its real business, the center of the Cisco mystique, the wellspring of this remarkable corporation, is the enterprise customer—and here sales are booming. Corporations are putting in networking upgrades like there is no tomorrow. Cisco is still golden, no matter how much all the pundits and naysayers want to find something wrong.

It may have been a bad year, but Cisco still has bragging rights to the network world. How much bigger its world can get is still unclear. But the answer is squarely on the shoulders of one good ol' boy from West Virginia. Is John T. Chambers big enough to lead his company out of the thicket of networking and into a much bigger world of his own creation? Or has he reached his limits?

Does he have any limits other than scientific know-how? Is that one too many at a technology company?

THIRTY MILES SOUTH of the shareholders' meeting, the city of San Jose's southern boundary ends in a field choked with weeds, in a desolate valley called Coyote. The now-abandoned agricultural valley once had greenhouses and row crops, but today it is the last undeveloped portion of the city. Through the center of the valley runs old Highway 101, the original north-south highway in California. Now the freeway has been moved a quarter of a mile to the east, and there is no longer much reason for traffic to head through the valley, which was once the site of the bloodiest stretch of roadway in the state. The old two-lane 101 highway, edged with eucalyptus trees, was known as Blood Alley for the thousands of head-on collisions that occurred along it.

Today there's nothing much left in Coyote Valley. To the north, what passes for a mountain in this low-slung part of California rises up—it is Coyote Peak, all 1,155 feet of it. At the intersection of the two main streets down in the flat center of the valley—Bailey Avenue and Santa Teresa Boulevard—

there is a fruit stand specializing in dried fruits of various kinds, and next to it is a junkyard. The only other signs of life in the desolate couple of square miles that make up the region are placards from optimistic realtors looking for customers and offering to "Build to Suit." It is a land that time forgot. Burned-out hulks of junked cars sit along the roadway, and cardboard and scrap shacks that are either abandoned, or should be, dot the landscape. This is a squatter's region, last stop on the opposite end of the scale from the Silicon Valley view visible from Cisco City and its squeaky-clean environment.

But the fortunes of Cisco and Coyote Valley are now closely intertwined, in a dance of development that has local environmentalists and the governments of neighboring towns angry—and the city of San Jose salivating over the $167 million in taxes the networking giant, and "good corporate citizen," will pay each year after constructing its proposed new campus. The $1.3 billion facility, if built, will supply everything except housing for the 20,000 new employees Cisco hopes to warehouse in the site. To stop criticism, the company agreed to leave much of the acreage untouched, as a wildlife preserve, and to pay a handful of formerly opposed environmental groups $3 million. Immediately, and characteristically, those left out of the deal cried foul and redoubled their efforts to stop the project.

It is probably a futile effort. Cisco has worked the political angles and garnered unanimous support from the San Jose City Council and the local newspaper, the San Jose *Mercury News*. Chambers has talked "openly," in that disarming way of his, about how "candidly, we could have gotten a much better deal in North Carolina or Boston, but we like it here in California, and if the people want us to stay we will." But there's more to it than political machinations and hardball. The environmentalists and local government are afraid, respectively, of damage to sensitive habitats and an influx of well-heeled valleyites who will change the rural character of the nearby towns.

In the hills a couple of miles to the west of Coyote Valley, is the ghost town of one of California's most important mines.

Once, it was every bit as essential to the development of California as the gold that was found 150 miles to the east. And it is particularly apt because it was a mine that had the same relationship to that gold rush as Cisco's routers, switches, and services do to the modern-day Internet Rush. It was called the New Almaden Mine, and it produced quicksilver, or mercury. Mercury was what adhered to the placer gold in the pans of the forty-niners and allowed them to separate it from the rocks and debris. In its heyday, in 1854, it was the largest mercury mine in the world.

Cisco's products are the quicksilver of the Internet and Information Ages. Its tools let entrepreneurs mine the Internet and let businesses find their gold in this New World.

But it is not just the proximity to the New Almaden Mine that makes this site so poetically, perhaps preternaturally, right for Cisco and John Chambers, as the company drives the worldwide data revolution and the man tries to put his mark on history. One hundred yards down the road from the new Cisco site there is a stand of trees, a windbreak of sorts. Beyond it is a driveway, without a gate, and a simple, single sign. It is the only other building in Coyote Valley. It was built in the 1960s, and it has the low, squat architecture of that era, a boxy four-story nondescript place with nothing remarkable about it.

Perhap's there's a siren's song wafting out of that building, and out of that company, that John Chambers cannot ignore. With the wind whistling through the tumbleweed and the goldenrod and the thistle, it's the song that he learned in his first job, at the company that he constantly refers to in his explanation for Cisco's business strategy. It's an American song, written by the greatest company of the last century, a company that Cisco emulates. The tune of the one company that Cisco could merge with, in a move that would guarantee John Chambers his place in history. The one merger that would create an eighty-year company, capable of truly dominating the development and the delivery of the lifeblood of the next century: the combination of networking and computing that will lead society into a new era.

The only other company in Coyote Valley is IBM, whose Santa Teresa laboratory is parked beyond those trees. It is a fabled place, where the disk drive was invented and the relational database was thought up. The irony is that Cisco would have to acquire IBM for those glory days to come back. Stranger things have happened in the New Economy.

And if not, can Chambers lead Cisco to more than just another quarter after quarter string of good numbers, lead them to a Brave New World with new businesses as big as networking? Can he lead the company across its own Isthmus of Panama to a whole new ocean? Then make them be successful in exploiting it? It will have to be built on something more than just networking.

And if he doesn't, and if the Coyote Valley adventure is the Edifice Complex, which strikes many corporate egos, and if Cisco fails to make its numbers, if it doesn't break away from all the rest of the pack? What then?

In that case all that will be left in Coyote Valley a few years from now will be another peeling and dilapidated realtor sign, in that same weed-choked field: "Future Home of Cisco Systems. Built to Suit."

Maybe Coyote Valley is where the future is going to be created. Maybe not. But it will happen on Internet time supplied by Cisco. John T. Chambers, and Cisco, have created the first great empire of the Information Age by selling pickaxes, Levis, and quicksilver to the early miners. Now they're going to try to sell them to everyone else too. In the process, they'll fulfill the vision that is printed on the plastic ID card that each of the 35,000 Cisco employees wears. It's a vision that came directly from John Chambers, one that elicited guffaws and derision when he first started using it five years ago. Very few are laughing anymore.

"We are going to change the way people work, live, play and learn."

Amen.

NOTES AND ACKNOWLEDGMENTS

ALMOST EVERYTHING IN THIS BOOK IS BASED ON MY OWN REPORTING.
My first taped interviews with John Chambers and Cisco executives date from 1997; the last material came from the November
2000 annual meeting. Over the years I conducted hundreds of interviews with competitors, employees, customers, observers, investors, and suppliers—too many to mention, especially since
more than a few of the most important insisted on anonymity.
Such is the power of a gigantic corporation like Cisco, and it most
affects those who know the company most intimately. Cisco itself
cooperated with me until spring 2000, when it decided to stop
further official contact or help.

Because most of the book concerns events that have occurred very recently, there is not much of a published record to
reference. However, one writer's work helped guide me and
should be consulted by anyone wanting to read more deeply in
this field; George Gilder first showed me how to think, and
write, about both transistors and telecommunications using a

much bigger stage. All his books are well worth reading, especially the classic *Microcosm* and the more recent *Telecosm*.

In terms of history, four books stand out in separate segments of the story: *City of Light,* by Jeff Hecht, tells the technical story of fiber optics up to the 1980s, albeit from a British point of view; *Making the Cisco Connection,* by David Bunnell and Adam Brate, does a good job of pulling together the published record about Cisco and adds some excellent early anecdotal history of the corporation; *On The Line,* Larry Kahaner's account of the divestiture of Ma Bell and the rise of the new telecommunications order in the 1980s, is a classic; and *Where Wizards Stay Up Late,* by Katie Hafner and Mathew Lyon, does a fine job of explaining the personalities, skirmishes, and hard work involved in creating the Internet we know today.

Many people helped me create this book. It starts with the members of CHICO (Chapel Hill Investment Company) in North Carolina and continues with Katrina Heron, Martha Baer, and Michael Noer at *Wired* magazine, who assigned me the story and turned it into such a powerful piece. But the real partner in the venture was the team at Prima Publishing, beginning with Ben Dominitz, president and founder, who believed in the book, was willing to tear up traditional contracts and forge a new relationship with a writer, and then held my feet to the fire in the face of extraordinary pressure to quit. His colleague, Steven Martin, Forum imprint publisher, shaped the book in far more ways than I can enumerate. He was midwife to this book, helped bring it into the world, argued and discussed with me endlessly the structure and flow of the story, always fought for more simplicity, left me alone when I needed it, and stayed with it to the end. Andi Reese Brady shepherded the project, and Ed McFadden and Joan Pendleton improved my writing.

Writing a book takes a personal toll. My family, especially my wife Janey, has borne the brunt of it. A handful of friends helped me rethink the story time and again, struggle through its disappointments, and celebrate successes with me; and they've held my hands during moments of doubt and kept me shuffling along toward the goal. Chief among them is Jim Forbes, a long-time colleague and a reporter's reporter, who has kept me grounded in the here and now, and John Champlin, who patiently listened to many of my most outlandish theories in their entirety before shooting them down.

In the end, all these people have tried to help me write a better, and more accurate and fair, book. Any errors that remain, and most of the opinions, are solely my responsibility.

INDEX